DO YOU HAVE WHAT IT TAKES? THE ART DIRECTORS CLUB
89TH ANNUAL

EDITORIAL DIRECTOR
Jennifer Larkin Kuzler

EDITOR
Lucas Stoffel

ASSISTANT EDITORS
Michael Waka
Whittney Suggs

AWARDS STAFF
Max Dunfey
Kris Hoover
Jennifer McClelland
Michael Waka

COPY EDITOR
Vanessa Levine-Smith

INTERIOR BOOK DESIGN
Lucas Stoffel
www.lucasstoffel.com

**PACKAGING, COVER CONCEPT AND
INFO GRAPHIC ILLUSTRATIONS**
Publicis New York
Rob Feakins
Roman Luba
Philip Arias
Tana Cieciora
Jin Hee Kwon
Jeremy Filgate
Catherine Somple

COMPANION DVD PRODUCTION
Noah Norman
Ancillary Magnet, LLC

PUBLISHER
RotoVision SA
Route Suisse 9
Ch-1295
Mies Switzerland

SALES AND EDITORAL OFFICE
Sheridan House
114 Western Road
Hove, East Sussex
BN3 1DD, United Kingdom
Tel: +44 (0) 1273 727268
Fax: +44 (0) 1273 727269
sales@rotovision.com
www.rotovision.com

DESIGN SOFTWARE
Adobe Creative Suite 5
Design Premium

THE ART DIRECTORS CLUB
106 West 29th Street
New York, NY 10001
United States of America
www.adcglobal.org

ISBN – 978-2-88893-147-8

TABLE OF CONTENTS

Change. Understanding it is the important thing. We change our light bulbs from incandescent to LEDs. We change our ideology from "buy new," to "mend and repair." We change our tools from a pencil to a computer to whatever is next. What remains consistent is our appreciation for a well-crafted idea that suits its purpose. We value its efficiency, it's relevance, it's newness, it's ties to culture. It's because in our hearts, we are artists. Artists are communicators.

This club was formed in 1920 in the defense of artists who crossed into corporate culture to create images for advertising. They weren't paid very well, and they weren't looked highly upon by those artists who were outside the system. I can fairly say that the former has changed, and we are making progress on earning the admiration of all.

Our mission at the Art Directors Club is to Connect, Provoke and Elevate world-changing individuals. Evidence of this can be found in all of our programming - YoungGuns, which celebrates talent 30 and under, Hall of Fame, and our recent addition GrandMasters, which recognizes educators. And this book is no different, as we recognize the top 1% of the field.

It is equally important to recognize that as awards shows come under continued scrutiny, I promise that we will change. Myself and the Board, along with the capable staff will in this coming year make changes that will improve the quality of the evaluation, growth and connecting of talent in our business to the clients, projects and products that need it most.

- Doug Jaeger
ADC Board President

With its prestigious 89-year legacy, the Annual Awards program is a major component of what the Art Directors Club is all about. But it's just one aspect of what ADC does throughout the year to Connect, Provoke and Elevate the international creative community.

The numbers tell a compelling story: out of 251 work days, the ADC Gallery was in use 203 of those days last year -- almost 80% of the time -- serving as home to a diverse range of awards presentations, exhibitions, lectures, panels and parties designed to bring creatives together, share ideas and grow careers.

ADC programs, events and activities span the entire length of the educational and professional career arc. There are educational programs such as the Henry Wolf Summer Photography Workshop for New York high school students and National Student Portfolio Reviews for those in college. There's ADC Young Guns for creatives under age 30, and Photography and Illustration Portfolio Reviews held annually at the ADC Gallery.

ADC also helps creatives pay tribute to those who lead with ADC GrandMasters, recognizing current and retired US-based educators, and the ADC Hall of Fame, honoring a diverse group of luminaries including Saul Bass, Leo Burnett, Jay Chiat, Walt Disney, Charles and Ray Eames, Milton Glaser, Andy Warhol and others.

Annual events that connect and provoke include ADC Designism, exploring the responsibilities of creatives to drive social, political and ecological change through their work, and ADC Reboot to help creatives expand career opportunities. There's Paper Expo and ADC's Holiday Party, as well as one-off events like the show of Eric Meola's arresting photos of India and a recent week-long seminar by the Berlin School. We've also expanded beyond our physical space, moving into the virtual world in partnership with YouTube to launch YouTube Show & Tell, a new gallery-style brand channel curated by ADC that showcases the best marketing examples on YouTube.

ADC enters its ninth decade as a dynamic, non-stop, multi-dimensional hub for bringing people together. It's a place to learn from the greats, view inspiring work, or simply have a good time and make new friends. It's been an exciting year, with even more on tap for our 90th. We hope you will join us.

- Olga Grisaitis
ADC Director

ADC**HALL OF FAME**

Since 1972, the Art Directors Club Hall of Fame has recognized and honored innovators who have made significant contributions to art direction and visual communications, and whose lifetime achievements represent the highest standards of creative excellence. An essay from the Board of Directors in the 51st Art Directors Annual reads, "This year we inaugurate the Hall of Fame. The nomination and election each year of these people will help to educate and inform not only the young people entering our business, but we hope will serve as an inspiration to all of us. In their hands, advertising and graphic communication [becomes] an art form." It is our pleasure to salute and pay tribute to this year's inductees. The lifetime achievements of these nine innovators represent the highest standards of excellence of the converging creative disciples that the Art Directors Club is proud to embrace.

- Chee Perlman & Janet Froelich
Co-chairs, 2010 Hall of Fame Selection Committee

ADC**HALL OF FAME**

1972
M.F. Agha
Lester Beall
Alexey Brodovitch
A.M. Cassandre
Rene Clarke
Robert Gage
William Golden
Paul Rand

1973
Charles Coiner
Paul Smith
Jack Tinker

1974
Will Burtin
Leo Lionni

1975
Gordon Aymar
Herbert Bayer
Cipe Pineles Burtin
Heyworth Campbell
Alexander Liberman
László Moholy-Nagy

1976
E. McKnight Kauffer
Herbert Matter

1977
Saul Bass
Herb Lubalin
Bradbury Thompson

1978
Thomas M. Cleland
Lou Dorfsman
Allen Hurlburt
George Lois

1979
W.A. Dwiggins
George Giusti
Milton Glaser
Helmut Krone
Willem Sandberg
Ladislav Sutnar
Jan Tschichold

1980
Gene Federico
Otto Storch
Henry Wolf

1981
Lucian Bernhard
Ivan Chermayeff
György Kepes
George Krikorian
William Taubin

1982
Richard Avedon
Amil Gargano
Jerome Snyder
Massimo Vignelli

1983
Red Burns
Seymour Chwast
Steve Frankfurt

1984
Charles Eames
Wallace Elton
Sam Scali
Louis Silverstein

1985
Art Kane
Len Sirowitz
Charles Tudor

1986
Walt Disney
Roy Grace
Alvin Lustig
Arthur Paul

1987
Willy Fleckhaus
Leon Friend
Shigeo Fukuda
Steve Horn
Tony Palladino

1988
Silas Rhodes
Ben Shahn
Bert Steinhauser
Mike Tesch

1989
Rudolph de Harak
Herschel Levit
Raymond Loewy

1990
Lee Clow
Reba Sochis
Robert Weaver
Frank Zachary

1991
Bea Feitler
Bob Gill
Bob Giraldi
Jim Henson
Richard Hess

1992
Eiko Ishioka
Rick Levine
Onofrio Paccione
Gordon Parks

1993
Bill Bernbach
Leo Burnett
Yusaku Kamekura
Robert Wilvers
Howard Zieff

1994
Alan Fletcher
Norman Rockwell
Ikko Tanaka
Rochelle Udell
Andy Warhol

1995
Robert Brownjohn
Paul Davis
Steve Heller
Roy Kuhlman
Jay Maisel

1996
Bill McCaffery
Erik Nitsche
Arnold Varga
Fred Woodward

1997
Allan Beaver
Sheila Metzner
B. Martin Pedersen
George Tscherny

1998
Tom Geismar
Chuck Jones
Paula Scher
Alex Steinweiss

1999
R.O. Blechman
Annie Leibovitz
Stan Richards
Richard Wilde

2000
Edward Benguiat
Joe Sedelmaier
Pablo Ferro
Tadanori Yokoo

2001/2002
Philip Meggs
Rich Silverstein
Giorgio Soavi
Edward Sorel

2003
Michael Bierut
André François
David Kennedy
Richard Saul Wurman

2004
Jerry Andelin
Jay Chiat
Muriel Cooper
Louise Fili
Al Hirschfeld
Tibor Kalman
Bruce McCall
Duane Michals
Edward Tufte

2006
Janet Froelich
Nicholas Negroponte
Issey Miyake
Nancy Rice
Art Spiegelman
Bert Stern

2008
Alex Bogusky
Ray Eames
Sir John Hegarty
Maira Kalman
John Maeda
R. Roger Remington
Bruce Weber

* Honorees pictured on
previous spread are in order
from left to right

The Art Directors Club
Hall of Fame

2010**SELECTION COMMITTEE**

Chee Pearlman
ADC Board Member; Principal, Chee Company

Janet Froelich
ADC Hall of Fame; ADC Board Member; Creative Director, *Real Simple*

Nicholas Blechman
ADC Member; Art Director, *The New York Times Book Review*

Rob Feakins
ADC Board Member; Chief Creative Officer/President, Publicis New York

Louise Fili
ADC Hall of Fame; Louise Fili Ltd

Doug Jaeger
President, ADC Board

Lisa Naftolin
ADC Member; Creative Director, Art + Commerce

Paula Scher
ADC Hall of Fame; Partner, Pentagram

Massimo Vignelli
ADC Hall of Fame; Vignelli Associates

Jeffrey Zeldman
ADC Member; Founder/Executive Creative Director, Happy Cog

As the founder and creative director of Baron & Baron, Fabien Baron has crafted identities for the fashion, cosmetic and fragrance world's most visible and influential brands. Baron's singular vision is evident in a broad range of award-winning advertising campaigns, package designs, logos and graphics. Baron has also applied his talents to the design of prominent magazines and books, and is renowned for his photography, as well as for directing groundbreaking television commercials and music videos.

FABIEN**BARON**

Baron was born in Paris in 1959 and studied at Ecole des Arts Appliques. He moved to New York in 1982 and shortly thereafter was hired as creative director for Barneys New York.

In 1988, Baron redesigned *Italian Vogue* under editor Franca Sozzani and two years later he became creative director of *Interview* magazine. After founding Baron & Baron, Inc. Baron relaunched *Harper's Bazaar* commencing an eight-year partnership with late editor-in-chief, Liz Tilberis. Simultaneously, in September 1992, Calvin Klein hired Baron as creative director. That same year, Baron art directed the arresting and provocative *Sex* book for Madonna. To the present day, Baron & Baron has continued to shape the image of the brand, creating iconic print, television and package designs for fashion and fragrances.

From 2000 to 2002, Baron worked as editor-in-chief and design director of *Arena Homme +*. In 2001, he debuted his first residential furniture line with Cappellini and in 2002 Baron introduced a contract furniture line with Bernhardt. The next year he became the creative director of *French Vogue* under editor-in-chief Carine Roitfeld. In October 2009, Baron rejoined Brant Publications' *Interview* and was named editorial director. He continues to work on a broad range of assignments for a select group of international clients.

a

R

BALENCIAGA, le fil PRODIGE

...sagesse du noir et *ivresse* de *total looks* réalisés sur *mesure* signent un *éloge* de la *féminité en surgonflement*, une allure suprême sur *laquelle* on se *retourne*. *Photographie* David Sims. *Réalisation* Marie-Amélie Sauvé.

s

f

feu sacré

a

Quintessence

W

denzel washington

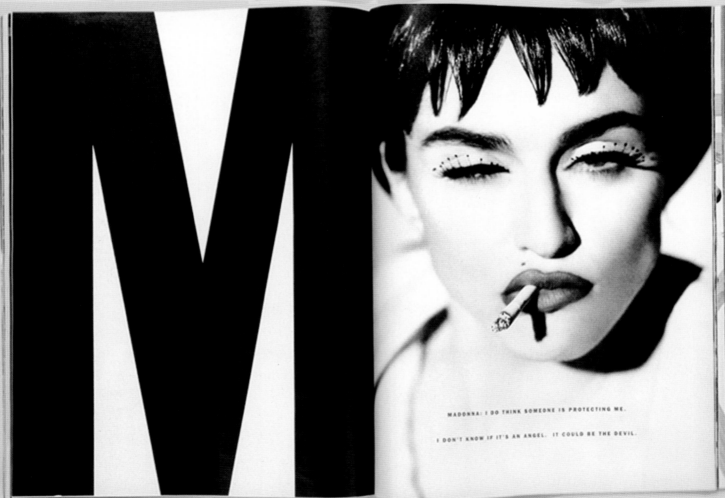

MADONNA: I DO THINK SOMEONE IS PROTECTING ME.

I DON'T KNOW IF IT'S AN ANGEL. IT COULD BE THE DEVIL.

dean
dick
stock
Well

b
o
wi
e

MADE
LENE
STO
WE

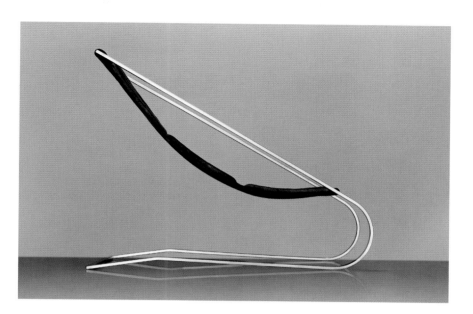

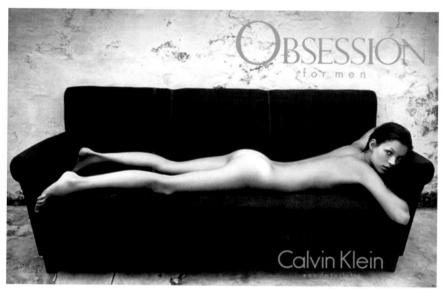

Matthew Carter was born and raised in England, son of the typographic historian Harry Carter. On leaving school in 1955, he spent a year at the Enschedé typefoundry in the Netherlands learning to make metal type by hand—a skill that proved to be commercially obsolete. To earn a living he had to adapt to drawing alphabets for modernist designers in London who were frustrated by the lack of contemporary sanserif typefaces in Britain at that time. His background, therefore, is a technical one; as a designer he is self-taught. If there is a

Georgia

Latin ABCDEFGHIJKLMNO
PQRSTUVWXYZ&abcdefghij
klmnopqrstuvwxyzæœfifl1234
567890$¢£ƒ¥@%.,-:;!?()*†‡

MATTHEW**CARTER**

Bell Centennial

1978. Commissioned by AT&T for the US telephone directories.

Name & Number

ABCDEFGHIJK LMNOPQRSTU VWXYZ&1234 567890abcdef ghijklmnopqrs tuvwxyz.,-:;!?

ABCDEFGHIJKLMNOPQRSTUVWXYZ & 1234567890 abcdefghijklmnopqrstuvwxyz .,-:;!? 6-point
ABCDEFGHIJKLMNOPQRSTUVWXYZ & 1234567890 abcdefghijklmnopqrstuvwxyz .,-:;!? 6.5-point
ABCDEFGHIJKLMNOPQRSTUVWXYZ & 1234567890 abcdefghijklmnopqrstuvwxyz .,-:;!? 7-point.

theme to his work over the past 50+ years, it is the relationship of design to technology during a period when the tools for making and setting type have changed more radically than at any other time in history. He has been able to make type by essentially all the methods ever used: metal by hand, metal by machine, photoset, digital, desktop, screen and woodtype for letterpress posters.

In 1965, Carter was hired by Mergenthaler Linotype in New York as staff designer with the job of exploring the implications of photocomposition, the change from type as a three-dimensional metal object to a two-dimensional photographic image. Snell Roundhand, designed in 1966, took advantage of the new medium by introducing a style of type, a joining script, that had been impossible to make in metal but worked well in film.

The next technology, digital type, proved to be a mixed blessing for the designer. In the 1970s, AT&T began to use pioneering high-speed digital systems to accelerate production of United States telephone directories. Their existing typeface performed badly under the new conditions. A replacement was commissioned from Mergenthaler to be "designed for printability." Since the new type was to be digital, Carter had to teach himself to work digitally. At that time there were no computer tools that could convert an analog image to a digital bitmap. Every single character of Bell Centennial, therefore, had to be drawn on graph paper, pixel by pixel, and encoded at a keyboard. This was an epic task of hands-on designing, but it paid off in the education it provided the designer.

Big Figgins Roman

ABCDEFGHIJKLMN
OPQRSTUVWXYZ&
abcdefghijklmnopqrstu
vwxyz 1234567890

Big Figgins Italic

ABCDEFGHIJKLM
NOPQRSTUVWXYZ
&abcdefghijklmnopqrs
tuvwxyz 1234567890

ITC Galliard Roman
ABCDEFGHIJKLMNOPQRSTUVWXYZ&ÆŒ
abcdefghijklmnopqrstuvwxyzæœfffiflffiffl ß &
1234567890$¢£€¥ƒ 1234567890 ⅛⅜⅝⅞ ½ ⅙⅚ ⅓⅔ ¼¾ ½
$¢1234567890,.-⁄$¢1234567890,.- 1234567890 (abdehilmnorstv)
& Q a ct ct d e h m n r R st t z

ITC Galliard Small Caps
ABCDEFGHIJKLMNOPQRSTUVWXYZ&ÆŒÇÐŁŠŽÞQ

ITC Galliard Italic
ABCDEFGHIJKLMNOPQRSTUVWXYZ&ÆŒ
abcdefghijklmnopqrstuvwxyzæœfffiflffifflfrßij
1234567890$¢£€¥ƒ 1234567890 ⅛⅜⅝⅞ ½ ¼¾ ½
$¢1234567890,.-⁄$¢1234567890,.- (abdehilmnorstv)
& Q a ct d e e g k m n nt sp st st t v z

Galliard was designed as a four-weight family for Mergenthaler Linotype in 1978. Three years later it was acquired by the International Typeface Corporation and re-released as ITC Galliard. The Carter & Cone digitization of the regular weight of Roman and Italic, done in 1992, includes the flourished final letters and other peculiars that were part of the original photocomposition fonts.

MANTINIA · MCMXCIII
CAPS AᴬBᴮCᶜDᴰEᴱFᶠGᴳHᴴ
AND IᴵJKᴷLᴸMᴹNᴺOᴼPQ
SUPERIOR RᴿSˢTᵀUᵁVᵛ
CAPS WᵂXˣYʸ&&ZᶻÆŒ
FIGURES 1234567890
SMALL CAPS ACEHIORSTUWYZ
LIGATURES TH V CT HE UP LA
TT CE TU TW TY ME MP MD MB E
ALTERNATIVES T & Y R R Q Q
TALL CAPITALS I T L Y
INTERPOINTS · · ·

Miller Display Roman

¶ABCDEFGHIJKLMNOPQRS
TUVWXYZ&ÆŒ&ÁÀÂÄÃÅÇÉ
ÈÊËÍÌÎÏÑÓÒÔÖØŠÚÙÛÜÝŸŽ
ÐŁÞABCDEFGHIJKLMNOPQRSTU
VWXYZ&ÆŒ&ÁÀÂÄÃÅÇÉÈÊËÍÌÎÏÑ
ÓÒÔÖÕØŠÚÙÛÜÝŸŽÐŁÞªºabcdefg
hijklmnopqrstuvwxyzæœfffiflffi
fflßáàâäãåçéèêëíìîïñóòôöõøšúùû
üýÿžðłþµ1234567890¼½¾12345
67890ªºe@$¢£¥ƒ€¤%‰•§*†‡®
©℗™.,:;-¡!¿?‘’“”„,'"°()[]{}/|¦\‹›«
»–—…_#+=÷−×¬~<>·´`ˆ¨˜¯˘˙˚

Shelley Volante

A B C D E F G
H I J K L M N
O P Q R S T U
V W X Y Z
&
abcdefghijklmnopqrs
stuvwxyz
1972

Verdana

Latin ABCDEFGHIJKLMNO
PQRSTUVWXYZ&abcdefghi
jklmnopqrstuvwxyzæœfifl
1234567890$¢£ƒ¥@%#+
Greek ΑΒΓΔΕΖΗΘΙΚΛΜΝΞ
ΟΠΡΣΤΥΦΧΨΩαβγδεζηθικλ
μνξοπρσςτυφχψω
Cyrillic АБВГДЕЖЗИЙКЛМ
НОПРСТУФХЦЧШЩЪЫЬЭ
ЮЯабвгдежзийклмнопрст
уфхцчшщъыьэюя

ABCDEFGHIJKLMNO
PQRSTUVWXYZ&ÆŒ
HEMBME1234567890
THE WALKER FONT
CONTAINS FIVE DIF-
FERENT "*SNAP-ON*"
SERIFS AND THREE
JOINING STROKES:
H H H H H H
H H H H H H
H H H H H H

Yale Design Roman & *Italic*
ABCDEFGHIJKLMNOPQRSTUVWXYZ&
1234567890 abcdefghijklmnopqrstuvwxyzæœfifl
ABCDEFGHIJKLMNOPQRSTUVWXYZ&
1234567890 abcdefghijklmnopqrstuvwxyzæœfifl

Yale Admin Roman & *Italic*
ABCDEFGHIJKLMNOPQRSTUVWXYZ&
1234567890 abcdefghijklmnopqrstuvwxyzææ
ABCDEFGHIJKLMNOPQRSTUVWXYZ&
1234567890 abcdefghijklmnopqrstuvwxyzææ

Yale Small Caps
ABCDEFGHIJKLMNOPQRSTUVWXYZ&
1234567890

Yale Street (for campus signs)
ABCDEFGHIJKLMNOPQRSTUVWXYZ&
1234567890 1234567890
abcdefghijklmnopqrstuvwxyzæœfifl

Georgia

Latin ABCDEFGHIJKLMNO
PQRSTUVWXYZ&abcdefghij
klmnopqrstuvwxyzæœfifl1234
567890$¢£ƒ¥@%.,-:;!?()*†‡
Greek ΑΒΓΔΕΖΗΘΙΚΛΜΝΞ
ΟΠΡΣΤΥΦΧΨΩαβγδεζηθικλμ
νξοπρσςτυφχψω
Cyrillic АБВГДЕЖЗИЙКЛМ
НОПРСТУФХЦЧШЩЪЫЬЭ
ЮЯабвгдежзийклмнопрсту
фхцчшщъыьэюя

Bell Centennial was more legible than the type it replaced. It also saved space in the directory columns. Nobody thought about saving trees in 1978, but AT&T did think about saving their paper bill and were very happy with the economical result. Bell Centennial was "accidentally ecological" before its time.

Carter, in a long association with the Linotype companies, designed ITC Galliard, Helvetica Compressed, Shelley Script, Olympian (for newspaper text) and faces for Greek, Hebrew and Devanagari. In 1981 he joined with three ex-Linotype colleagues to start Bitstream, a digital typefoundry, in Cambridge, Massachusetts. He worked there for ten years, leaving with one of his co-founders, Cherie Cone, to start Carter & Cone Type in 1992. At that date the personal computer and, as importantly, open font formats, were making independent typefounding a viable business. It became possible to design typefaces and make fonts in much the same spirit that punchcutters had worked in the early centuries of type's history. For Carter, whose temperament considers "designing" and "making" virtually inseparable, the last 18 years have been the most rewarding.

In addition to retail fonts for general license (Mantinia, Sophia, Big Figgins, Big Caslon, Miller), typefaces have been commissioned by *Time*, *Newsweek*, *U.S. News & World Report*, *Sports Illustrated*, *BusinessWeek*, *The Washington Post*, *The Boston Globe*, *The Philadelphia Inquirer*, *The New York Times* (the paper and the magazine), *The Guardian* and *Le Monde*. Other custom types have been designed for the Walker Art Center, Yale Universit, and the Museum of Modern Art.

In the mid-'90s, Carter started working with Microsoft to develop the "screen fonts" Verdana and Georgia whose priority was legibility in the inhospitable technical environment of computer monitors. A profile in *The New Yorker* of December 5, 2005, began: "Matthew Carter is often described as the most widely read man in the world. Carter designs typefaces." If this is true, it is because Verdana and Georgia, distributed freely by Microsoft, have become ubiquitous in contemporary screen-based visual culture.

Georgia

ABCD

f one word could describe Philip Harrison Hays, it would be glamour, the old Hollywood kind. He had looks, style, and ambition, and he came of age near the end of an era when illustration still dominated advertising and publishing, and when great illustrators were stars.

Born in Sherman, Texas on May 14, 1930, Phil spent his formative years in Louisiana, joined the Air Force in 1950, and in 1952 enrolled at the Art Center College of Design in Pasadena. "I had this gut feeling I wanted to get serious about art so I drove to L.A. It only took that one trip and a stroll through the student gallery to convince me."

PHIL**HAYS**

In 1955, Hays moved to New York and enjoyed immediate success, stretching the conventions for romantic illustrations in magazines such as *Seventeen*, *Cosmopolitan*, *Redbook* and *McCalls*. "His early watercolor approach, partly inspired by Vuillard, was often quite loose but also extremely detailed," wrote Steven Heller, who described him as "one of a young band of expressive and interpretative illustrators, including Robert Weaver, Jack Potter, Tom Allen and Robert Andrew Parker who, rather than paint or draw literal scenes based entirely on an author's prose, interpreted texts with an eye toward expressive license. Hays said that representational illustration was an art of nuance, and his work routinely dug below the surface, drawing on Impressionist, Expressionist and Surrealist influences."

Silas H. Rhodes, a founder and president of the fledgling School of Visual Arts, was looking for strong new talent, and, in 1957, hired Hays to teach and later chair the Illustration Department. Younger than many of his students who were attending on the G.I. Bill, Hays introduced novels, plays and films as a way to increase visual and verbal literacy.

By the mid-1960s Hays' work for fiction in *Esquire* and visual reportage in, *Sports Illustrated* "had become darker and more serious," observed friend and artist James McMullan, and in the 1970s his emotionally arresting portraits of musicians from blues singers Bessie Smith and Billie Holiday to rock and roll legends Elvis Presley, Jerry Lee Lewis and Eric Clapton, set a new standard for LP albums and the covers of Rolling Stone.

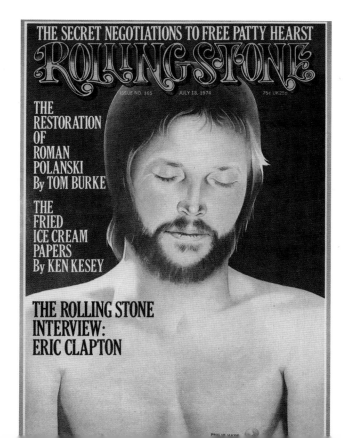

For nearly 24 years, Phil Hays lived the life of a consummate New Yorker in a penthouse apartment on Central Park West where he threw parties, a home in Huntington, Long Island where he liked to ride horses, and finally in a loft in Noho as an intrepid pioneer of "downtown." His circle of friends included movie actors Ben Piazza and Rita Gam, artist Andy Warhol and restaurateur Johnny Nicholson.

"I'm proud of that period of my life and all that work," says Hays, "But there came a time where I was working nights and weekends and thinking it had gone on long enough. I pulled a Garbo and quit. I felt complete with what I had accomplished and it was easy to move on." In 1978 Hays accepted an invitation from Art Center to head its Illustration Department and moved back to California.

For the next 24 years, Hays proved to be as much of a force in education as he had been in illustration. Art Center presented him with the Don Kubly Award for Professional Attainment in 2002 with the statement that "Phil's second great talent—his affinity for teaching—was waiting to be more fully expressed and is reflected in the creative talents of the many students who have sought and found inspiration during his years in the classroom."

"Philip Hays probably inspired more successful artists than any other teacher I can think of. He welcomes experimentation and innovation," said Paul Davis of his mentor and friend when Hays received the Society of Illustrators 2000 Distinguished Educators in the Arts award. "His favorite expression is 'Why not?'"

"I gain tremendous pleasure from my students' work," said Hays, "as much pleasure as I found in my own." He retired in 2002, and, besides Davis, well known former students include Robert Hagel, Norman Green, Matt Mahurin, Doug Aitken, The Clayton Brothers, Esther Watson, Jeffrey Smith, Jason Holley, Alex Gross, Greg Raglund, Sam Martine, Joo Chung and Caldecott Medal winner, David Shannon.

Philip Hays died on October 24, 2005 at age 74. Aitken wrote, "In a quiet and mysterious way, Hays' work slid under the door of popular culture and affected it like sand falling in the cracks of a machine…the glamour of the subjects fade and their flaws and vulnerability appear… revealed is our beautiful disintegration as we're faced with the inevitable race toward mortality."

"I never wanted to be anything but an illustrator," Hays once said. "There were those who separated fine art from illustration, looking down their noses at the latter. Sometimes people would ask if I ever wanted to do my own work. I always replied, 'Everything I do is my own work.' I loved working against a hard edge, getting an assignment and turning it into my own—pleasing the client and myself. I was never tempted to be a painter. Andy Warhol, Ben Shahn and Richard Lindner were heroes of mine, primary influences. They instigated the movement and if I am considered part of the next generation that helped revive the aesthetics of illustration, I am proud.

- **Myrna Davis**

George Nelson has been called the "Designer of Modern Design." Born in 1908 in Hartford, Connecticut, he studied architecture at Yale University and earned a fellowship to study at the American Academy in Rome from 1932-34. A prolific writer, designer and creative thinker, Nelson's work includes architecture, furniture, lamps, clocks, exhibits, identity programs, graphics, urban development, numerous books, articles and visual documentaries. He was the lead designer for the 1959 American National Exhibition in Moscow for the 1959 U.S.S.R.–U.S.A. exchange, and introduced America to the Russian people.

GEORGE**NELSON**

the herman miller collection

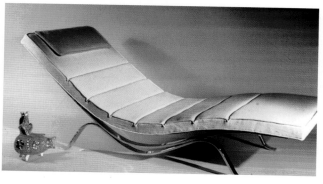

When writing on his own remarkable 50-year career, George described a series of creative "zaps" — moments of out-of-the-blue inspiration "when the solitary individual finds he is connected with a reality he never dreamed of."

An early zap came when he was at the American Academy in Rome. Before returning home, an idea struck him: He would travel Europe and interview leading modern architects, hoping to get the articles published in the United States. He succeeded, and in the process introduced the United States design community to the European avant-garde. This set in motion a sequence of what he called "lucky" career breaks that were really the inevitable outcomes of his brilliance as an observer, designer, teacher and author.

The first break was being named an editor of *Architectural Forum* magazine. Working on a story in 1942, he was looking at aerial photos of blighted cities when—zap!—he developed the concept of the downtown pedestrian mall, which was unveiled in the *Saturday Evening Post*. Dubbed "The Greening of Main Street," this led the way to much urban revitalization.

Soon after, another zap led to the Storagewall, the first modular storage system and a forerunner of systems furniture. The Storagewall showcased in a 1945 *Life* magazine article, caused a sensation in the furniture industry. Herman Miller, founder of D.J. DePree, saw the article and was so impressed that he paid a visit to Nelson in New York and convinced him to be his director of design, which spurred Nelson to found his design firm, George Nelson & Associates. The warm personal and professional relationship between Nelson and DePree yielded a stunning range of products, from the playful Marshmallow Sofa to the first L-shaped desk, a precursor of today's workstation.

Nelson once wrote that Herman Miller "is not playing follow-the-leader." That's one reason why George Nelson & Associates worked with Herman Miller for over 25 years as they shepherded design into the modern era.

During this same period, George Nelson & Associates also created many landmark designs of products, showrooms and exhibitions for a variety of companies and organizations.

Nelson said that for a designer to deal creatively with human needs, "he must first make a radical, conscious break with all values he identifies as antihuman." Designers also must constantly be aware of the consequences of their actions on people and society. In fact, he declared that "total design is nothing more or less than a process of relating everything to everything." So he said that rather than specializing, designers must cultivate a broad base of knowledge and understanding.

George died in 1968. At his memorial service, Tom Pratt, former senior vice president of Herman Miller, long-time associate and friend of George said this:

He was incredulous at the thought that design would have any other purpose than to improve the quality of life in the built environment. He believed that designers didn't so much create as discover, and that to address a problem by starting out to innovate was a sure-fire way to miss the solution altogether. He cautioned about being too serious in the pursuit of design excellence lest one miss the joy of the activity. He fretted about the inaccurate use of words that confused the real content of one's meaning. He fought narrow views and closed-mindedness and struggled to keep the minds of those he cared about open. He disagreed loudly with the notion of growth equaling progress and worked hard to point out that, in fact, though counterintuitive in our society, it might be just the opposite. He believed that revolutionary research started many times with throwing out what was known and starting over with the unknown. He loathed the notion that any man would truly believe that he held the truth, exclusive of any other man.

Christoph Niemann was born in Waiblingen, Germany in 1970. Between 1991 and 1997 he studied Graphic Design at the State Academy of Fine Art in Stuttgart, Germany, with Heinz Edelmann. The Art Directors Club of Germany awarded his master thesis with the Talent of The Year Award.

CHRISTOPH**NIEMANN**

His first stints in New York were internships for Paul Davis in 1995, and for Paula Scher at Pentagram in 1996, when he also did his first drawings for *Rolling Stone* and *The New York Times Book Review*. After his graduation from The Art Academy in Stuttgart in 1997 he moved to New York and started working as an editorial Illustrator.

He quickly became a regular contributor to most major magazines and newspapers. His illustrations have appeared on the covers of *The New York Times Magazine*, *Wired*, *Time*, *Newsweek*, *Fast Company*, *Atlantic Monthly* and *The New Yorker*. Even though he has illustrated almost every conceivable content, his obsession with politics, economics and culture have made him a staple on the pages of *The New York Times* Op-Ed Page and The Book Review, as well as the financial page of *The New Yorker*, which has featured his drawings since 1999.

He was asked to illustrate ads for Nike, Microsoft, The Royal Mail, MoMA and Amtrak and has created popular animations for Google.

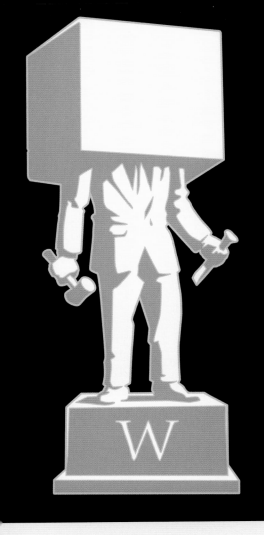

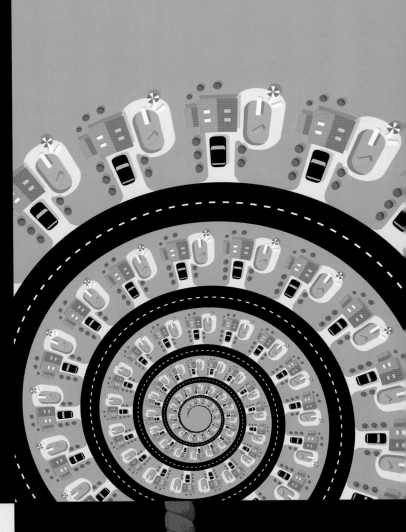

RISK

Regular Tree

Cloud Tree

Cloud-That-Actually-
Resembles-a-Car Tree

1957-Ford-Thunderbird Tree

Christoph has written and illustrated many books, among them *The Pet Dragon*, a book that teaches Chinese characters to young children, and *I LEGO N.Y.*, in which he has created ultra-abstract miniature sculptures of all things New York, from the famous to the mundane. With Nicholas Blechman, a frequent collaborator, he is the creator of the art book series 100%.

In 2008, he started Abstract City a visual blog for the website of *The New York Times*. In this very personal series he explores his obsessions with New York, pop culture, food, music and family life by using a wide range of media — from drawing with coffee on napkins, to Lego, from hand sewn voodoo puppets, to autumn leaves.

Christoph's work has garnered awards from all major design organizations, like the Art Directors Club, SPD, AIGA and American Illustration, and he has lectured at design conferences in the United States, Mexico, Europe, South Africa, Japan and Australia. At the age of 29, he became the youngest member of AGI (Alliance Graphique Internationale).

Christoph and his wife, the art historian and journalist Lisa Zeitz, have three sons. In 2008, they moved to Berlin, where Christoph continues to draw, write and animate for clients around the globe.

Ernie and Birch

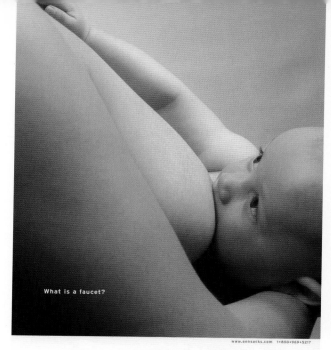

What is a faucet?

ANN SACKS
tile stone plumbing

www.annsacks.com 1•800•969•5217

After graduating from the University of Oregon, Dan spent a few years in public relations before he applied his writing talent to the advertising business. 28 years ago, Dan was a copywriter at a small Portland agency working on the Nike account with his partner, David Kennedy. Phil Knight came to Dan and David and explained that he wasn't too thrilled with the agency but appreciated their talent and wondered if they had ever thought of starting up their own agency. Shortly after that conversation, Dan and David went out on their own with one small client and three other employees. And so Wieden+Kennedy was born in 1982.

DAN**WIEDEN**

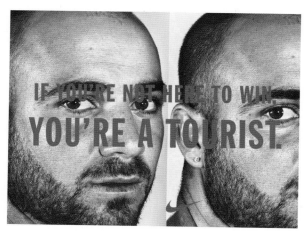

Almost three decades later the legacy is still unfolding, and the company that started with five employees now has offices in Portland, New York, London, Amsterdam, Tokyo, Shanghai and Delhi, with nearly 1,000 employees working 24 hours a day, around the world.

Its projects are as varied as branding international companies, producing sports documentaries and releasing some of Japan's best music through W+K Tokyo Lab.

In 2008, Wieden+Kennedy was chosen by *Adweek* magazine as their Global Network of the Year, further proof that Dan's vision of an independent, creatively led agency can make meaningful, progressive and challenging work for our clients. And that it can be profitable. In 2009, Wieden+Kennedy reported $2.08 billion annual capitalized billings working with a diverse client base that includes some of the world's most recognizable brands, such as Nike, Target, Levi's, ESPN, Coca-Cola, Electronic Arts, Honda, P&G and Nokia.

The growth has been nice, but that has really never been what motivates Dan. His goal was to start a different type of advertising agency. An agency where people could perform at their best without the structures and bureaucracies that plague larger agencies. An agency that wouldn't lose its creativity as it grew. Sure, Dan has won a slew of awards and attention, but deep down he is just a regular guy trying to make a difference. And being that regular guy is what our clients most appreciate and value in Dan. What really differentiates Dan is his relentless ability to dream and inspire. In an age where integrity is seldom seen in the advertising business, Dan's fight to remain independent and continue to provide a place where fellow dreamers can work has resulted in some of the best work of our time, and an environment where people and brands can both flourish.

Jessica Helfand and William Drenttel are partners at Winterhouse, a design studio in northwest Connecticut. Their work focuses on print and online publishing, educational and cultural institutions, and design programs of social impact.

They are the 2009-10 recipients of Rockefeller Foundation funding to develop a global initiative around design and social innovation; the winners of a 2010

WINTER**HOUSE**

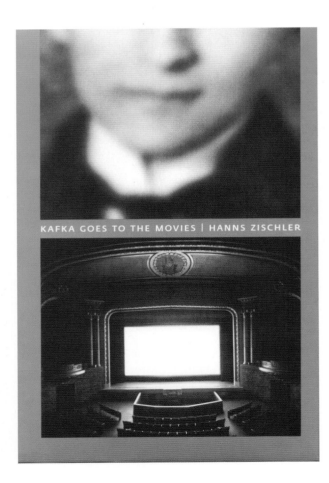

Sappi "Ideas That Matter" grant; and were appointed in 2010 as the first Henry Wolf Residents in Graphic Design at the American Academy in Rome.

They are co-founding editors of Design Observer, the leading international website for design, visual and cultural journalism online.

In 2006, they founded the Winterhouse Institute. Among its initiatives, the Institute created the AIGA Winterhouse Awards for Design Writing and Criticism (a yearly $10,000 prize for design writing). More recently, it created the Polling Place Photo Project, a national initiative to document citizen experiences at polling places, conducted during the 2006-08 election cycles.

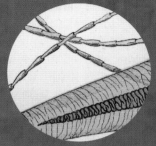

BUBONIC PLAGUE

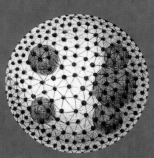

ALGAE

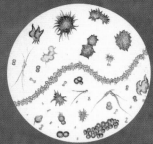

URINE

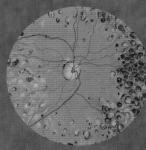

EYEBALL

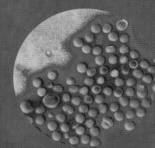

DIARRHEA

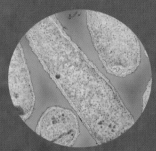

HAIR

CORK

PARASITE

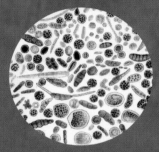

AIR SPORES

E. COLI

MONSTERS

EARTH

A BETTER WORLD BY DESIGN

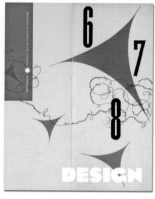

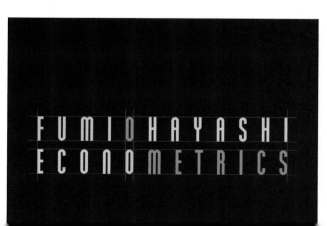

Helfand and Drenttel have been visiting critics at many design and academic programs, and have lectured internationally at AIGA Design Biennials, Andy Warhol Museum, Annenberg Center for Public Policy, Aspen Design Summit, Brno Design Biennial, Carnegie Mellon University, Cooper-Hewitt National Design Museum, Cranbrook Art Center, Indaba Design Festival, Library of Congress, Ljubljana Design Biennial, Netherlands Design Institute, San Francisco Museum of Contemporary Art, School of Visual Arts and Walker Art Center, among others.

Jessica Helfand has been senior critic in the graduate program in graphic design at Yale School of Art since 1996. She also teaches the Yale College freshman art seminar — Art 001: Studies in Visual Biography — inspired by her book, *Scrapbooks: An American History*, published by Yale University Press.

She is the author of three other books on design and cultural criticism: *Reinventing the Wheel* (2002), *Screen: Essays on Graphic Design, New Media and Visual Culture* (2001), and *Paul Rand: American Modernist* (1998). She has written for many publications including *Aperture*, *Communications Arts*, *Eye Magazine*, *Los Angeles Times Book Review*, *Print* and *The New Republic*.

In 2006, Helfand was appointed by the Postmaster General to the U.S. Citizens Stamp Advisory Committee, where she chairs the design subcommittee. She is a life fellow of the American Antiquarian Society.

Prior to founding Winterhouse, Helfand was an award-winning editorial and interaction designer, working with leading publications and newspapers. She is a graduate of Yale University, where she received a B.A. in Architectural Theory, and an M.F.A. in Graphic Design.

William Drenttel is the editorial director of Design Observer, and directs the Winterhouse Institute and its recent work at the intersection of design and social innovation.

He is the design director of Teach For All, an international initiative working towards educational equality globally. Previously, he served as the creative director of two large literary foundations, Poetry Foundation and Nextbook. He has also published and designed over 20 books under the Winterhouse imprint, many of them co-published with leading academic publishers.

He is president emeritus of the American Institute of Graphic Arts, a senior faculty fellow at Yale School of Management, and a fellow of the New York Institute of the Humanities at New York University. He has served on the boards of the Cooper-Hewitt National Design Museum, Lingua Franca, Mayo Clinic Center for Innovation, Poetry Society and Susan Sontag Foundation.

Prior to founding Winterhouse, Drenttel was president of Drenttel Doyle Partners and a senior vice president of Saatchi & Saatchi. He is a graduate of Princeton University, where he received a B.A. in Film and European Cultural Studies.

French photographer Brigitte Lacombe has built an illustrious career as a portrait photographer, as a photographer documenting films from "behind-the-scenes," and as one of the world's most recognized travel photographers.

After first serving as an apprentice in the black & white lab of Elle in Paris, she attended the Cannes Film Festival in 1975 and met actors Dustin Hoffman and Donald Sutherland, who invited her to the film sets of *Fellini's Casanova* and *All the President's Men*. Later that year, she worked On Steven Spielberg's *Close Encounters of the Third Kind*, and for seven years was the first and only staff photographer for the Lincoln Center Theater in New York.

BRIGITTE**LACOMBE**

Lacombe works with directors Martin Scorsese, Mike Nichols, Sam Mendes, Michael Haneke, David Mamet, Quentin Tarantino and Spike Jonze, on many of their films including: The Invention of Hugo Cabret, Shutter Island, The Departed ,The Aviator, Gangs of New York, Inglourious Basterds, Nine, The Road, Revolutionary Road, The Reader and Doubt.

She is also a renown travel photographer, winning the Einsenstaedt Award for travel photography in 2000. Under contract with Condé Nast Traveler magazine, for the last 25 years, her recent assignments include visits to Lebanon, Oman, Cuba, Haiti, Senegal, Egypt, Mozambique, Syria, Jordan, Bosnia, and India.

Lacombe contributes to many publications, including Vanity Fair, The New Yorker, The New York Times Magazine, Time, GQ, German Vogue, and Paris Vogue.

Her advertising clients include Prada, Hermés, Nespresso, Lancôme, Movado, Rolex, The Metropolitan Opera, HBO, Paramount Pictures, and The Weinstein Company.

Earlier this year, in support of their fight against AIDS, Lacombe directed video portraits of 30 actors and musicians for PROJECT (RED). She has produced a pair of books: "Lacombe anima | persona," her retrospective of photographs from 1975-2008 published by SteidlDangin with an essay by Frank Rich (2009), "Lacombe cinema | theater," published by Schirmer/Mosel with essays by David Mamet and Adam Gopnik (2001).

ADC **WINNERS BY CATEGORY**

There were 265 winners in total. Here the winning work is represented visually, by category.

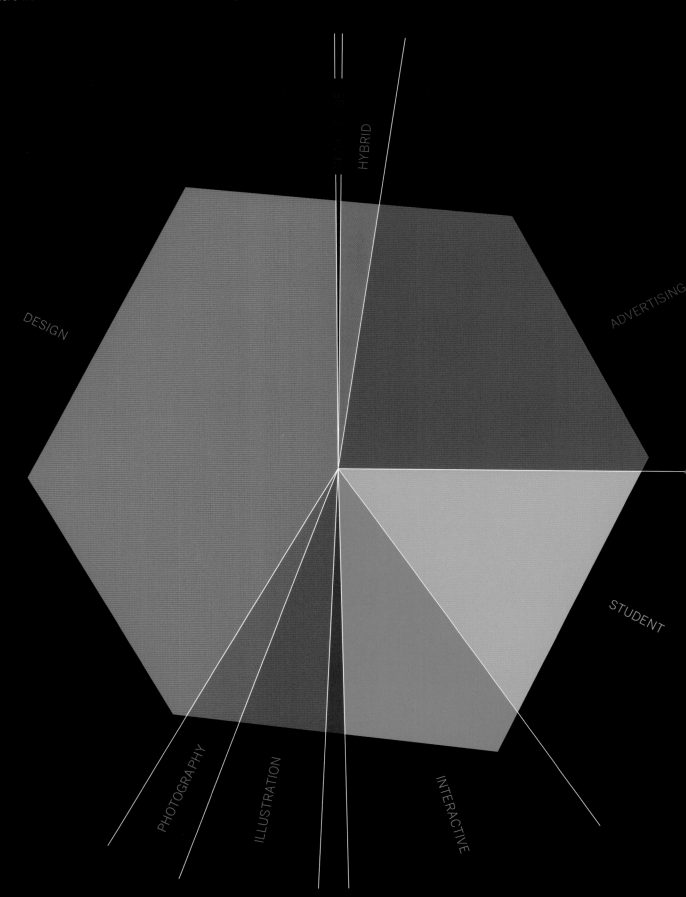

BRONZE 16% of all awards given

MERIT 24% of all awards given

GOLD 3% of all awards given

SILVER 7% of all awards given

DESIGN

It was an absolute honor to serve as the ADC Design Jury Chair for the 89th Annual Awards. It is always a fascinating and mind opening experience to see work from the world that you would not normally have the chance to see. From the latest in digital experiences to exquisite craftsmanship in traditional media, the winning is certainly a testament that design touches all parts of our lives. Taken as an ag the body of work from this and past Annual Awards demonstrates how design pivotal role in helping to shape, connect and define society as a whole. I hope th find the work on the following pages inspiring and I encourage all of you to cont support for the ADC.

- Chris C
Executive Creative Director,
ADC Design

DESIGN FIRM OF THE YEAR:
NEW YORK TIMES MAGAZINE

ADC**DESIGN JURY**

CHRIS
CAMPBELL
INTERBRAND

As executive creative director, Chris is charged with leading Interbrand's creative resources in New York and partnering with executive leadership to continue to build a network of creative excellence across North America. He also plays a key role in the firm's overall strategic planning and development.

Chris' expertise includes the development of strategic branding solutions, including corporate identity, corporate literature, marketing communications and advertising. With more than 20 years of design experience, he has created award-winning work recognized by organizations including the Art Directors Club, Communication Arts, the Advertising and Design Club of Canada, the American Institute of Graphic Arts, and ReBrand 100.

Chris' work is part of the permanent design collection of the Smithsonian Institution's National Museum of Design in New York. He has also served on the board of directors for The Society of Graphic Designers of Canada.

Chris is an honors graduate of the Communication and Design program at the Ontario College of Art and Design, Toronto.

Chris has developed creative solutions for clients such as: AT&T, TD Ameritrade, Microsoft, McDonald's, Xerox, eBay, Thomson Reuters and Victoria's Secret, among others.

VANESSA ECKSTEIN
BLOK

Throughout her career, Vanessa Eckstein has found herself drawn to thinking and creating across genres and borders. Through BLOK, her design studio headquartered in Mexico City, she has worked on projects for Nike, Pepsi, The Miami Art Museum, Museo Tamayo, Club Monaco, Roots and UNICEF among others. Vanessa has recently turned her focus to two new initiatives: the launch of a children's publishing house and a public awareness effort dedicated to social, political and environmental issues around the world.

The recipient of numerous awards, such as the Clio, The Art Directors Club of New York, The Type Directors Club of Tokyo, The One Show, ID, Brno Biennale of Graphic Design Russia, Trnava Poster Triennial (Slovakia), The Advertising & Design Club of Canada, and the Type Directors Club, among many others. BLOK´s work is featured in the permanent collection of the Royal Ontario Museum of Canada.

SEAN SAYLOR
MTV INTERNATIONAL

Sean Saylor is vice president of creative for MTV and VH1 Latin America, Tr3s and MTV International. In this role, Saylor is responsible for managing the creative vision, services and promotional strategies across all brands.

In 2008, Saylor played a key role in the development of MTV International's World Design Studio (WDS) based in Argentina. Under his leadership, the WDS has produced ground breaking campaigns for shows including *16 & Pregnant* and the 2009 MTV Europe Music Awards. This year, his team was also recognized by *The New York Times* for their innovative global campaign tied to the MTV US hit Jersey Shore.

Most recently, Saylor also served as executive producer of the music video "Wavin' Flag", Coke's 2010 World Cup anthem. As creative director, Saylor's artistic talents also graced the cover of the Latin Grammy® winning Alejandro Sanz MTV Unplugged album.

Previously, Saylor was art director for MTVN Latin America.

WEBSITE BEHANCE.NET/SAYLORS

MICHELLE DOUGHERTY
IMAGINARY FORCES

Born in Mexico City and raised in California, Michelle Dougherty started painting at an early age. She attended Art Center College of Design in Pasadena, California, earning a degree in graphic design where her love for design evolved to include motion and film.

As a director at Imaginary Forces, Michelle has enjoyed the opportunity to collaborate with the leading artists, animators, directors and producers in the industry.

She has designed and directed campaigns for Microsoft, Pontiac, Lexus, Dove, and Nokia, and main title sequences for *The Legend of Zorro* and *The Number 23.* She earned an Emmy nomination and her work has been recognized by the Art Director's Club, The One Show and the AIGA. She has been featured in numerous publications including *IdN, HOW, Communication Arts, I.D. Magazine,* and *Creativity.*

WEBSITE IMAGINARYFORCES.COM

OMAR VULPINARI
FABRICA

Since 1998, Omar Vulpinari has been head and creative director of Visual Communication at Fabrica, the Benetton Group communication research center in Treviso, Italy.

Directing advertising and communication design projects for the United Nations, Witness, Amnesty International, Reporters Without Borders, United Colors of Benetton, Coca-Cola, Istituto Luce, Porsche, Vespa, *The New Yorker* and Fox International. Fabrica's visual communication work under his direction has been featured in major international media and dedicated exhibitions at the Centre Pompidou in Paris, La Triennale in Milan, the Shanghai Art Museum, the Shiodomeitalia Creative Centre in Tokyo and the MAK Vienna.

Recently winner of the Graphis Platinum G advertising award for the UNWHO-UNICEF Global Child Injury Prevention campaign. He is advisor for the United Nations World Health Organization and Regional Ambassador for INDEX: Design to Improve Life Awards.

Vulpinari teaches Communication Design at the IUAV University of Venice in San Marino. He is currently vice president of Icograda-International Council of Graphic Design.

TODD ST. JOHN
HUNTERGATHERER

Todd St. John is an artist, designer and animator living in New York City. St. John produces both commercial and experimental work through HunterGatherer, the studio/workshop that he founded in 2000. He has created animations, illustrations and graphics for everyone from MTV to Money Mark to *The New York Times*. In 1994, he was included in the 2003 Cooper-Hewitt National Design Triennial and was nominated in 2008 for an Emmy for the short "Circle Squared". In addition to his studio, he also teaches as a graduate critic at the Yale School of Art.

KATIE JAIN
HATCH DESIGN

Katie Jain is a co-founder and creative director of Hatch Design, a San Francisco based graphic design firm centered on one powerful idea: the best design is honest, hands-on and human. Since opening their doors, Hatch has created award-winning identity, packaging, collateral, advertising, promotional and interactive design for companies including: Apple, Coca-Cola, GE, Johnson & Johnson, Harrah's, Hilton, Starbucks and many others.

Katie was raised in the Pacific Northwest, studied design at the California College of Arts and Crafts, and then began her career at Templin Brink Design, where she created work for clients such as American Eagle Outfitters, MTV, Peace Cereal, Quiksilver and Williams-Sonoma. Her work has been recognized for excellence in virtually every major design competition around the world. In 2008, she and the Hatch team successfully launched their first "hatchling," JAQK Cellars, a wine brand born out of a passion for design.

TWITTER HATCHDESIGN
WEBSITE HATCHSF.COM

JOHN MICHAEL BOLING
RHIZOME

John Michael Boling is the Associate Director of Rhizome, a new media arts organization based in the New Museum in New York. Boling, a leading figure in creative technology and internet art, was a founding member of the internet surfing club Nasty Nets, (http://www.nastynets.com) and creator of the infamous website 53 o's (http://www.gooooooooooooooooooooooooooooooooooooooooooooooooooooogle.com).

His work has been shown internationally at institutions, festivals and DIY spaces, including The New Museum of Contemporary Art in New York, Galerie West in Den Haag, Seventeen Gallery in London, and the Sundance Film Festival.

TIM HETHERINGTON
PHOTOGRAPHER

Tim Hetherington is a photographer and filmmaker who has reported on conflict and social issues since the 1990s. His diverse work has ranged from digital projections at the Institute of Contemporary Art in London, to fly-poster exhibitions in Lagos, to handheld device downloads. His awards include a Fellowship from the National Endowment for Science, Technology and the Arts (2000-04), the World Press Photo of the Year (2008), and the Grand Jury Prize at the 2010 Sundance Film Festival (for the documentary *Restrepo*, co-directed with Sebastian Junger). He lives in New York and is a contributing photographer for *Vanity Fair* magazine.

WEBSITE TIMHETHERINGTON.COM

NATE WILLIAMS
ILLUSTRATOR/ARTIST

Nate Williams has worked extensively in various facets of the illustration and design industry with a wide variety of clients. His hand drawn lettering and illustration work has been geared to both adults and children and has appeared in magazines, advertising, publishing, music, fashion, textiles, home decor, merchandise, posters and newspapers. His work has been published, exhibited or reviewed in the United States, Europe, South American and Asia.

Nate has worked with the charity organization Art with Heart, which unites volunteers from the arts to serve children in crisis by empowering them through self-expressionand creativity. His illustration has been honored by American Illustration, Communication Arts, Society of Illustrators, The Type Director's Club, The ADDY'S and SILA. In addition to his illustration and fine art work, Nate conceived, designed, programmed, launched and maintains the highly successful illustration community portals http://www.illustrationmundo.com and http://www.letterplayground.com.

TWITTER N8W
WEBSITE N8W.COM
WEBSITE ALEXANDERBLUE.COM

DIRK
BARNETT
MAXIM

Dirk Barnett is currently the creative director of *Maxim* magazine. Previously, he was the creative director for *Blender* magazine, *Key*, *The New York Times Real Estate Magazine*, *Play*, *The New York Times Sports Magazine*, *Premiere* magazine and *Popular Science*. Barnett's work has been recognized by the American Institute of Graphic Arts, The American Society of Magazine Editors, the Type Director's Club, the Art Directors Club, British Design and Art Direction Awards, and the Society of Publication Designers.

He teaches at the School of Visual Arts and is currently the vice president of the Society of Publication Designers. He lives in New York City with his wife and son.

WEBSITE DIRKBARNETT.COM

LOUIS
GAGNON
PAPRIKA

Louis Gagnon co-founded Paprika in 1991. Since then, Gagnon's relentless pursuit of essence, refinement and beauty has racked up more than 500 national and international awards for the Montreal design firm.

Gagnon's style is characterized by stunning graphic themes balanced by a clear rationality that fuses innate elegance to intelligent utility.

Paprika was the first North American agency featured in a *Design & Designers* book, a prestigious collection that profiles the most influential figures in international design (Pyramyd Publishers, Paris). And there is a show in Paris (spring 2010) that will be devoted to the Paprika oeuvre.

Louis Gagnon has taught at the École de Design at the Université du Québec à Montréal since 2005.

TWITTER PAPRIKAMONTREAL
WEBSITE PAPRIKA.COM

ROBERT
MURDOCK
METHOD

As chief creative officer, Robert is charged with shaping the creative vision for Method's studios and clients. Working closely with the Experience Design team, he's responsible for crafting much of Method's groundbreaking work across brand and digital experiences for some of the most respected brands worldwide. Robert's holistic approach to design and innovation has allowed him to work on projects ranging from interface design for products, brand identity and communications design to interactive design for web and evolving platforms.

Over the course of his tenure at Method, Robert has served as creative director on work for Autodesk, TED, Nokia, Nike and Comcast. Most recently, he's been working with Nokia to redefine their approach to creating new services and engaging with customers across platforms and devices. Robert believes in a collaborative approach, creating work that engages and inspires, but also addresses business objectives and moves clients toward their goals. He believes that exceptional design has the ability to meet these objectives, transcend the ephemeral, and make a meaningful connection with its audience.

Robert boasts more than 15 years of brand and interactive experience. Prior to Method, he founded Coato, a small design studio focusing on innovative skunk-works User Interface prototypes for Automotive and Consumer Electronics clients across the United States, Asia and Europe. During his time at Coato, several of the team's concepts were converted from visions of the future into fully developed products still being used today.

Early on, Robert broadened his expertise at several interdisciplinary studios, including Fitch and Addwater, where he worked with a variety of brands, from Levis to Sun Microsystems.

CARIN
GOLDBERG
CARIN GOLDBERG DESIGN

GARRICK
HAMM
WILLIAMS MURRAY HAMM

Carin Goldberg was born in New York City and studied at the Cooper Union School of Art. She began her career as a staff designer at CBS Television, CBS Records and Atlantic Records before establishing her own firm, Carin Goldberg Design, in 1982. Over the following two decades Carin designed hundreds of book jackets for all the major American publishing houses. In recent years, her image, making has expanded to publication design, brand consulting and editorial illustration.

Carin is one of the first recipients of the Art Directors Club GrandMasters Award for Excellence in Education (2008), and in September 2009, she was awarded the prestigious AIGA Gold Medal.

In 2009, she received The Cooper Union President's Citation for "exceptional contributions to the field of graphic design…" In 2008, Carin completed a two-year term as president of the New York Chapter of the American Institute of Graphic Arts. She is a member of the Alliance Graphique Internationale and served on its board of directors from 2006-09.

Carin has taught Third Year Typography and Senior Portfolio at the School of Visual Arts in New York City for 27 years.

WEBSITE CARINGOLDBERG.COM

A graduate of Somerset College of Art in 1989, Garrick joined Williams and Murray in 1999 after a chance meeting at a wedding reception and has never looked back.

Amongst other projects, he has been the creative cirector on the WMH's re-launch of Fortnum & Mason's packaging and identity and, more recently, helped launch Jamie Oliver's new Recipease store in Clapham, which picked up a Gold Lion at Cannes.

As a former president of D&AD and a Fellow of the RSA, Garrick has a keen interest in design education, facilitating workshops in both the United Kingdom and Asia. He has been profiled in the *Financial Times* and *The Observer*. In his spare time, Garrick is an avid filmmaker; his first short film, "Lucky Numbers," was nominated at the Chlotrudis Awards, United States. His second, "The Man Who Married Himself," starred Richard E Grant and Emilia Fox was screened at BAFTA earlier this year.

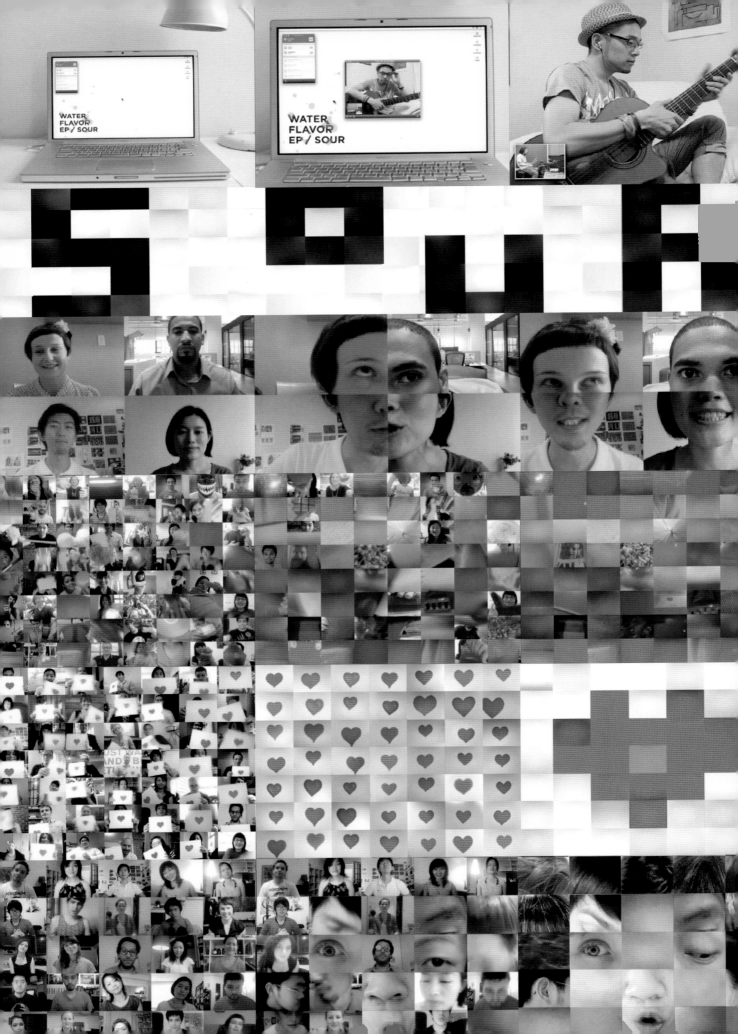

GOLD | TELEVISION AND CINEMA DESIGN |
MUSIC VIDEO

SOUR'S 'HIBI NO NEIRO' (TONE OF EVERYDAY)
MASA & HAL & MAGICO & MASAYOSHI

**MASA
& HAL**

**MAGICO
& MASAYOSHI**

Director Masashi Kawamura, Hal Kirkland, Magico Nakamura,
Masayoshi Nakamura
Music Sour
Agency Masashi & Hal & Magico & Masayoshi
Client Zealot Co.,Ltd, Neutral Nine Records

Sour's "Hibi No Niero" is a music video that is filmed entirely via
webcams. The 80 plus cast members were sourced from the
band's international fan base. Each animation sequence relies
on the precise choreography of up to 64 people at a time, each
webcam screen representing one pixel in a larger image. With a
production budget of $0, the entire production relied solely on the
enthusiasm and time donated by the fans themselves.

Country United States

Additional Awards

⬡ **ADVERTISING BRONZE**
NON - BROADCAST MEDIA

GOLD | CORPORATE AND PROMOTIONAL DESIGN |
IDENTITY PROGRAM

EFFP
IDENTITY
PURPOSE

**LOUISA
PHILLIPS**

**ADAM
BROWNE**

**STUART
YOUNGS**

**PAUL
FELTON**

Creative Director Stuart Youngs, Rob Howsam
Art Director Adam Browne
Designer Paul Felton
Project Manager Louisa Phillips
Agency Purpose
Client EFFP (English Farming and Food Partnerships)

EFFP is a consultancy for the agricultural and food industries.
They strive to build bonds between these two industries, to make
both more efficient. EFFP needed help to differentiate themselves
from other consultants in the sector. The resulting black and
white identity is bold, pioneering, confident and revolutionary, all
attributes to which EFFP aspires. We have created a full suite of
stationery and marketing materials, including corporate leaflets,
folders, a website and their magazine, *VIEW*.

Country United Kingdom

Additional Awards:

● **DESIGN BRONZE**
TRADE MAGAZINE | FULL ISSUE

VIEW

Conversations for a Smarter Planet: 11 in a Series

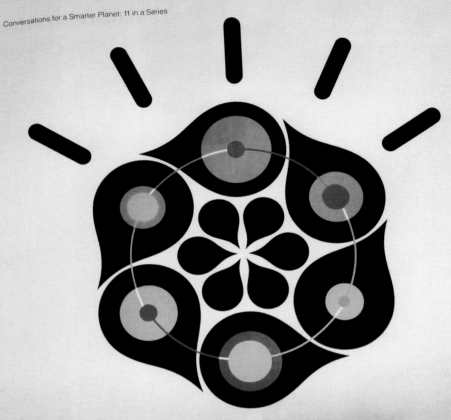

Smarter resources to fuel a smarter planet.

Advances in science have made it possible to envision a planet that's powered in very new ways, creating electricity from the sun, the wind, waves, the atom or some combination thereof. But we also know it won't happen overnight—not profitably or on a global scale. For decades to come, we'll need to continue extracting energy stored in matter lying far beneath the Earth's surface—also known as fossil fuels.

In fact, in the near term we'll need to extract more oil and natural gas than ever before. Projections show energy consumption increasing by 50% in the next 25 years. As we move toward a renewable future, we need to shape our hydrocarbon present in ways that are more efficient, affordable and protective of the environment.

Today, we can only extract about one-third of the oil in an existing reserve, leaving billions of barrels in reservoirs. That's unfortunate, since it can cost $100 million to drill a single new well. Just a 1.5% increase in recovery from existing wells would yield enough oil for half a year's global consumption, lowering the cost of fuel—which would mean lower prices for travel, homes, food and consumer products.

Put simply, we need smarter oil and gas fields. And that means gathering and managing real-time data from across the entire production stream, in vast quantities. One oil field alone can generate the equivalent of 200 DVDs' worth of data per day. Making sense of all this information is critical for better decision making—about exploration, production and management.

Smarter exploration means integrating and processing geophysical and other relevant data to develop 3-D models of reservoirs. It means finding previously inaccessible oil and gas reserves embedded beneath difficult terrain or the deepest ocean waters. Repsol, in partnership with scientists from around the world, is using advanced seismic imaging technology from IBM to reveal oil and gas deposits that traditional imaging techniques can't see.

Smarter production means capturing information about the volume and quality of oil and gas reservoirs before a new well is drilled. It means minimizing the drilling footprint and exploration risk while improving the safety and reliability of operations. One U.S.-based firm is using seismic data and rock physics inversion to create a comprehensive, integrated view of potential resources.

Smarter reservoir management makes use of sensors embedded across pipes, pumps and an entire field, generating data that can be compared against historical trends and applied to help optimize well performance. An intelligent field can even monitor itself while being run by a team of "virtual" experts around the world. Norway's StatoilHydro is linking real-time sensing capabilities in the field with collaborative analytics systems that increase the recovery rates of its oil and gas fields.

And being smarter is not just about management. It's also about anticipating problems before they occur—and, in some cases, adjusting automatically to prevent them, thereby reducing the risks to people and the environment. We have the ability today to infuse the system by which we find, extract and produce our energy resources with intelligence, and to make the most of every single drop.

Let's build a smarter planet. Join us and see what others are thinking at **ibm.com**/think

THINK

SMARTER PLANET
OFFICE - JASON SCHULTE DESIGN

JASON SCHULTE

Vice Chairman, Creative Chris Wall (Ogilvy & Mather)
Executive Creative Director Susan Westre (Ogilvy & Mather)
Creative Director Greg Ketchum, Tom Godici (Ogilvy & Mather)
Art Director Jason Schulte (Office), Tom Godici, Lew Willig (Ogilvy & Mather)
Copywriter Greg Ketchum, Rob Jamieson, Mike Wing (Ogilvy & Mather)
Designer Rob Alexander, Will Ecke, Jason Schulte
Agency Office - Jason Schulte Design
Client Ogilvy & Mather, NYC

We created a visual vocabulary for IBM's "Smarter Planet" campaign, which was based on a vision to help solve the world's biggest problems.

The campaign featured essays describing thought-provoking solutions for dozens of issues — from reducing road traffic and city crime, to improving food safety and local water supplies. Our challenge was to create a bold graphic language that illustrated these complicated solutions in a simple, approachable, but still visually arresting and distinctive way that could be understood around the world.

We were inspired by the creative vision that designers Eliot Noyes and Paul Rand developed for IBM in 1955, when they defined how the "most advanced electronics company" should look. Based on those same principles, we developed a visual vocabulary defined by IBM's spirit and aspiration. The icons are as bold, modern, provocative and relevant as the ideas they represent.

Country United States

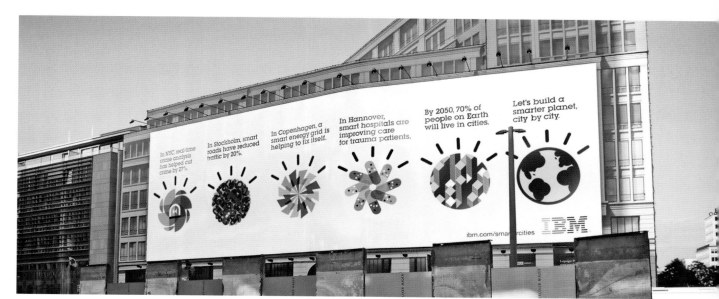

GOLD | ENVIRONMENTAL DESIGN |
WAYFINDING SYSTEMS, SIGNAGE, DIRECTORY

THE COOPER UNION
PENTAGRAM

ABBOTT
MILLER

Art Director Abbott Miller
Designer Abbott Miller, Jeremy Hoffman, Brian Raby, Susan Brzozowski
Photographer Chuck Choi, Iwan Baan
Agency Pentagram Design
Client The Cooper Union

In September 2009, The Cooper Union for the Advancement of Science and Art opened its new Thom Mayne-designed academic building in New York's East Village. Abbott Miller and his team at Pentagram developed a unique program of environmental graphics for the building that is fully integrated with the architecture. The signage typography is set in the font Foundry Gridnik, chosen for its resemblance to lettering on the façade of the school's original 1859 building. The typography has been physicalized in different ways, engaging multiple surfaces of the three-dimensional signs, appearing extruded across corners, or cut, extended and dragged through the material. The building canopy features optically extruded lettering that appears correct when seen in strict elevation, but distorts as the profile of the letter is dragged backwards in space.

Country United States

GOLD | PHOTGRAPHY |
MAGAZINE EDITORIAL

OBAMA'S PEOPLE
THE NEW YORK TIMES MAGAZINE

**NADAV
KANDER**

**GAIL
BICHLER**

**AREM
DUPLESSIS**

**KATHY
RYAN**

Creative Director Arem Duplessis
Art Director Gail Bichler
Designer Leo Jung, Hillary Greenbaum
Photographer Nadav Kander
Director Kathy Ryan
Editor Gerry Marzorati
Photo Editor Kira Pollack, Kathy Ryan
Publisher The New York Times
Agency The New York Times Magazine

Country United States

GOLD | PHOTGRAPHY |
MAGAZINE EDITORIAL

GREAT
PERFORMERS
THE NEW YORK TIMES MAGAZINE

**PAOLO
PELLEGRIN**

**AREM
DUPLESSIS**

**GAIL
BICHLER**

**KATHY
RYAN**

Creative Director Arem Duplessis
Art Director Gail Bichler
Designer Leo Jung
Photographer Paolo Pellegrin
Director Kathy Ryan
Editor Gerry Marzorati
Photo Editor Kira Pollack
Publisher The New York Times
Agency The New York Times Magazine

Country United States

SILVER | TELEVISION AND CINEMA DESIGN |
ANIMATION

SHAN
SHUI
JWT SHANGHAI

**LILLIE
ZHONG**

**RAFAEL
FREIRE**

Creative Director Sheung Yan Lo, Yang Yeo
Art Director Lillie Zhong, Yang Yong Liang
Copywriter Jacqueline Ye, Rafael Freire
Designer Sean Tang
Illustrator, Photographer Yang Yong Liang
Print Production Liza Law, Joseph Yu, Tao Shen
Account Service Betty Tsai
Agency JWT Shanghai
Client CEPF

Country China

SILVER | EDITORIAL DESIGN |
SPECIAL TRADE BOOK

THE END
PILOT NY

**DAVID
MEREDITH**

Art Director David Meredith
Copywriter Walter Thomas
Designer David Meredith
Photographer Rodney Smith
Producer Kim Blanchette
Publisher Blanchette Press, Seven Editions
Agency Pilot NY
Client Rodney Smith

The End is a visual and literary play on the surreal notion of photographic reality. The images are that of photographer, Rodney Smith, who shoots entirely with film in the middle of this digital age. The camera's point-of-view, combined with that of the photographer, brings a sense of whimsy and playfulness to the seemingly impossible pictures. *The End* further plays on this thread by ending with the beginning.

Country United States

SILVER | EDITORIAL DESIGN |LIMITED EDITION,
PRIVATE PRESS or SPECIAL FORMAT BOOK

JOURNEY
TO SOUTH
ADK JAPAN

JIRO
AOKI

Creative Director, Illustrator, Editor Jiro Aoki
Art Director Jiro Aoki, Yasuo Enokida
Copywriter Kayano Shinonome
Designer Yasuo Enokida, Miyuki Shinohara
Photographer Oida Hideo
Producer Toshihiro Kaneyuki, Shunsuke Kaga
Publisher WWD
Agency ADK JAPAN
Client Levi Strauss Japan

Our objective was to push the product to highly fashion-
conscious consumers on the Internet, while considering capital
outlay costs. Since the goal was to create a buzz within the
Internet community, we looked into strategies that would offer
the antithetical elements of reality and scarcity value. The brand
book was made available at those bookstores frequented by
Japan's most fashion-conscious customers in a limited edition
of 30 copies. The B1 pages were used un-cut to give a roughness
to the finish. The choice of the timeworn silkscreen printing
process was intended to convey the timelessness and dynamism
of denim, with its classic-but-new image, and to give the product
premium as a work of art. We succeeded in getting exposure on
29 different media, far higher than the 16 achieved through TV
commercials that were aired the previous autumn. There was
also a whopping approximately 2.5-fold increase in traffic through
the brand's official website.

Country Japan

SILVER | CORPORATE AND PROMOTIONAL DESIGN |
ANNUAL REPORT

BORALEX 2008
ANNUAL REPORT
PAPRIKA

**RENÉ
CLÉMENT**   **LOUIS
GAGNON**

Creative Director Louis Gagnon
Art Director René Clément
Copywriter Lefebvre Communications Financière Inc.
Designer René Clément
Photographer Monic Richard, Raphaël Helle, Boralex
Director Jean Doyon
Agency Paprika
Client Boralex

Boralex is a private electricity producer. The company awarded
us the mandate of creating an annual report reflecting their
dynamism and expertise in renewable energy (wind power,
hydroelectricity and wood residue energy).

We created a simple black and white grid with a twist; colored
pages that are binded at different angles, suggesting the rotary
motion of a wind turbine.

Country Canada

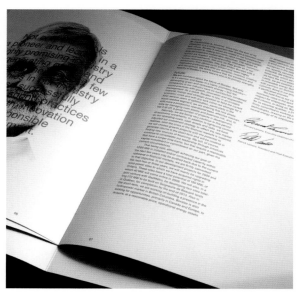

RSD

2008
Report on Sustainable
Development

Cascades

GREEN BY NATURE

CASCADES' 2008 REPORT ON SUSTAINABLE DEVELOPMENT
PAPRIKA

SÉBASTIEN BISSON   **LOUIS GAGNON**

Creative Director Louis Gagnon
Art Director, Designer Sébastien Bisson
Copywriter Cascades Communication Department
Photographer Guillaume Simoneau, Monic Richard, Sylvie-Diane Rhéault, Martin Morissette, Marcel Lefebvre
Director Jean Doyon
Agency Paprika
Client Cascades

Resource reusability has been basic to Cascades since it was founded in 1964. The report, which is distributed internally to shareholders, business partners and the environmental sector, should feature design that strongly reflects its published content.

We were asked to graphically represent Cascades' commitment to a smaller ecological footprint. We emphasized three axes of sustainable development: environment, society and the economy. Each has a section with a distinct color and page width, which makes the document easy to browse. The report is printed in two colors with vegetable-based inks, and on experimental environmental paper produced by Cascades. Sustainable development is part of the company's DNA, so we had to design a communications tool with more environmentally friendly materials. It was important both to improve functionality and reduce waste. A good example is the paperboard cover that allowed it to be distributed without extra wrapping.

Country Canada

WE'RE WITH STUPID.

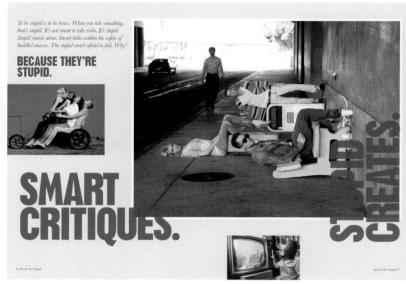

To be stupid is to be brave. When you risk something, that's stupid. It's not smart to take risks. It's stupid. Stupid stands alone. Smart hides within the safety of huddled masses. The stupid aren't afraid to fail. Why?

BECAUSE THEY'RE STUPID.

SMART CRITIQUES. STUPID CREATES.

SILVER | CORPORATE AND PROMOTIONAL DESIGN | BOOKLET or BROCHURE

BE STUPID.
ANOMALY COMMUNICATIONS

CHRIS WHALLEY

Head of Operations Chris Whalley
Executive Creative Director Mike Byrne
Creative Director Kevin Lyons
Art Director Ian Toombs, Andrea Gustafson, Coral Garvey
Copywriter Sean McLaughlin
Agency Anomaly Communications
Client Diesel

Stupid is a wonderful thing. It's a way of life. It's how we, Diesel, think you should love. The world would be a much happier place if we were all a bit more stupid. Stupid is not advertising; it's a movement. And this is the manifesto of stupid – delivered to the whole world as a big, ridiculous oversized bible in every Diesel store across the globe.

Country United States

BE STUPID.

DIESEL
FOR SUCCESSFUL LIVING

SILVER | CORPORATE AND PROMOTIONAL DESIGN |
IDENTITY PROGRAM

THE NATURAL FERMENTATION, HOMEMADE BAKERY, DAICHI NO MI
ANOMALY COMMUNICATIONS

YUICHI MUTO

Creative Director, Copywriter Yuichi Muto
Art Director Yumiko Yasuda
Designer, Illustrator Tomohiro Okazaki, Maya Matsumoto
Production Company ayrcreative
Agency ayrcreative
Client Daichi no Mi

The natural fermentation, homemade bakery, Daichi no Mi:
A bakery devoted to making each item by hand, and with loving care.

Even our posters, pamphlet, calendar and paper bags are handmade, using a sheet-by-sheet mimeograph printing method. There, we explain the Daichi no Mi dedication to baking in easy-to-understand terms for children and adults alike. We believe the posters, pamphlet, calendar and paper bags help convey to our customers our great passion for genuine, homemade quality.

Country Japan

パンのお父さん

パンのお母さん

天然酵母の手づくりパン　大地の実

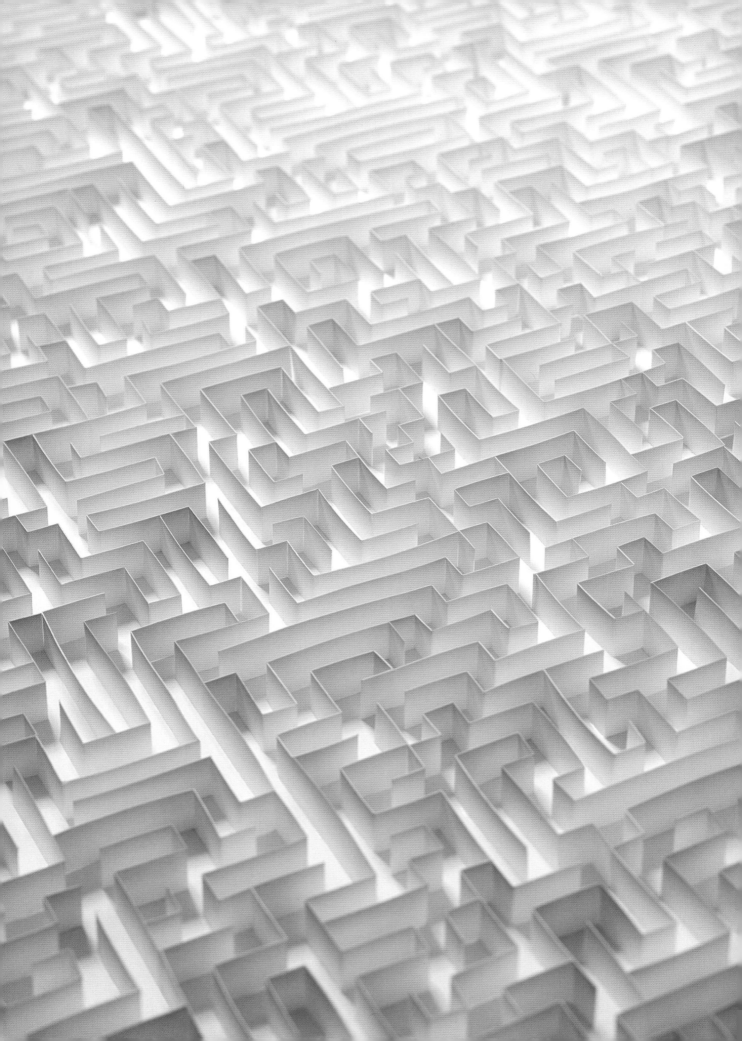

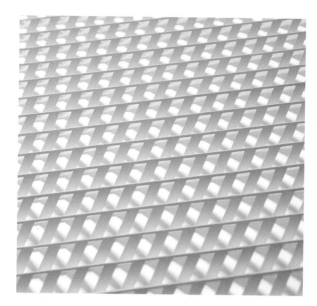

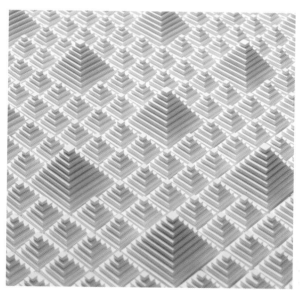

SILVER | POSTER DESIGN | PROMOTIONAL

CUTTER ART OF OLFA
DENTSU INC.

HIDETO YAGI

Creative Director Yu Sato
Art Director Hideto Yagi
Designer Kentaro Kasahara, Masaru Ooba, Keiji Isobe
Photographer Shinichi Masumoto
Director Kentaro Kasahara
Editor Ryuji Tomonaga
Agency Dentsu Inc. Tokyo/Ad Dentsu Osaka Inc.
Client OLFA Corporation

Brief:
Executive the act of cutting paper in a free and creative manner. Present the product not merely as a tool for cutting, but as one for creation.

Solution:
We challenged how far we could go in transforming paper and polystyrene board into art with a single Olfa paper cutter. The act of cutting straight lines, which is what a cutter does best, was repeated over and over to create geometrical patterns. We spent an entire year cutting paper. The paper cutter actually used in the process is laid out in the lower white space of the poster. In order to highlight the product name, OLFA = Snap-Off Blade, each poster shows a cutter with a blade snapped off.

Country Japan

SILVER | POSTER DESIGN |
PUBLIC SERVICE or NON-PROFIT

GLOBAL
WARMING
LEO LIN DESIGN

**CHUN-LIANG
LEO LIN**

Art Director, Designer Leo Lin
Production Company Leo Lin Design
Client TPDA

Country Taiwan, ROC

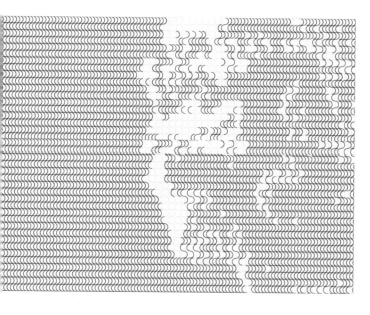

GRAPHIC TRIAL 2009, REPETITION ON SURFACE
DRAFT CO., LTD.

RYOSUKE UEHARA

Art Director Ryosuke Uehara
Designer Aya Iida
Agency DRAFT Co., Ltd.
Client Toppan Printing Co., Ltd.

These posters are designed for a poster exhibition featuring printing technique, held by Toppan Printing Co., Ltd. in Tokyo. I attempted to express the images of human beings with units of a simple pattern made of several dots. The repetition of the unit shows the graphic images and also the humanity of the motif. And I also attempted to express depth using printing techniques such as a varnish, white ink and silver ink. I am really grateful to Toppan Printing for its help.

Country Japan

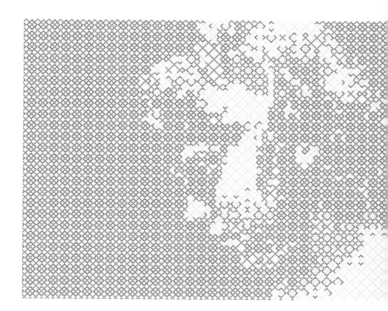

ELYJAH:
PLANET, PLANET.
ZWÖLF

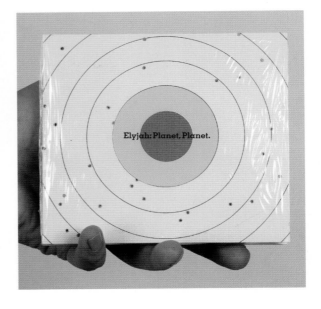

**BJÖRN
WIEDE**

**STEFAN
GUZY**

Designer Stefan Guzy, Björn Wiede
Photographer Norman Konrad
Producer Kieran Joel, Marcus Lisse
Styling Leena Zimmermann
Agency Zwölf
Client Klimbim Records

The songs on Elyjah's debut album are both playful and
atmospheric. It leaves a lasting impression. To ensure that the
message was conveyed to the customer, we fired pellets at
all 2,000 covers. They circle like planets around a fixed point.
Returning to a time in which men had morals in their hearts and
cloth handkerchiefs in their trouser pockets, we put the band in
Herr von Eden suits and then printed the large-format photos by
hand. Typographically, we continued this theme with two
typefaces from that time period: Memphis, from Emil Rudolph
Weiß (1929) and the Wieynck Gotisch from Heinrich Wieynck
(1926) were put into use on an old Heidelberg printing machine.

Country Germany

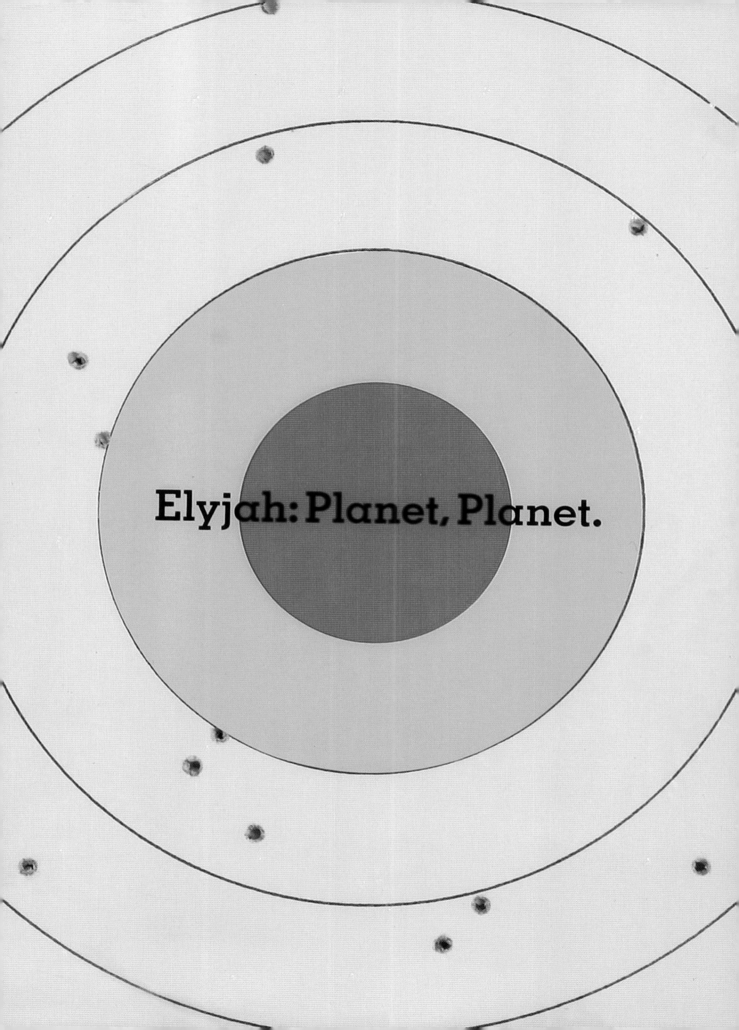

Elyjah: Planet, Planet.

SILVER | ENVIRONMENTAL DESIGN |
WAYFINDING SYSTEMS, SIGNAGE, DIRECTORY

"LE MUSÉE GRANDIT"
(THE MUSEUM IS GROWING)
PAPRIKA

RENÉ
CLÉMENT   **LOUIS**
                              GAGNON

Creative Director Louis Gagnon
Art Director René Clément
Designer René Clément, François-Xavier St-Georges
Director Jean Doyon
Agency Paprika
Client Montreal Museum of Fine Arts

Under the signature "Le Musée grandit" (The Museum is growing), we produced temporary signage for the Montreal Museum of Fine Arts to hide construction areas inside and out. The project's name speaks to both the expansion of Museum space and improved services (a concert hall and new galleries will open in a fourth pavilion).

With yellow, one of the Museum's corporate colors, as a thematic link, we used barricade tape—a fixture in the building industry—to explore the institution's permanent collection in relation to the ongoing construction, as well as sounds and noises connected to this world.

Country Canada

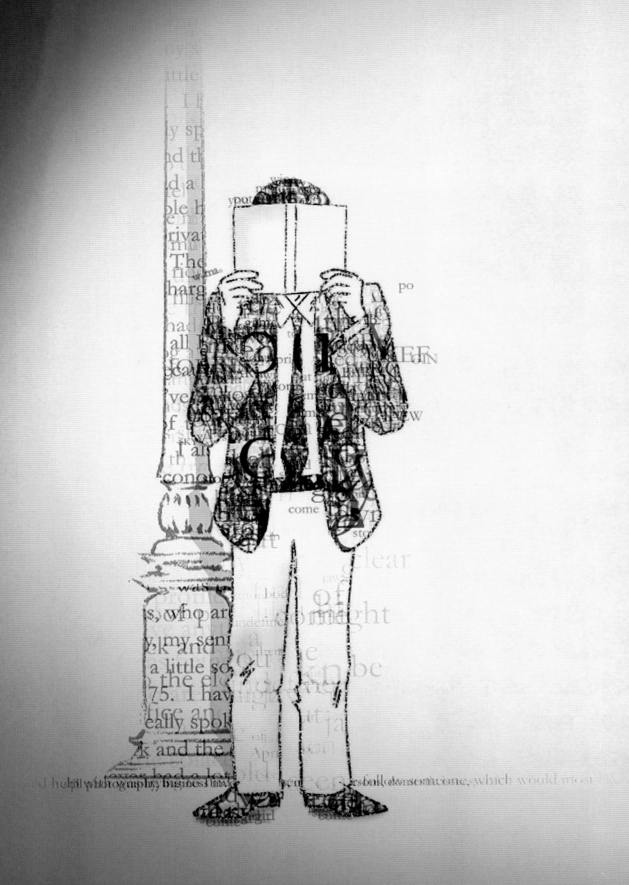

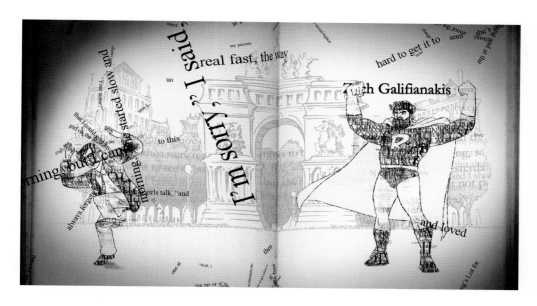

SILVER | TELEVISION AND CINEMA DESIGN |
IDENTITIES, OPENINGS, TEASERS

BORED
TO DEATH
CURIOUS PICTURES

TOM
BARHAM

Designer, Director Tom Barham
Editor Nicole Turney
Head of Production John Cline
Executive Producer Mary Knox
Producer Paul Schneider
Agency Producer Anna Dokoza, Brad Carpenter
Production Company, Agency Curious Pictures
Client Dakota Pictures

The idea for the "Bored to Death" title sequence was literally to create a metafictional world by placing the protagonist, a writer, in a world of his imagination built with his own words.

To do this we combined traditional animation with after effects and 3-D to create characters and backgrounds that were comprised of the very text used in the original *McSweeney*'s short story. Each character is composed of words and phrases that delineate who they are and what they do.

A book was the logical vehicle for the opening, and flipping the pages served as the transitional device from scene to scene. Like chapters, lines from the pages assembled or revealed characters and locations with each new title.

Country United States

SILVER | TELEVISION AND CINEMA DESIGN |
IDENTITIES, OPENINGS, TEASERS

AMTV
ID'S
MTV NETWORKS

**DAVID
MCELWAINE**

CROBIN

Senior Creative Director Jeffrey Keyton, Romy Mann
Creative Director David McElwaine
Copywriter David McElwaine, Crobin
Designer, Director, Editor Crobin
Director of Photography Ed David
Animator Chris Gallagher
Producer Ross Jeffcoat
Line Producer Kimie Kimura-Heaney
Production Company MTV Design
Agency MTV Networks
Client MTV

AMTV is a six-hour block of music videos on MTV, promoted as a morning destination for viewers getting ready for the day. Since viewers were typically watching only 30-40 minutes at a time, we needed IDs that would grab their attention, add brand value and have attitude, but not in an in-your-face kind of way. With music being a vital part of our audience's morning routine, we paired pop stars with breakfast and created IDs in which MTV artists miraculously appear in people's food: Imagine half-eaten eggs that reveal Taylor Swift's face, or Lil' Wayne showing up in pancake syrup. Ultimately these IDs helped increase time spent viewing the block.

Country United States

COLUMBIA PICTURES PRESENTS

ZOMBIELAND

ABIGAIL BRESLIN

SILVER | TELEVISION AND CINEMA DESIGN |
TITLE DESIGN

ZOMBIELAND
LOGAN MEDIA

**MARIA
ESQUIVEL**

Agency Logan Media
Client Sony Pictures

Country United States

INFRASTRUCTURE!
THE NEW YORK TIMES MAGAZINE

**THOMAS
DOYLE**

**AREM
DUPLESSIS**

**GAIL
BICHLER**

**KATHY
RYAN**

Creative Director Arem Duplessis
Art Director Gail Bichler
Designer Leo Jung
Illustrator IC4 Design, Thomas Doyle
Photographer Tom Schierlitz
Director Kathy Ryan
Editor Gerry Marzorati
Photo Editor Luise Stauss
Publisher The New York Times
Agency The New York Times Magazine

Country United States

THE ARCHITECTURE ISSUE

The New York Times Magazine

JUNE 14 2009

INFRASTRUCTURE!*

*(IT'S MORE EXCITING THAN YOU THINK, ACTUALLY.)

SILVER | PHOTOGRAPHY |
MAGAZINE ADVERTISING

FURNITURE
MESSAGES
GRABARZ & PARTNER
WERBEAGENTUR GMBH

**HEIKO
NOTTER**

**OLIVER
BRKITSCH**

Executive Creative Director Ralf Heuel
Creative Director Dirk Siebenhaar, Tom Hauser
Art Director Oliver Brkitsch
Copywriter Heiko Notter
Photographer Patrice Lange
Lithographer Sven Hagmeister
Agency Grabarz & Partner Werbeagentur GmbH
Client IKEA

When it comes to working with their hands, not all people
are as talented as they would like to be. Our campaign
shows what happens when these people try to assemble
IKEA furniture by themselves anyway: shit, oops and a silent
cry for help from completely misassembled furniture. The
solution is very simple:

Next time: IKEA Assembly Service.

Country Germany

BRONZE | PHOTOGRAPHY | BOOK

TOKYO
UNTITLED
RENATO D'AGOSTIN

RENATO D'AGOSTIN

Creative Director, Copywriter Renato D'Agostin
Designer Renato D'Agostin, Greta Bizzotto
Agency Renato D'Agostin
Client MC2 Gallery

Country United States

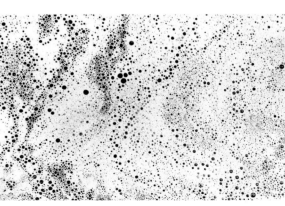

BRONZE | ILLUSTRATION |
MAGAZINE EDITORIAL

ANXIETY!
THE NEW YORK TIMES MAGAZINE

**AREM
DUPLESSIS**

**GAIL
BICHLER**

Creative Director Arem Duplessis
Art Director Gail Bichler
Copywriter, Publisher The New York Times
Designer Gail Bichler, Leslie Kwok
Illustrator Mickey Duzyj
Editor Gerry Marzorati
Agency The New York Times Magazine

Country United States

BRONZE | ILLUSTRATION |
BOOK DESIGN

VISUAL CIRCUS
NANYANG TECHNOLOGICAL UNIVERSITY

I-HSUAN CINDY WANG

Designer, Illustrator, Editor I-Hsuan Cindy Wang
Publisher Garden City Publishers
Production Company GraphicHome Advertisement & Arts Co., Ltd
Agency Nanyang Technological University
Client Garden City Publishers

This book aims to establish an intimate relationship between prints and illustration. By bringing alive the information through these techniques; I wish that the viewer will be able to have a better imagination through the interaction.

Country Singapore

BRONZE | ILLUSTRATION |
POSTER or BILLBOARD ADVERTISEMENT

LUTZKA ESCAPES
SAATCHI & SAATCHI LA

RYAN JACOBS

Executive Creative Director Mike McKay
Creative Director Ryan Jacobs
Art Director Mike Czako, Abe Cortes
Copywriter Bob Fremgen
Illustrator Tavis Coburn
Senior Print Producer Rachel Dallas-Noble
Art Producer Angee Murray
Production Company Primary Color
Agency Saatchi & Saatchi LA
Client Toyota Motor Sales U.S.A., Inc.

Toyota sponsors three athletes that perform during the Dew Action tour: a BMX vertical specialist (Jamie Bestwick), and two skaters (Bob Burnquist and Greg Lutzka.) These posters were printed so that athletes could sign something for fans who visited the Toyota booth.

The goal was to create something that didn't reek of sponsorship so that fans would hang the posters on their walls.

The posters were a big hit among a crowd that can be very "sell out" skeptical.

Country United States

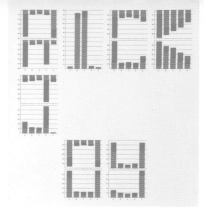

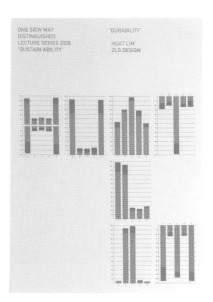

BRONZE | EDITORIAL DESIGN | BOOK JACKET |

ONG SIEW MAY DISTINGUISHED LECTURE SERIES BOOK COVER
HANSON HO

**HANSON
HO**

Creative Director, Designer Hanson Ho
Editor Erik G L'Heureux
Agency Hanson Ho
Client Department of Architecture, National University of Singapore

The Ong Siew May Distinguished Lecture Series is a series of talks by renowned architects. It is documented by this commemorative set of booklets, one book for each speaker. The talks are based on the theme of Sustainability, but we wanted to avoid the whole cliché of using the usual "go green" graphics as not all the speakers were pro-sustainability.

Finally, we used bar charts to represent the discussion of Sustainability, since the subject is so quantifiable and statistical. Much to my delight, the bar charts also doubled up as type that could be used to express the names of the individual speakers.

Country Singapore

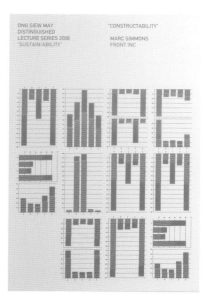

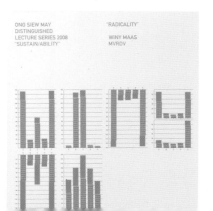

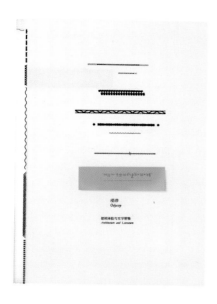

BRONZE | EDITORIAL DESIGN | GENERAL TRADE BOOK |

ODYSSEY: ARCHITECTURE & LITERATURE
CHINA YOUTH PRESS

XIAO MAGE

CHENGZI

Creative Director Xiao Mage, Chengzi
Art Director Xiao Mage, Chengzi
Copywriter Ou Ning
Designer Xiao Mage, Chengzi
Illustrator Xiao Mage, Chengzi
Director Xiao Mage, Chengzi
Editor Huimin Ma
Production Company Beijing Shuncheng Color Printing Co.,Ltd
Agency China Youth Press

This book is entitled *Odssey*, but in fact it has nothing to do with myth. The editor of this book invited nine famous writers to tour nine interesting architectural locations and write nine stories relevant to these spaces. The designer used the abstract point, line and plane to express the concept of roaming; the pieces of paper of different sizes and types expressed the concept of buildings; the reserved format arranged the stories; and the sticker on the chapter page represented the relation of architecture and literature.

Country China

BRONZE | EDITORIAL DESIGN |
GENERAL TRADE BOOK

UNS
ICH ER
PRILL & VIECELI

Copywriter Beat Gloor
Designer Tania Prill, Alberto Vieceli
Publisher Salis Verlag Zurich, Switzerland
Production Company fgb, Freiburg, Germany
Agency Prill & Vieceli
Client Beat Gloor

Separation hurts. Separation is liberating. Either way, we often later regret the absence of something of which we were once certain. The result is uncertainty.

Beat Gloor separates words. Sometimes according to orthigraphical rules, sometimes not. As a labourer in the field of words and letters, his job is the use of language. 20 years in the making, the collection *uns ich er* aims to be a standard reference on the subject of German word breaks. According to the author, the book contains at least 90% of all the linguistically interesting word breaks in the German language.

uns: us, our
ich: I
er: he
unsicher: uncertain
Example in English: surf ace | surface

Country Switzerland

BRONZE | EDITORIAL DESIGN | LIMITED EDITION,
PRIVATE PRESS, or SPECIAL FORMAT BOOK

SMALL
STUDIOS
PRILL & VIECELI

JIANPING
HE

Creative Director Jianping He
Art Director Jianping He
Designer Jianping He
Editor Jianping He
Publisher Hesign (Berlin & Hangzhou)
Production Company Hesign (Berlin & Hangzhou)
Agency Hesign
Client Hesign (Berlin & Hangzhou)

Small Studios is a compilation of 100 international small studios.
Because they are young and small, they are assumed to be rude,
disrespectful and aggressively competitive. They run the risk of
being boycotted, forgotten and envied...

However, small studios exist. They are fresh, flexible and full of
creativity.

Country Germany

BRONZE | EDITORIAL DESIGN | LIMITED EDITION,
PRIVATE PRESS, or SPECIAL FORMAT BOOK

SVA UNDERGRADUATE
CATALOG 2010/11
VISUAL ARTS PRESS, LTD.

**MICHAEL J.
WALSH**

Creative Director Anthony P. Rhodes
Art Director Michael J. Walsh
Designer E. Patrick Tobin, Brian E. Smith, Suck Zoo Han,
Anthony Bloch
Agency Visual Arts Press, Ltd.
Client School of Visual Arts

The objective of the School of Visual Arts' undergraduate catalog,
Proof, is to show prospective students why SVA is the preeminent
training ground for the next generations of artists. We want to
prove that SVA, located in New York City, is the best art school to
attend.

Our solution to that objective was to present visual and factual
evidence—proof—first by giving dozens of facts about New
York City, SVA and its students, and then by presenting literally
hundreds of examples of student work throughout the book.

The catalog's design aspires to create an object worthy of such
an art school. We created a reversible cover/poster and stickers
to suggest interactivity throughout, and we chose the paper
specifically to provide a maximum number of pages to showcase
art, while keeping it lightweight enough to ship economically.

Country United States

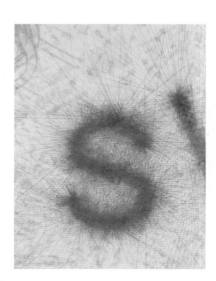

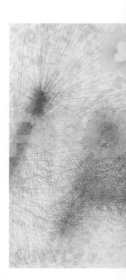

**SVA students have
interned at over 700
NYC companies:** ABC; America Greetings; Apple, Inc; Art & Commer
Art Directors C; *Artforum*; BBDO; Bill Plympton; C
Pizza; CBS; Ce us Films; *Charlie Rose Show*; Come
ral; Condé Nast; Cooper-Hewitt onal Design Museum; *Cosmogirl*;
LaChapelle; DC Comics; *Details* mazine; Deutsch; DeVito/Verdi; Epic
Esquire magazine; *Forbes* magaz *Fortune* magazine; Fox Broadcast
any; *Graphis*; Grey Advertising; perCollins; *Harper's Bazaar*; HBO;
eractive; *Instyle* magazine; Jim H on Company; *Late Night with Cona*
ifetime Television; *MAD* magazin Magnum Photos; Marvel Comics; M
Magazine; McCann Erickson; Mira x; MTV Networks; NBC; New Line
he New Yorker; *The New York Ti* s; Nickelodeon Animation Studios;
Mather; Penguin Putnam; Penta m; *Premiere*; *Print*; Publicis; RCA
hinoFX; *Rolling Stone*; Saatchi & atchi; *Saturday Night Live*; Sesame
op; Scholastic Inc.; Sony BMG; magazine; *The Daily Show with Jo*
; The Weinstein Company; *Tee eople* magazine; *Teen Vogue*; Time

BRONZE | EDITORIAL DESIGN |MUSEUM,
GALLERY, or LIBRARY BOOK

WEI JIA
2004-2008
CHINA YOUTH PRESS

**XIAO
MAGE**

CHENGZI

Creative Director Xiao Mage, Chengzi
Art Director Xiao Mage, Chengzi
Copywriter Wei Jia
Designer Xiao Mage, Chengzi
Illustrator Xiao Mage, Chengzi
Director Xiao Mage, Chengzi
Editor Fang Fang
Agency China Youth Press
Client Star Gallery

Country China

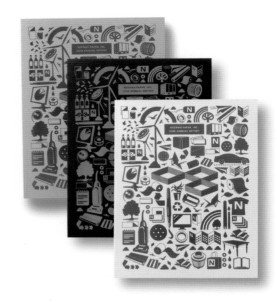

BRONZE | CORPORATE AND PROMOTIONAL DESIGN |
ANNUAL REPORT

NEENAH PAPER 2008
ANNUAL REPORT
ADDISON

**RICHARD
COLBOURNE**

**JASON
MILLER**

Creative Director Richard Colbourne
Art Director, Designer Jason Miller
Copywriter Edward Nebb
Illustrator, Photographer Multiple
Agency Addison
Client Neenah Paper, Inc.

Neenah Paper's directive to us was to communicate all the
ways in which the company had executed its strategic plan in
becoming a more focused and agile fine paper company. The
annual report needed to express both the specialized niche focus
of Neenah's products and culture, as well as the straightforward
accountability of their strategic planning and execution. We
found that, in many ways, the qualities that made Neenah a more
interesting and competitive company also positioned them to
weather the economic downturn.

We developed a typographic solution, based on a series of terms
that communicate these differentiators—which are simple
and direct—and then executed the typography in unique and
surprising ways, relevant to each topic. It is very straightforward
in message, yet at the same time highly expressive from a visual
standpoint.

Country United States

BRONZE | CORPORATE AND PROMOTIONAL DESIGN |
ANNUAL REPORT

TMB 2008 PROJECTES, PERSPECTIVES AND DREAMS
BIS DIXIT

Creative Director www.bisdixit.com
Editor Transports Metropolitans de Barcelona
Production Company Grafiques Trema
Agency Bis Dixit
Client Transports Metropolitans de Barcelona (TMB)

Transports Metropolitans de Barcelona asked us to develop
an annual report targeted to the users of public transportation
instead of partners, political staff or managers of the corporation.
We divided the book into three parts. The visual section uses
design to explain the company's ten major goals in a visual way.
The social part is made by the people for the people; photos from
Flickr illustrate small stories from the Metro users. The third and
last part of the book included the annual statistics as a graphic
interpretation of data hidden in Japanese foliage.

Country Spain

BRONZE | CORPORATE AND PROMOTIONAL DESIGN |
ANNUAL REPORT

END THE
LIES
DESIGN ARMY

**JAKE
LEFEBURE**

**PUM
LEFEBURE**

Creative Director Pum Lefebure, Jake Lefebure
Art Director Pum Lefebure
Designer Sucha Becky
Agency Design Army
Client Human Rights Campaign

The Human Rights Campaign was in full force for 2009, with
many high-profile projects and endorsements. The theme
"End the Lies" was a way to raise awareness with a very direct
approach—using the words of those speaking out, for and
against the HRC. The oversized self-mailer format and lightweight
enviro-friendly papers helped drive the design, but the HRC09
report also uses visual verbiage to convey the thoughts, issues
and other challenges facing the HRC. Direct quotes set in bold
typographics convey the impact and importance of the report,
while the distinct color scheme gives a little softness (and
uniqueness) to the otherwise text-heavy report.

Country United States

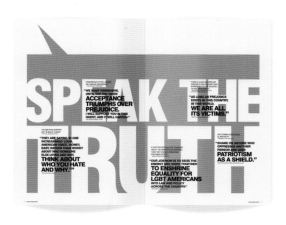

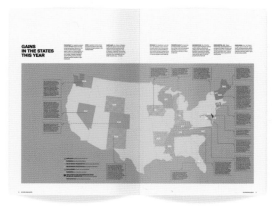

BRONZE | CORPORATE AND PROMOTIONAL DESIGN |
IDENTITY PROGRAM

GÖTEBORGSTRYCKERIET
IDENTITY

HAPPY FORSMAN & BODENFORS AB

OSKAR
ANDERSSON

LISA
CAREBORG

Creative Director Lisa Careborg
Art Director Oskar Andersson
Photographer Marcel Pabst
Account Director Anna Sparredal
Account Manager Linda Almström, Jessica Wallin
Agency Happy Forsman & Bodenfors AB
Client Göteborgstryckeriet printing house

Göteborgstryckeriet was established in 1918 and is one of the leading printing houses in Sweden. Their new identity highlights technical creativity and the desire to experiment. The logo includes an updated version of a lion—the company's brand in its early days. Every item, from labels and business cards to boxes and samples, are high quality and technically advanced, and incorporate unconventional solutions. E g prints visualize different techniques (screen, varnish, etc.) that depict the identity colors in physical form, and delivery boxes that become a book shelf filled with Göteborgstryckeriet's printed portfolio.

Country Sweden

BRONZE | CORPORATE AND PROMOTIONAL DESIGN |
IDENTITY PROGRAM

CORPORATE IDENTITY
OF THE 4TH BIENNIAL OF SLOVENE
VISUAL COMMUNICATIONS
ILOVARSTRITAR

**JERNEJ
STRITAR**

**ROBERT
ILOVAR**

Creative Director, Designer Robert Ilovar, Jernej Stritar
Copywriter Inge Pangos
Illustrator Robert Ilovar
Editor Inge Pangos, Tomato Košir
Agency IlovarStritar
Client Brumen Foundation

Country Slovenia

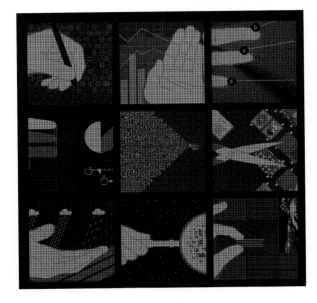

BRONZE | CORPORATE AND PROMOTIONAL DESIGN |
IDENTITY PROGRAM

ICOGRADA WORLD DESIGN
CONGRESS 2009 BEIJING VI
SCHOOL OF DESIGN,
CHINA CENTRAL ACADEMY
OF FINE ARTS

**HE
JUN**

Creative Director He Jun
Art Director He Jun
Designer He Jun, Liu Yinchuan, Huang Zhixian, Zha Yin, Li
Jingjing, Teng Yi, Luo Xue, Lou Xiaoyi, Liang Chen, Chen Dong
Agency School of Design, China Central Academy of Fine Arts
Client Icograda World Design Congress 2009 Beijing

Country China

BRONZE | CORPORATE AND PROMOTIONAL DESIGN |
MISCELLANEOUS

IGI V. THERAPEUTIC PLAY KIT
PIVOT DESIGN, INC.

Creative Director Brock Haldeman, Liz Haldeman
Designer April Weaver, Kate Longstein, Jason Thompson
Agency Pivot Design, Inc.
Client Baxter International, Inc.

In collaboration with Baxter, a family living with Primary Immune Deficiency (PI) and a child life specialist, we created and developed this one-of-a-kind therapeutic play kit specifically for families living with PI. The kit is built around a doll character we created named Igi V., a whimsical spin on IGIV (immune globulin intravenous), the blood plasma therapy used to treat PI. The kit helps children with PI learn about and communicate their thoughts and feelings about the infusion experience through structured play. The program has been a huge success and we are currently developing additional character extensions to the brand. More than most, this design exercise was really about changing lives in a truly meaningful way. We know our creative solution was successful because we have been able to hear directly from the families positively touched by the kit.

Country United States

BRONZE | CORPORATE AND PROMOTIONAL DESIGN |
MISCELLANEOUS

CHARLES DARWIN STAMPS
ROYAL MAIL GROUP LIMITED

JIM SUTHERLAND

Head of Design Marcus James
Design Manager Susan Gilson
Creative Director Jim Sutherland, Gareth Howat
Designer Ben Christie
Agency Royal Mail Group Limited (Stamp Designs)
Client Stamp Design, Royal Mail Group Ltd

This set of six stamps commemorates both the bicentenary of the birth of Charles Darwin and the 150th anniversary of the publication of *The Origin of Species*. To convey the concept of the many different areas of science that Darwin bestrode and the idea that they were interlinked, we used the graphic concept of the jigsaw puzzle. The design physically connects the portrait of Darwin with different images representing zoology, ornithology, geology, botany and anthropology. Mixing modern photography with historic imagery, not only creates vibrant contrast and visual interest but also hints at how Darwin's conclusions are still relevant today. His concepts are reflected in the similar framing and positioning of Darwin's portrait to the Orangutan. This is only the third time Royal Mail has produced a die-cut stamp issue.

Country United Kingdom

BRITISH DESIGN
CLASSICS STAMPS
ROYAL MAIL GROUP LIMITED

PIERRE
VERMEIR

Head of Design Marcus James
Design Manager Catharine Brandy
Creative Director Pierre Vermeir (HGV Design)
Photographer Jason Tozer
Agency Royal Mail Group Limited (Stamp Designs)
Client Stamp Design, Royal Mail Group Ltd

This stamp issue started with the 50th anniversary celebrating
the first Mini rolling off the Longbridge production line. The Mini
is the most popular British-made car in the world. A further nine
equally iconic 'British Design Classics' were required to create
a set of ten. All had to be considered instantly recognizable and
icons of their era, honoring the design not the invention. Each
of the chosen designs featured on these stamps have come to
symbolize the spirit of a particular British era.

Two major criteria determined the final design approach—
simplicity and authenticity. The specially commissioned
photography portrays them as heroes, stripping away any
distractions. The framing and simplicity brings a cohesive style
to disparate objects, creating a strong graphic quality. Sourcing
pristine originals to photograph was a monumental task, and
it also presented a variety of challenges to create a unified
photographic result.

Country United Kingdom

1ST Anglepoise Lamp
Designed by George Carwardine

1ST Concorde
Designed by Aérospatiale-BAC

1ST London Underground Map
Designed by Harry Beck

1ST Routemaster Bus
Design team led by AAM Durrant

1ST Supermarine Spitfire
Designed by RJ Mitchell

1ST Mini Skirt
Designed by Mary Quant

1ST K2 Telephone Kiosk
Designed by Sir Giles Gilbert Scott

1ST Polypropylene Chair
Designed by Robin Day

WA INTERNATIONAL FABRIC COLLECTION 2010

BRONZE | POSTER DESIGN |
PROMOTIONAL

WA FABRIC COLLECTION 2010
702 DESIGN WORKS

Creative Director, Director Gaku Ohsugi
Designer Tetsuya Namaizawa
Producer Fumiko Shirahama
Agency 702 Design Works Inc.
Client WA LTD.

This poster announced a new line of window interiors and fabric curtains. Our client, WA LTD., is a fabric manufacturer and importer that specializes in curtain materials.

Country Japan

BRONZE | POSTER DESIGN | PROMOTIONAL

ALL-CLEAR POSTER
DDB NEW YORK

REUBEN HOWER

GERARD CAPUTO

CHUCK TSO

Creative Director Eric Silver
Art Director Chuck Tso, Gerard Caputo
Copywriter Reuben Hower
Designer Chuck Tso
Photographer Matt Karas
Producer Ralph Navarro, Alyssa Dolman
Agency DDB New York

We were tasked with creating an announcement for this year's Bill Bernbach Diversity Scholarship, to be distributed throughout various college campuses. This program awards five students hefty scholarships based on diversity, but just as importantly, on creative merits. It was important to practice what we preached—creativity matters. To create the clear poster, we played with various transparent substrates to find a durable material that, while colorless, would still catch the eye when placed over colored backgrounds. We then silkscreened a clear varnish over the acetate to create our translucent message. The posters directed viewers to a website where students could submit applications and creative portfolios for consideration.

Country United States

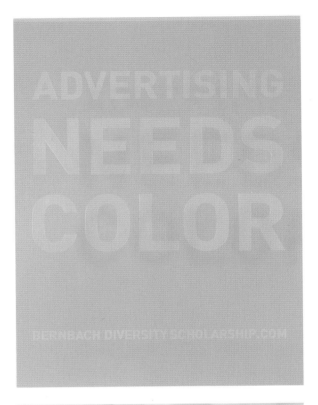

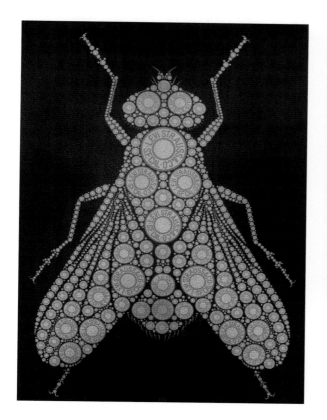

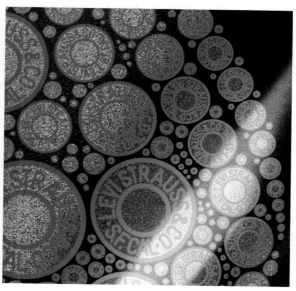

BRONZE | POSTER DESIGN |
PROMOTIONAL

BUTTON
FLY
SAGMEISTER INC.

**RICHARD
THE**

**STEFAN
SAGMEISTER**

Creative Director Stefan Sagmeister
Designer Richard The, Joe Shouldice
Illustrator Richard The
Agency Sagmeister Inc.
Client Levi Strauss & Co.

Country United States

BRONZE | POSTER DESIGN |
PROMOTIONAL

LESS AND
MORE TOKYO
SHIMADA DESIGN INC.

Creative Director Hajime Nariai
Art Director Tamotsu Shimada
Copywriter Shinya Kamimura
Designer Tamotsu Shimada, Miyuki Amemiya
Producer Keiko Ueki
Agency Shimada Design Inc.
Client Fuchu Art Museum

Country Japan

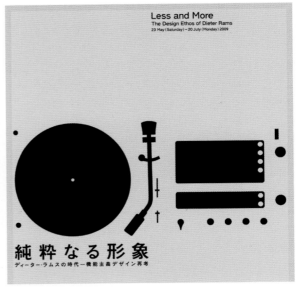

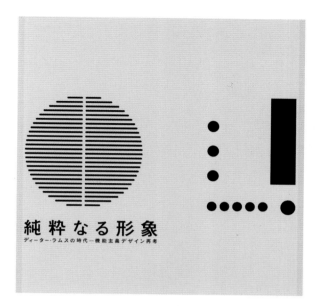

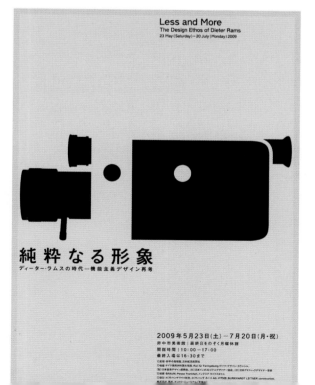

BRONZE | POSTER DESIGN |
PUBLIC SERVICE or NON-PROFIT

RETURN OF
THE ORNAMENT
HAPPY FORSMAN & BODENFORS AB

**OSKAR
ANDERSSON**

**LISA
CAREBORG**

Creative Director Anders Kornestedt, Lisa Careborg
Art Director Oskar Andersson
Account Director Robert Axner
Account Manager Madeliene Sikström
Agency Happy Forsman & Bodenfors AB
Client The Swedish Museum of Architecture

Ornaments are decorative elements with no function. This
exhibition is one example of a recurrent trend; playing with
architectonic aesthetics. Stickers were used to "ornament" 350
unique posters. We allowed the ornaments to climb into—or
out of—the posters to further illustrate the recurrence of the
ornament in urban space.

Country Sweden

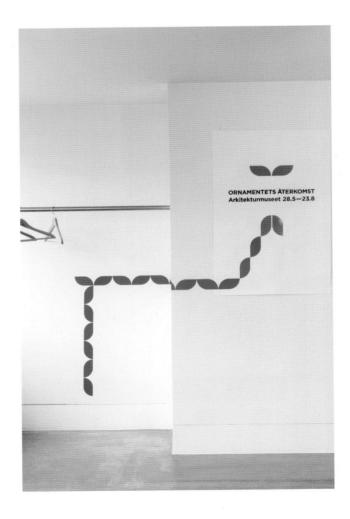

11. SEP. 2001

THE 9.11 ATTACKS TO WTC
PRE ORGANIC COTTON×DESIGN
T-SHIRTS PROJECT BY KURKKU

THE CHERNOBYL DISASTER
PRE ORGANIC COTTON×DESIGN
T-SHIRTS PROJECT BY KURKKU

PRE-ORGANIC COTTON THE DAY T-SHIRTS PROJECT
GOOD DESIGN COMPANY

MANABU MIZUNO

Art Director Manabu Mizuno
Designer Mari Kuno
Agency good design company
Client kurkku

THE FALL OF BERLIN WALL
PRE ORGANIC COTTON×DESIGN
T-SHIRTS PROJECT BY KURKKU

There are many problems that we can solve if we look at things not from one angle but from many. We believe the world can be a place where all might feel hope.

The Pre-Organic Cotton program supports cotton farmers in India who cultivate organic cotton fields. "Pre-Organic Cotton" (POC) is the term given to cotton crops during the first, transitional three years that they are farmed without chemicals of any kind. Good design company not only made logo marks and an advertisement, but also established a fashion brand that is made by POC.

We produced a t-shirt with a design using historical events that have had a great impact on humankind. These posters used the same image as the t-shirt. Through fashion, the brand attracts people from all walks of life.

Country Japan

BRONZE | POSTER DESIGN |
PUBLIC SERVICE or NON-PROFIT

WHAT GOES AROUND
COMES AROUND
BIG ANT INTERNATIONAL

**FRANK
ANSELMO**

**JESEOK
YI**

**WILLIAM
TRAN**

**RICHARD
WILDE**

**ALFRED S.
PARK**

Executive Creative Director Alfred S. Park
Creative Director Richard Wilde
Art Director Frank Anselmo, Jeseok Yi
Copywriter Francisco Hui, William Tran
Agency Big Ant International
Client Global Coalition for Peace

This simple outdoor poster campaign focused on the spiraling
cycle of war, reminding viewers that the violence perpetrated
abroad will breed the hatred that fuels tomorrow's violence—
What Goes Around Comes Around.

Country United States

Additional Awards:

ADVERTISING MERIT
PUBLIC SERVICE NON-PROFIT | CAMPAIGN

PLUGS
BBDO NEW YORK

**JAMES
CLUNIE**

**KARA
GOODRICH**

**PIERRE
LIPTON**

Chief Creative Officer David Lubars, Bill Bruce
Senior Creative Director Kara Goodrich
Creative Director James Clunie, Pierre Lipton
Art Director James Clunie
Copywriter Pierre Lipton
Illustrator Nick Dewar
Art Buyer Kathy Lando
Retoucher Steve Lakeman
Agency BBDO New York
Client The Economist

Country United States

BRONZE | ENVIRONMENTAL DESIGN |
GALLERY, MUSEUM EXHIBIT or INSTALLATION

LG FIVE
SHIMONI FINKELSTEIN DRAFTFCB

**KOBI
BARKI**

**REUVEN
GIVATI**

Creative Director Kobi Barki
Art Director Reuven Givati, Liat Tzur, Daphne Orner
Copywriter Kobi Barki, Maayan Karniel
Designer Amidov, DesignMill, Umami, XtazaSdom, Mesila
Director Kobi Barki, Reuven Givati
Producer Emanuel Raz, Boaz Meiri
Curator Maya Dvash
Agency Shimoni Finkelstein Draftfcb
Client H.Y. GROUP

Our challenges and key objectives:
1. To find an original and stimulating way for people to engage with the LG product (screens), the product experience (a digital experience) and most importantly, the brand, by integrating the product into the format of a 'popular' culture exhibition.
2. To position LG as a brand leader with something meaningful to contribute to popular culture.

The solution:
We gave five leading product-design groups the LG screen as raw material and challenged them to create an experience around it. The idea was to provoke the general public to re-think their relationship with screens and the way that they blur the boundaries between the 'virtual' and the 'real'.

The result was "LG Five," a free exhibition featuring five diverse installations in five ancient spaces, aimed at provoking the general public to re-think their relationship with digital screens, and 'virtual' and 'real' experiences.

Country Israel

BRONZE | TELEVISION, AND CINEMA DESIGN | IDENTITIES, OPENINGS, TEASERS

TED 2009
CONFERENCE OPEN
TROLLBÄCK+COMPANY

Creative Director Jakob Trollbäck, Joe Wright
Designer Peter Alfano, Paul Schlacter
Producer Whitney Green
Sound Design Sacred Noise
Agency Trollbäck+Company
Client TED

For the opening sequence for TED's 25th anniversary conference, The Great Unveiling, we created a piece that plays off the "unveiling" idea, evoking each of TED2009's 12 different themes with a symbolic movement particular to each word: REBOOT, DISCOVER, ENGAGE, INVENT, SEE, PREDICT, DARE, RECONNECT, GROW, DREAM, REFRAME, FULFILL. The sum of these forms adds up to one final reveal: THE GREAT UNVEILING.

Country United States

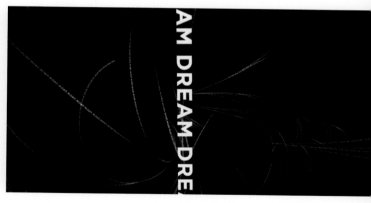

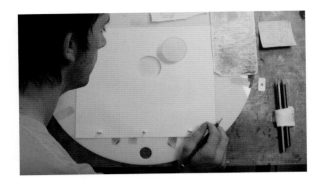

BRONZE | TELEVISION AND CINEMA DESIGN | ANIMATION

OIAF SIGNAL FILM
HEAD GEAR ANIMATION

JULIAN GREY

Creative Director, Director Julian Grey
Animator Julian Grey, Isaac King, Sean Branigan
Producer Kathryn Rawson
Agency Head Gear Animation
Client Ottawa International Animation Festival

Head Gear designed the opening "Signal Film" for the 2009 Ottawa International Animation Festival, joining a rich tradition of animation-themed trailers going back to the 70s. This year sees the old bouncing ball cliché expanded upon in unusual and compelling mediums.

Country Canada

BRONZE | TELEVISION AND CINEMA DESIGN |
IDENTITIES, OPENINGS, TEASERS

WORLD SCIENCE FESTIVAL 2009 OPEN

TROLLBÄCK+COMPANY

Creative Director Jakob Trollbäck
Designer Peter Alfano, Emre Veryeri, Tolga Yildiz
Sound Design Sacred Noise
Producer Whitney Green
Agency Trollbäck+Company
Client World Science Festival

We have been honored to create the opening for the World
Science Festival in New York two years in a row. This time, we
started with an idea of a very abstract piece. We wanted to use
organic transitions to string together the most beautiful, natural
and scientific elements we could imagine. In the end, the physics
of motion and animation just happened to line up the scenes in a
way that told a story about our evolutionary journey.

Country United States

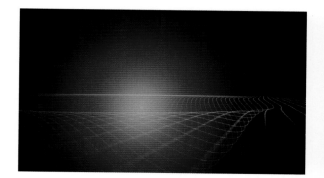

BRONZE | TELEVISION AND CINEMA DESIGN |
ANIMATION

THE WILDE
ONES
SCHOOL OF VISUAL ARTS

Creative Director David Rhodes
Art Director Richard Wilde
Copywriter Richard Wilde, Benita Raphan, Richard Pels
Designer Hoon Chong
Director Benita Raphan
Editor Catherine Gionfriddo, Clayton Hemmert
Producer David Rhodes
Agency School of Visual Arts
Client School of Visual Arts

The Wilde Ones is a 17 minute piece dedicated to Richard Wilde's
tenure as chair at the School of Visual Arts, and to his leading
the department of Graphic Design and Advertising to success
upon success. The opening of the film features all of Richard's
collections and shows the toys coming together to play follow-
the-leader, with Richard leading.

Country United States

BRONZE |TELEVISION AND CINEMA DESIGN |
ANIMATED LOGO

SYFY
IDS

SYFY

Creative Director Michael Engleman, Dan Witchell
Art Director Dan Witchell, Amie Nguyen
Designer, Director Mike Alderson, Tim Swift
Producer Kate Leonard, Roger Whittlesea
Production Company ManvsMachine
Agency Syfy, ManvsMachine, Proud Creative
Client Syfy

When the Sci Fi Channel changed its name to Syfy, the whole
look and feel of the network changed too, and a new tactile brand
aesthetic was adopted. The logo was especially designed to
look like something one could reach out and touch – a physical,
hands-on representation of imagination itself. To emphasize
this important aspect of the Syfy brand, and to illustrate the
network's exceptional capacity for creative storytelling, a series of
idents were developed to reinforce the new name. Brought to life
by simple but premium visuals, the resulting campaign has been
instrumental in conveying Syfy's identity both on-air and off, and
continues to enjoy popularity almost a year later.

Country United States

JAQK
CELLARS
HATCH DESIGN

**KATIE
JAIN**

**JOEL
TEMPLIN**

Creative Director Katie Jain, Joel Templin
Copywriter Vinnie Chieco
Designer Eszter Clark, Ryan Meis
Agency Hatch Design
Client JAQK Cellars

JAQK Cellars is a collaboration between Hatch Design founders and a renowned Napa Valley winemaker. Named after the Jack, Ace, Queen and King in a deck of cards, it is a new wine company dedicated to "play." The packaging of all eight wines in the inaugural offering evoke the allure and sophistication of the world of gaming: High Roller, Soldiers of Fortune (the Jacks), Black Clover (Clubs), Pearl Handle (the derringer that tamed the gambling saloons), 22 Black (roulette), Bone Dance (dice), Her Majesty (the Queen) and Charmed (the luckier the better).

Country United States

BRONZE | BRANDING | CAMPAIGN NON-PROFIT |

D&AD AWARDS CEREMONY
NB STUDIO

BEN STOTT

DANIEL LOCK

Creative Director Ben Stott, Nick Finney, Alan Dye
Copywriter Scott Perry
Designer Daniel Lock
Animator Ed Wright
Agency NB Studio
Client D&AD

Country United Kingdom

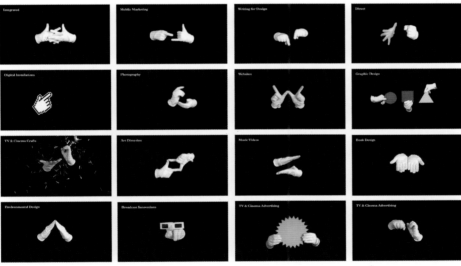

MERIT | PHOTOGRAPHY |
BOOK

THE OTHER HALF
OF THE SKY
POWERHOUSE BOOKS

LILI
ALMOG

Creative Director, Photographer Lili Almog
Art Director, Designer Mine Suda
Producer Craig Cohen
Agency powerHouse Books
Client Lili Almog

Country United States

MERIT | PHOTOGRAPHY |
MAGAZINE EDITORIAL

I AM THE
WORLD
ACHIM LIPPOTH
PHOTOGRAPHYPHY

ACHIM
LIPPOTH

Photographer Achim Lippoth
Agency Achim Lippoth Photography
Client kid's wear

Country Germany

MERIT | PHOTOGRAPHY |
SELF-PROMOTION

CATHERINE LEDNER
2009 PROMO
**CATHERINE LEDNER
PHOTOGRAPHY**

**SEAN
CORRIGAN**

Photographer Catherine Ledner
Designer Todd Richards at Tar Studio
Agency Catherine Ledner Photography

Country United States

PEOPLE

 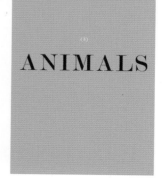

ANIMALS

MERIT | PHOTOGRAPHY |
NEWSPAPER ADVERTISEMENT

THE
UNSEEN
BBDO GERMANY GMBH

Creative Director Toygar Bazarkaya, Carsten Bolk
Art Director Jake Shaw
Copywriter Florian Birkner
Photographer Matt Barnes
Agency BBDO Germany GmbH
Client SPUK Pictures

Country Germany

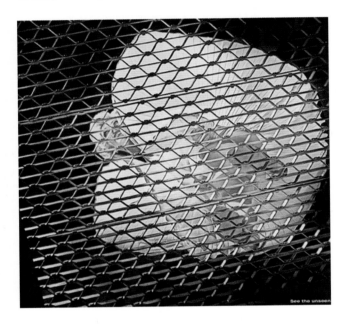

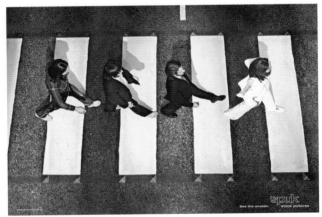

MERIT | ILLUSTRATION |
BOOK JACKET

CHINUA ACHEBE
BOOKS
EDEL RODRIGUEZ STUDIO

EDEL RODRIGUEZ

Art Director John Gall
Designer Helen Yentus
Illustrator Edel Rodriguez
Publisher Random House
Agency Edel Rodriguez Studio
Client Random House / Anchor Books

These are a series of covers for books by the African author Chinua Achebe. The stories deal with civil war, strife and colonialism in Nigeria. I wanted the covers to be part of a cohesive series, yet convey a sense of the book's individuality.

Country United States

MERIT | ILLUSTRATION |
CARTOON or COMIC BOOK

RED RIDING HOOD REDUX
NORA KRUG ILLUSTRATION / PARSONS THE NEW SCHOOL FOR DESIGN

NORA KRUG

Designer Nora Krug, Serge Baeken
Illustrator Nora Krug
Publisher Bries
Agency Nora Krug Illustration / Parsons The New School for Design
Client Bries Books

Red Riding Hood Redux is a series of wordless picture books, representing the inner world and point of view of each character in the original fairy tale: Red Riding Hood, the wolf, the mother, the grandmother and the hunter.

The characters' stories overlap and only by reading all five books simultaneously, is this new version of the story understood. Moments left untold in the original tale are revealed.

For example, pages 44 and 45 in each book tell a different angle of the same moment in the story: Red Riding Hood is eaten by the wolf, while the grandmother is exploring the wolf's stomach's mysterious fauna and flora. Simultaneously, the hunter, passing by the grandmother's house looking for deer to shoot, hears Red Riding Hood scream and the sound of her cracking bones, while the mother is in her car, on the way to visit her husband, who is in prison for accidentally having shot the grandmother's husband.

Country United States

MERIT | ILLUSTRATION | MISCELLANEOUS

THE BOOKMARK PROMOTION
SCHOLZ & FRIENDS HAMBURG GMBH

SUZE BARRETT
DENNIS LUECK

Creative Director Suze Barrett, Dennis Lueck, Matthias Schmidt, Stefan Setzkorn
Art Director Joanna Broda
Copywriter Vicky Jacob-Ebbinghaus
Graphic Designer Katharina Uelsberg
Illustrator Carmen Segovia, Romy Bluemel, Gisela Goppel, Andrea Ventura, Pietari Posti, Katharina Gschwendtner, Tina Berning
Agency Producer Eva Kannemann
Agency Scholz & Friends Hamburg GmbH
Client Felix Jud & Co. KG Verlagshaus und Buchhandlung

Country Germany

MERIT | ILLUSTRATION | SELF-PROMOTION

THE PATTERNS FOUND IN SPACE
MIKE PERRY STUDIO

MIKE PERRY

Agency Mike Perry Studio

Country United States

MERIT | ILLUSTRATION |
NEWSPAPER ADVERTISEMENT

PANDA
SERIES
BBH CHINA

Creative Director Johnny Tan
Art Director Yinbo Ma
Copywriter Carol Ong, Leo Zhang
Illustrator Jianfeng Pan
Other Jasmine Huang, Ken Wang
Agency BBH China
Client WWF China

Country China

MERIT | ILLUSTRATION |
POSTER or BILLBOARD ADVERTISEMENT

OPPOSITE
EARTH
YOUNG & RUBICAM

Global Creative Director Graham Lang
Creative Director Guillermo Vega, Icaro Doria, Menno Kluin
Art Director Guillermo Vega, Menno Kluin
Copywriter Icaro Doria
Account Management Lucy Harries
Agency Young & Rubicam
Client Land Rover

The brief was to come up with new executions on the long-running Go Beyond campaign for Land Rover. We illustrated situations in work, family and life that people want to escape from, both literally and figuratively. Land Rover allows you to get as far away from it all as possible.

Country United States

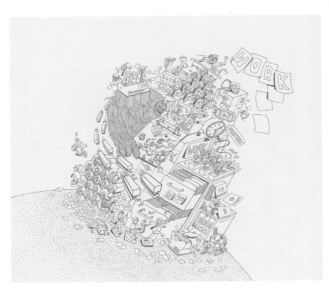

MERIT | ILLUSTRATION |
POSTER or BILLBOARD ADVERTISEMENT

DEW ACTION SPORTS TOUR
SAATCHI & SAATCHI LA

RYAN JACOBS

Executive Creative Director Mike McKay
Creative Director Ryan Jacobs
Art Director Mike Czako, Abe Cortes
Copywriter Bob Fremgen
Illustrator Tavis Coburn
Senior Print Producer Rachel Dallas-Noble
Art Producer Angee Murray
Production Company Primary Color
Agency Saatchi & Saatchi LA
Client Toyota Motor Sales U.S.A., Inc.

Toyota sponsors three athletes that perform during the Dew Action tour. They are a BMX Vertical specialist (Jamie Bestwick), and two skaters (Bob Burnquist and Greg Lutzka.) These posters were printed so that athletes could sign something for fans who visited the Toyota booth.

The goal was to create something that didn't reek of sponsorship so that fans would hang the posters on their walls.

The posters were a big hit among a crowd that can be very "sell out" skeptical.

Country United States

MERIT | EDITORIAL DESIGN |
MAGAZINE, CONSUMER | FULL ISSUE

COLORS 76
FABRICA S.P.A.

ERIK RAVELO

BARBARA SOALHEIRO

Creative Director Erik Ravelo
Art Director Saulo Casals
Designer Joshua Levi, Bryce Licht
Photographer Alexander Basta, Kitra Cahana, Elena Chernyak,
Director Paolo Landi
Photography Consultant Piero Martinello
Photo Editor Anna Grassi, Mauro Bedoni
Kenzaburo Fukuhara, Yann Gross, Jennifer Osborne
Interaction Designer Julian Koschwitz
Executive Editor Fabio Amato
Managing Editor Erica Fusaro
Editor Barbara Soalheiro, Benjamin Joffe-Walt
Associate Editor C.M. Koseman, Elena Favilli
Contributor Ramon Pezzarini, Giulia De Meo
Video Executive Editor Bryce Licht
Video Editor Chiara Andrich, Heloisa Sartorato, Riccardo Pittaluga, Hanna Abi-Hanna
Producer Mauro Bedoni
Production Company United Colors of Benetton
Agency Fabrica S.p.A.

Working on Colors 76 was a big challenge for two reasons. It was the first time we made an entire issue opening the participatory platform www.colorsmagazine.com to worldwide contributors who submitted pictures, stories and ideas. We came up with a 'Web-to-print' concept: we published all the stories on the website, and the best ones got featured in the printed magazine. At the same time, we were the first to experiment with Augmented Reality, an Open Source technology connecting print content and Web in an easy-to-use way. Not only can video play inside the magazine, but the magazine itself becomes a 'key' to meet the people featured through uncut interviews and behind-the-scenes footage. Colors 76 took the dynamic qualities of the Web and combined them with printed matter: from Web to print with the contents and back to the Web to make the magazine alive.

Country Italy

MERIT | EDITORIAL DESIGN |
BOOK JACKET

THINGS WE DIDN'T
SEE COMING
MENDELSUND DESIGN

**PETER
MENDELSUND**

Art Director, Designer Peter Mendelsund
Editor Shelley Wanger
Publisher Pantheon Books
Agency Mendelsund Design
Client Pantheon Books

Country United States

MERIT | EDITORIAL DESIGN |
BOOK JACKET

DORORO
MENDELSUND DESIGN

Art Director, Designer Peter Mendelsund
Illustrator Osamu Tezuka
Editor Yani Mentzas
Agency Mendelsund Design
Client Vertical Press

Country United States

We Things V
See Didn't S
ing Comi
ven by Stev
am Amsterda

The

of

MERIT | EDITORIAL DESIGN |
BOOK JACKET

THE BOOK OF PENGUIN
RADLEY YELDAR LTD

Creative Director, Designer Robert Riche
Copywriter Duncan Campbell, Rebecca Sinclair, Rob R
Illustrator Heather Briggs, Robert Riche
Photographer DK Images, Henry Thomas, Robert Riche
Account Director Simon Hutley
Agency Radley Yeldar Ltd
Client Penguin Group

Country United Kingdom

MERIT | EDITORIAL DESIGN |
UNIVERSITY PRESS BOOK

ABSTRACT
07/08
SAGMEISTER INC.

**STEFAN
SAGMEISTER**

**JOE
SHOULDICE**

Creative Director Stefan Sagmeister
Designer Joe Shouldice, Richard The, Daniel Harding
Editor Scott Marble
Agency Sagmeister Inc.
Client Columbia Graduate School of Architecture Planning and
Preservation

Columbia University asked the studio to design their annual
publication, Abstract, a yearbook for the Graduate School of
Architecture, Planning and Preservation.

The content is divided into three different color-coded books
that insert into each other to form their own pyramid-shaped
architecture. The smallest book contains only photos of staff and
students, the middle book contains only text, and the large book
showcases student work. An extensive cross-reference system
directs users to related content between the books.

Country United States

MERIT | EDITORIAL DESIGN |
BOOK JACKET

3/4 POLAR
COLLECTION
PAPRIKA

Creative Director Louis Gagnon
Art Director, Designer David Guarnieri
Agency Paprika
Client Éditions Les Allusifs

Les Allusifs is a firm that likes to distinguish itself from the more commercial, less art-oriented publishing houses. The company publishes serious works of fiction by internationally renowned authors in Europe and North America. Our mandate was to create covers for the new *3/4 Polar* (literally, "3/4 Detective Novels") collection of detective novels. Les Allusifs wanted this new collection to be very different from all their other publications.

Our primary goal was to render the expression "3/4 Polar" in typographical form. The name of this romans noirs collection evokes the balance of the psychological, historical and sociological themes in each novel. To make this collection stand out from competing titles in bookstores, we decided to give the covers a "French retro look." The typography, paper color and binding were carefully selected to reflect this tradition.

Country Canada

MERIT | EDITORIAL DESIGN | MAGAZINE,
CONSUMER | COVER

THE SECRET FORMULA THAT
DESTROYED WALL STREET
WIRED MAGAZINE

Creative Director, Designer Scott Dadich
Design Director Wyatt Mitchell
Agency Wired Magazine
Client Wired Magazine (Condé Nast)

Country United States

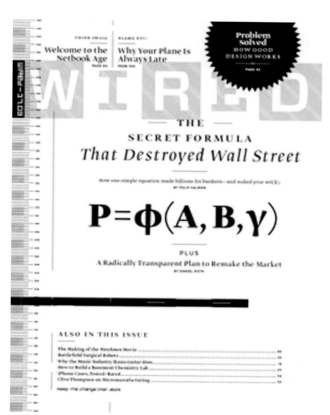

MERIT | CORPORATE AND PROMOTIONAL DESIGN |
ANNUAL REPORT

SAMSUNG
PROFILE 2009
THE CORPORATE
AGENDA

DAVID
RODRIGUEZ

Creative Director Dan Koh
Copywriter Dan Bollin
Designer David Rodriguez
Photographer Bruce Lum, Sajinmoon Studio
Agency The Corporate Agenda
Client Samsung Group

Since Samsung Group is not required to publish an annual report, we've created the "Profile" which highlights key achievements of the Group and its affiliates throughout the year. While best known for its consumer electronics division, the Group's 59 subsidiaries touch nearly every aspect of Korean industry, from life insurance to construction.

This year's theme, Step Forward, acknowledges the challenges from 2009—a volatile global economy, shifts in leadership, sputtering commercial markets and uncertainty—yet provides a reason to celebrate and look towards the future. Together, we work, play and share in ways that were unimaginable even 20 years ago. Ideas and inspiration spring from every corner of the world. Individual voices bind to form collective movements. The march of science and technology have answered longstanding questions and sparked new, exciting curiosities. The road ahead promises kinship and chaos, stress and liberation, excitement and trepidation.

Country United States

MERIT | EDITORIAL DESIGN |
SPECIAL TRADE BOOK

FUTURETAINMENT
FROST* DESIGN

Creative Director Vince Frost
Art Director Vince Frost
Designer, Quan Payne
Photographer Mike Walsh
Publisher Phaidon
Author Mike Walsh
Agency Frost* Design
Client Phaidon Press/Mike Walsh

In his book *Futuretainment*, digital expert Mike Walsh follows the consumer-led revolution in media and entertainment. In a bid to move away from the traditional 'business book,' the design element played an important function in visually communicating the forward-thinking content. The main challenge was in designing a book about the future that wouldn't date. The solution lay in modernist design from the 50s and 60s, as its futuristic aesthetic is removed enough to stand up to our contemporary views of the future. Arrows are used throughout to emulate the forward movement of time and the progression of the industries documented in the book, acting as both figurative and literal pointers to the future that lies ahead.

Country Australia

MERIT | CORPORATE AND PROMOTIONAL DESIGN | BOOKLET or BROCHURE

WE MAKE LIGHT
ALT GROUP LTD

**ANNA
MYERS**

**DEAN
POOLE**

Creative Director Dean Poole
Copywriter Dean Poole, Ben Corban, Felicity Stevens
Designer Anna Myers
Photographer Duncan Cole, Michael Ng, David St George,
Michael Woods, Getty Images
Agency Alt Group Ltd
Client Selecon

Philips Selecon is a leading international theatre and architectural
lighting design and manufacturing company based in New
Zealand. The purpose of the brand book was to assist in
communicating company values and direction internally
and externally. The brand book was part of a broader brand
development program for the company that assisted in the
articulation of its vision, mission and values. The brand book
became a central part of the project, documenting the results of
the initial discovery stages and articulation of strategy in a visual
form. The book was used to communicate within the company
domestically and internationally, and served as a reference point
for all external communications.

Country New Zealand

MERIT | CORPORATE AND PROMOTIONAL DESIGN | BOOKLET or BROCHURE

ELLERY'S THEORY OF NEO-CONSERVATIVE CREATIONISM – CATALOGUE
BROWNS

JONATHAN ELLERY

Designer Jonathan Ellery, Claire Warner
Copywriter Dr. Jules Wright
Artist Jonathan Ellery
Publisher Browns Editions
Agency Browns
Client Jonathan Ellery / The Wapping Project

Artist Jonathan Ellery unveiled his fourth solo show at The Wapping Project, London, in November 2009. Ellery's Theory of Neo-conservative Creationism combined materials to produce a three-element, multi-sensory show. Suspended brass sculptures depicting a series of ambiguous artworks responded to floating books and offset a digital sound installation. The one-color catalogue was commissioned to accompany the show and represent the artist to a cultural audience.

Country United Kingdom

MERIT | CORPORATE AND PROMOTIONAL DESIGN | CALENDAR or APPOINTMENT BOOK

26&26
THE CHASE CREATIVE CONSULTANTS

LI RUI

BEN CASEY

Creative Director Ben Casey, Lionel Hatch
Designer Li Rui
Agency The Chase Creative Consultants
Client Font Shop, Font Works and Atomic Type

This year, our week-by-week calendar, 26&26, was designed for Font Shop, Font Works and Atomic Type. It consists of 53 pages, each page featuring a type character—26 lower case, 26 upper case and an ampersand. We allocated an individual character to 53 of the country's leading designers and typographers, we asked them to choose their favorite typeface for that character, and to write 25-50 words on why they like it so much.

Country United Kingdom

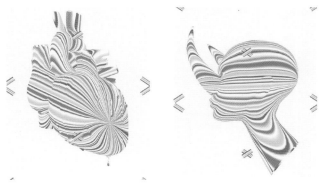

MERIT | CORPORATE AND PROMOTIONAL DESIGN |
IDENTITY PROGRAM
20TH MACAO ARTS FESTIVAL
HONG CHONG IP DESIGN

**HONG
CHONG IP**

Designer Hong Chong Ip, Victor Hugo Marreiros, Leong Chi Hang
Illustrator Hong Chong Ip, Ha Tin Cheong
Photographer Hong Chong Ip
Agency Hong Chong Ip Design
Client Cultural Affairs Bureau of the MACAO S.A.R. Government

Serving the visual image of this festival, the "Heart" can best represent our utmost dedication and passion for the arts. Four fluorescent colors were chosen to create a "sugar coating" for the "bloody heart." Therefore, on one hand, we softened the concept of "bloody" for the public and on the other hand, portrayed the conflicts between innocent and bloody; sweet and painful; realistic and unrealistic.

Country Macau

MERIT | CORPORATE AND PROMOTIONAL DESIGN |
IDENTITY PROGRAM

SEEDS OF
THE CITIES
SENSETEAM

Creative Director Hei Yiyang
Designer Hei Yiyang, Ii Junrong, Peng Jun, Yuan Wei
Agency SenseTeam
Client HSA

This is the visual identity system for Huasen Architecture Company's touring exhibitions. Perforated characters on the Visual Identity System are from the LED Indicating System of the exhibitions. Characters on the LED screen are made up of and shown by dots. They can change at any time.

Country China

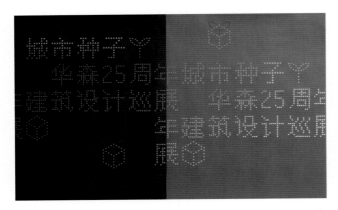

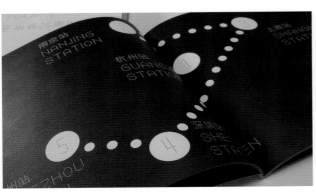

MERIT | CORPORATE AND PROMOTIONAL DESIGN |
IDENTITY PROGRAM

BIG
BUSINESS
SENSETEAM

Creative Director Hei Yiyang
Art Director Hei Yiyang
Designer Hei Yiyang, Wang XiaoMeng
Illustrator Wang XiaoMeng
Production Company SensePubli
Agency SenseTeam
Client SensePubli

The visual identity system we created promotes Big Business through a logo, a book, typography, advertising and posters.

Country China

MERIT | CORPORATE AND PROMOTIONAL DESIGN |
IDENTITY PROGRAM

X EXHIBITION
SENSETEAM

Creative Director Hei Yiyang
Designer Hei Yiyang, Liu Zhao, Zhao Meng, Zhan Ting, Huang Muqiu, Li Jia
Photographer Zhang Qing
Agency SenseTeam
Client SGDA & LOOOK

X exhibition is an international graphic design exhibition, which employs the light character as the principal design element.

The whole space mixes music, video and 3-D works/ environmental devices together, enriching the time-space transformation of the 3-D space. As an exhibition that displays the talents of 11 young designers from five countries around the world, the lights symbolize the spurt of creative ideas. Additionally, the passages made by modulating tubes separate various exhibitors. The colorful light gives a magic atmosphere to the opening ceremony.

Country China

MERIT | CORPORATE AND PROMOTIONAL DESIGN |
COMPLETE PRESS or PROMOTIONAL KIT
CASS ART KIDS
PENTAGRAM DESIGN

Art Director, Designer Angus Hyland
Illustrator Marion Deuchars
Agency Pentagram Design
Client Cass Art

Country United Kingdom

MERIT | CORPORATE AND PROMOTIONAL DESIGN |
SELF-PROMOTION

HANDLE WITH CARE
WINE BAGS
PENTAGRAM DESIGN

Creative Director Louis Gagnon
Art Director, Copywriter René Clément
Agency Paprika

Paprika sends a Holiday Season gift to clients and friends each year. This year, we decided to play on the all-too-common "bottle of wine" gift idea.

The joke was that our gift came with no bottle and no wine... just a big box with eight thought-provoking, smile-inducing wine bags inside—each one a concept on its own, such as:
• In case of emergency, pull the handle...but be careful. It may contain traces of cheap wine.
• Did you know it takes ten minutes of skipping to burn off the calories in a single glass of wine? Fortunately the string on the handle can be used as a skipping rope.
• A kick from champagne...before they're pulled, the handles are shaped like a champagne flute.

It's all there and more. We wouldn't string you along. Honest!

Country Canada

MERIT | CORPORATE AND PROMOTIONAL DESIGN |
CALENDAR or APPOINTMENT BOOK

ROSE
DRAFT CO.,LTD.

Creative Director Satoru Miyata
Art Director Yoshie Watanabe
Designer Yoshie Watanabe, Kazuya Iwanaga
Illustrator Yoshie Watanabe, Kazuya Iwanaga
Agency DRAFT co., ltd.
Client D-BROS

Country Japan

MERIT | CORPORATE AND PROMOTIONAL DESIGN |
LOGO or TRADEMARK

THE COOPER UNION
DOYLE PARTNERS

Creative Director Stephen Doyle
Designer Jason Mannix
Agency Doyle Partners
Client The Cooper Union

"Provocative" is the word that was the genesis of a new logo for Cooper Union, and it was Milton Glaser's. It summarized his ideas about how to represent such a pivotal hotbed of curiosity and accomplishment. Complementing this, and coinciding with a 150th anniversary, a new logo could graphically signal Cooper's vitality, its complexity, its energy and its unity. The school's president said a new logo should "transcend history, tradition and culture, and embrace the future." Other members of the logo committee wanted the logo to "push boundaries," or represent "light, motion and transparency." I wanted the new logo to somehow address the difference of science and art, as well as their union. For me, it seemed like the two sides of the brain... different thinking, but inextricably linked and mutually dependent—and just so much fun when you put them together.

Country United States

MERIT | CORPORATE AND PROMOTIONAL DESIGN |
LOGO or TRADEMARK

WALK UP PRESS LOGO
VILLE

JOSEPH TRAYLOR **ELIZABETH DIGIACOMANTONIO**

Creative Director Joseph Traylor
Designer Joseph Traylor, Elizabeth diGiacomantonio
Agency Ville
Client Walk Up Press

Walk Up Press is a greeting card and paper goods company based in Brooklyn, New York.

Country United States

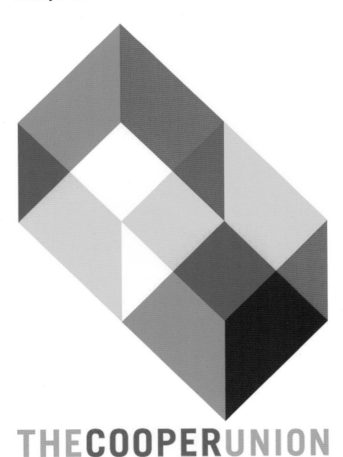

THE**COOPER**UNION

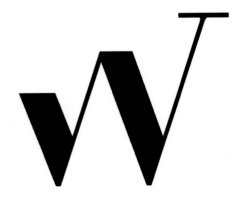

MERIT | CORPORATE AND PROMOTIONAL DESIGN |
CALENDAR or APPOINTMENT BOOK

HANAMOTO 29NO-HI WEEKLY CALENDAR
PENGUIN GRAPHICS

Creative Director Kazuto Nakamura, Tomiko Nakamura
Art Director Kazuto Nakamura, Tomiko Nakamura
Copywriter, Illustrator Tomiko Nakamura
Designer Kazuto Nakamura, Tomiko Nakamura, Shuji Nagato
Agency Penguin Graphics
Client Hanamoto

The calendar of the butcher's shop. As for 2 of the number, "ni" 9 pronounces "ku" meet "niku" in Japanese.
A notice poster of a butcher shop to assume point double service day every month for 2nd, 9th, and 29th. An original weekly calendar of 2010 to announce it.
The illustration presents the form of the nose of the stamp by a different illustration to a base entirely for 365 days on "niku days" (meat day).
It did it to the device which became happy by fun contents every day through one year to watch.

Country Japan

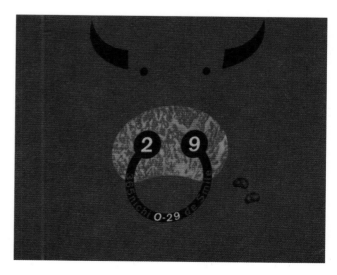

MERIT | CORPORATE AND PROMOTIONAL DESIGN | MISCELLANEOUS

EARTH HOUR 2009
HOYNE DESIGN

Creative Director Dan Johnson
Designer, Illustrator Walter Ochoa
Finished Artist Darren Rochford
Agency Hoyne Design
Client Australia Post

Hoyne was briefed to design a series of stamps for Australia Post to promote Earth Hour 2009. The stamps should appeal to a broad audience and be recognizable as a second 'environmental' series to Australia Post customers.

We focused on three simple actions for Earth Hour: turning lights out, switching power points off and saving energy (by unplugging). The two local stamps featured illustrations of nocturnal animals to highlight the 'lights out' message. The international stamp included an orangutan, a species endangered by humanity's cavalier approach to the environment.

The general public responded in a very positive way to the embedded messaging and playful tone. The stamps successfully raised awareness for Earth Hour and encouraged the public to get involved and take action.

Country Australia

MERIT | CORPORATE AND PROMOTIONAL DESIGN | SELF-PROMOTION

ROHNER LETTERPRESS AND ENGRAVING 2010 PROMOTIONAL
50,000FEET, INC

Creative Director 50,000feet, Inc
Agency 50,000feet, Inc
Client Rohner Letterpress and Engraving

50,000feet collaborated with Rohner Letterpress and Engraving to build awareness with their clients and inspire them to act. The direct mail communication employed an artisanal approach to represent a variety of printing techniques, all delivered with a personal touch. Its appeal was direct to the senses, playfully exploring how words can sometimes take the shape of the sounds they make. The result combined sight, sound and touch into a simple, but impactful, series.

Country United States

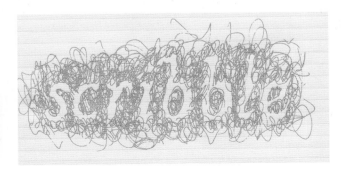

MERIT | CORPORATE AND PROMOTIONAL DESIGN | STATIONARY

LET'S START

DENTSU YOUNG & RUBICAM LTD. (Y&R Thailand)

Creative Director Phayungsak Jaruphun
Art Director Veris Na Songkhla (Graphic Group Head)
Illustrator Visionary
Account Manager Pavara Tanboonchit
Agency Dentsu Young & Rubicam Ltd. (Y&R Thailand)
Client Glammer Education

Country Thailand

MERIT | POSTER DESIGN |
PROMOTIONAL

ACUPUNCTURE NEEDLES
NIPPON DESIGN CENTER

**YASUHIDE
ARAI**

**SHINJI
HOSONO**

Art Director, Designer Yasuhide Arai
Photographer Shinji Hosono
Retoucher Yoshimasa Shimizu
Acupuncturist Masamichi Takahashi
Agency NIPPON DESIGN CENTER
Client Nihon Sogo Ryoji

These posters are for an acupuncture company, and show acupuncture needles on human's back. The needle positions represent musical charts and notes, suggesting that its treatment eases your pain, as though you feel like humming with joy.

I am very honored to be given such a prestigious award like this. I cannot stop thanking people who supported me in this project, especially the photographer, Mr. Hosono. I am also proud of my family for always showing an understanding of my work. Above all, I would like to dedicate this precious award to my dearest daughter, just born last year.

Country Japan

MERIT | POSTER DESIGN |
PROMOTIONAL

SANSAN FARM CO POSTER
MOC

Art Director, Designer Kaoru Morimoto
Production Company Migration
Agency MOC
Client SANSAN FARM

This poster was made to promote a port processing and sales company. A pig sacrifices its life and says EAT ME so that it may become MEAT, and we may eat and exist. Meat becomes the script. The script becomes a message from the pig.

Country Japan

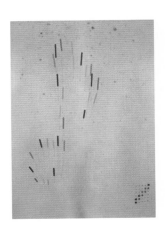
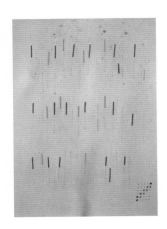
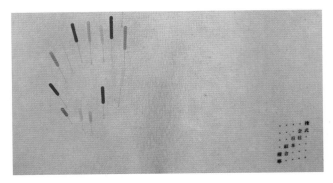

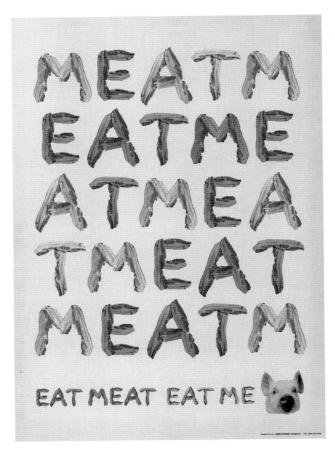

MERIT | CORPORATE AND PROMOTIONAL DESIGN |
POSTCARD, GREETING, INVITATION

WEDDING
INVITATION
PURPOSE

**NATHAN
WEBB**

**PHIL
SKINNER**

Creative Director Stuart Youngs, Rob Howsam
Designer Nathan Webb, Phil Skinner
Project Manager Louisa Phillips
Agency Purpose
Client Jasmine and Tim Plowright

Our objective was to create a unique wedding invitation, personal to both individuals.

Jasmine is from the city and Tim is from the seaside. My Other Half stationery brings the two together for their wedding.

Country United Kingdom

MY OTHER HALF

MERIT | POSTER DESIGN |
PUBLIC SERVICE or NON-PROFIT

SEA _ SIGNALS / RAILROAD CROSSINGS / STREET LIGHTS / PARKING LOTS
DENTSU TEC INC.

HIROSHI KUMABE

FUSANARI MASUDA

Creative Director Hiroshi Kumabe
Art Director, Designer Fusanari Masuda
Copywriter Yuya Kikuchi
Photographer Kayo Yamashita
Photo Editor Chihiro Bekku
Printing Director Takashi Iwamoto, Nobuo Yoshimatsu
Producer Tsuyoshi Kogure
Agency DENTSU TEC INC.
Client WWF Japan

Country Japan

MERIT | PACKAGE DESIGN |
FOOD, BEVERAGE

GUT OGGAU WINE
BOTTLES & WINE BOX
JUNG VON MATT/DONAU
WERBEAGENTUR GMBH

Creative Director Andreas Putz, Volkmar Weiss, Thomas Niederdorfer
Art Director Volkmar Weiss
Designer Iris Dominek
Copywriter Thomas Niederdorfer, Dietmar Voll
Illustrator Anje Jager
Producer Joerg Guenther
Agency Jung von Matt, Donau Werbeagentur GmbH
Client Eduard Tscheppe, Gut Oggau

The Oggau Estate is an Austrian wine growing estate that produces nine wines that differ in character and age. It was our task to design labels and packaging for those wines. Since every wine, like every person, has a unique character, we assigned a face, a story and a name to each wine. Eventually, this led to a typical family clan with grandparents, parents and children.

Country Austria

MERIT | POSTER DESIGN |
POINT-OF-PURCHASE

DRAGON
NOODLE
DAVID AND GOLIATH

Chief Creative Officer David Angelo
Creative Director Colin Jeffery, John Kieselhorst
Copywriter Greg Smzurlo
Designer John Kieselhorst
Agency David and Goliath
Client MGM Mirage, MCC Group

Country United States

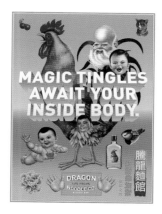

THE OFFICIAL NYC
INFORMATION CENTER
LOCAL PROJECTS

**JAKE
BARTON**

**CLAIRE
WEISZ**

Principal in Charge Jake Barton, Claire Weisz
Creative Director Jake Barton
Art Director Katie Lee
Designer Claire Lin, Benjamin Bours
Photographer Paul Warchol
Video Producer, Videographer Ariel Efron
Producer Tiya Gordon
Sound Designer Jim Aveni
Interaction Designer Ian Curry
Developer David Lu, Brian House, Jack Kalish, Veronique Brossier
Production Company Local Projects, WXY Architecture
Agency Local Projects
Client NYC&Co.

Country United States

BMW EFFICIENTDYNAMICS
JOY IS BMW
BLUE SCOPE
COMMUNICATIONS GMBH

**ANDREAS
STEPHAN**

**CHRISTOPH
SCHMUCK**

Creative Director Andreas Stephan, Christoph Schmuck
Designer Jens Flintrop, Raphaela Meis, Andreas Riemer, Gregor Siber, Christine Weiner, Jörg Zeppezauer, Catharina Zintl
Director Uwe Prell
Producer Mischa Schulze, Sylvia Demes
Film Production gate 11, Christian Künstler, Conny Krause, Arnd Buss v. Kuk
Agency Blue Scope Communications GmbH
Client BMW AG

In our concept design and implimention of the BMW stand, our goal was to make the press and the general public experience responsibility and emotions, as well as solid solutions and joy.

Efficiency and dynamics are two sides of the same coin for BMW. The image: The agile white BMW EfficientDynamics fleet driving on the 280 meter track. The banked curve represents dynamics, the fuel consumption efficiency across all model series.

Movement, architecture, light and interactive media are linked with elements of joy (drinks, motor sounds, classic cars, shows and vehicle handovers).

Country Germany

MERIT | ENVIRONMENTAL DESIGN | ENVIRONMENT

CHOCOLATE RESEARCH FACILITY - WHEELOCK PLACE
ASYLUM CREATIVE

CHRIS LEE

CHERIN TAN

Creative Director Chris Lee
Designer Cherin Tan
Photographer Edwin Tan (Lumina)
Agency Asylum Creative
Client Chocolate Research Facility Pte Ltd

The concept for Chocolate Research Facility was derived from its product offering of chocolate bars in 100 flavors. It was the world's first attempt at having such an array of choices, and we wanted to express the obsession of the owners. Therefore, we came up with the idea of "taking fun seriously" and decided that the research process would be a great theme to carry the brand.

The design is groundbreaking in concept. We took unexpected elements that are serious, and combine them with food and experimentation. Different playful elements, such as the overflowing chocolate wall and the slab tables, make it accessible to consumers of all ages. The design of the brand is completely thought out from its concept to execution. No detail is spared in the creation of this project.

Country Singapore

MERIT | ENVIRONMENTAL DESIGN | ENVIRONMENT

RADIO FREE EUROPE/RADIO LIBERTY SCULPTURE SIGN
C&G PARTNERS

Creative Director Steff Geissbuhler
Designer Steff Geissbuhler, Mariano Desmaras
Photographer PRIMA Blansko
Agency C&G Partners
Client Radio Free Europe/Radio Liberty

The commission was to design a sign at the new Radio Free Europe/Radio Liberty Headquarters in Prague, Czech Republic that would project the mission of the organization. Words were selected to communicate the urgent nature of the news broadcasting to countries with limited freedom of the press. The ten-foot-high, custom-drawn, dimensional letterforms create a sculptural installation that changes language depending on direction of approach, either "LIBERTY" or the same word with the same amount of letters in Czech, "SVOBODA."

The piece functions as a graphic sign, public art and sculpture, as well as an extension of the brand.

Country United States

MERIT | ENVIRONMENTAL DESIGN | ENVIRONMENT

GREY GROUP SIGNAGE AND ENVIRONMENTAL GRAPHICS
PENTAGRAM DESIGN

PAULA SCHER

Art Director Paula Scher
Designer Paula Scher, Andrew Freeman
Photographer Peter Mauss, Esto
Agency Pentagram Design
Client Grey Group

In December 2009, Grey Group relocated to a new, state-of-the-art headquarters in the former International Toy Center in the Flatiron District. Pentagram developed a playful program of environmental graphics for the space to promote the creativity of the company's various divisions and to tie the loft-like floors of the new headquarters together into a cohesive environment. The interiors were designed using different materials for each division or department on each floor. The environmental graphics use these same materials—wood, glass, metal and polymer—in ways that suggest the personalities of the different divisions. The signage mixes the materials with elements of reflection, transparency, lighting and pattern to create a series of optical illusions that sets each department apart.

Country United States

MERIT | ENVIRONMENTAL DESIGN | ENVIRONMENT

HARLEY-DAVIDSON MUSEUM SIGNAGE AND ENVIRONMENTAL GRAPHICS
PENTAGRAM DESIGN

MICHAEL BIERUT

Art Director Michael Bierut
Designer Michael Bierut, Katie Barcelona
Photographer Paul Warchol, Timothy Hursley
Agency Pentagram Design
Client Harley-Davidson Motor Company

The Harley-Davidson Museum in Milwaukee, Wisconsin showcases the history, culture and engineering of an American icon. Pentagram designed the architecture, exhibitions, signage and environmental graphics for the 130,000 square-foot museum that sits on a 20 acre reclaimed industrial site in downtown Milwaukee. The museum consists of three interconnected buildings, conceived of as an urban factory with space for permanent and temporary exhibitions, the company's extensive archives, a restaurant called Motor, a café called Racer, and a retail store called The Shop.

Country United States

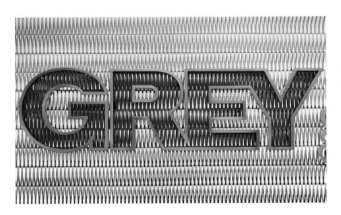

VOESTALPINE
STAHLWELT
KMS TEAM GMBH

**MICHAEL
KELLER**

**ARMIN
SCHLAMP**

Creative Director Michael Keller
Art Director Marc Ziegler, Birgit Rose Vogel
Designer Susana Frau, Moritz Pongratz
Director Armin Schlamp
Client Manager Christine Schauer
Project Manager Katrin Schiese
Consulting Christian P. Árkay-Leliever (KMS TEAM NY)
Documentational Photographer Michael Haegele
Partner Agency Jangled Nerves
Agency KMS TEAM GmbH
Client voestalpine AG

The voestalpine Stahlwelt is a brand museum, that introduces visitors to the Voestalpine Steel Group and to the steel material in the context of a didactic concept of experience and knowledge using a variety of multimedia exhibition elements.

The program of the Stahlwelt exhibition begins with the experience of steel and progresses to impart knowledge regarding processing, products and the company. The experience is enjoyed in a "crucible," in which 80 chrome-plated steel spheres of a diameter of up to 2.5 meters are arranged in accordance with the molecular structure of iron and are surrounded by a variously programmed 700 square meter LED mantle. Knowledge is communicated in the adjacent "tower": a vertical conveyor belt transports steel exhibits that illustrate the value creation chain of the material.

Country Germany

FUKUTAKE
HOUSE 2009
FLAME, INC.

Art Director Masayoshi Kodaira
Designer Masayoshi Kodaira, Yukiharu Takematsu
Photographer Mikiya Takimoto, Fumihito Katamura
Producer Soichiro Fukutake
Agency FLAME, Inc.
Client Fukutake Foundation for the Promotion of Regional Culture

Country Japan

MERIT | ENVIRONMENTAL DESIGN |
GALLERY, MUSEUM EXHIBIT, INSTALLATION

THE L!BRARY INITIATIVE
PENTAGRAM DESIGN

MICHAEL BIERUT

Creative Director Michael Bierut
Designer Michael Bierut, Josh Berta, Rion Byrd-Gumus, Kai Salmela, Rafael Esquer, Maira Kalman, Christoph Niemann, Stefan Sagmeister, Yuko Shimizu, Charles Wilkin
Photographer Peter Mauss, Esto, Kevin Chu, Jessica Paul
Agency Pentagram Design
Client Robin Hood Foundation

Since 2002, Pentagram has contributed to a visionary effort by the Robin Hood Foundation: an initiative to build new school libraries in elementary schools throughout New York City. A range of talented architects have designed the libraries; private companies have donated books and funds; and Pentagram has provided the graphic design, including signage, wayfinding and a masterbrand, that ties all the sites together.

The libraries are usually located in older buildings with high ceilings, but the shelves in the libraries can't be built higher than kids can reach. This means there is a space between the top shelf and the ceiling just begging for something special. That something turned out to be murals. The results can now be seen in schools all over New York, including five new libraries in the Bronx, which feature murals by Rafael Esquer, Maira Kalman, Christoph Niemann, Stefan Sagmeister and Yuko Shimizu, and Charles Wilkin.

Country United States

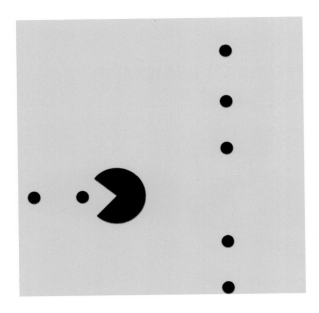

MERIT | TELEVISION AND CINEMA DESIGN |
IDENTITIES, OPENINGS, TEASERS

NETWORK IDS
MRS. K

MITCH MONSON

Creative Director Jeanne Kopeck, Mitch Monson
Art Director, Designer Mitch Monson
Animation Andimages, Engine Room
Producer Lauren Worth, Mary Daisey
Agency Mrs. K
Client Best Buy

Best Buy approached us to create television IDs that brought a quirky and playful personality to the in-store network within Best Buy stores. These IDs played both domestically and internationally so the concepts had to be simple and register quickly in any market. The concept for each ID was to start with a very simple, flat graphic construct, and then transform that into a dynamic dimensional experience (in various genres) and then resolve back to a simple Best Buy iconic tag. This creative solution for the IDs was so successful that they also found placement in commercial tags and network transitions both on-air and in stores for Best Buy.

Country United States

HOUSE OF IMAGINATION
SYFY

Copywriter Brett Foraker (4 Creative), Tom Tagholm (4 Creative)
Designer Brett Foraker (4 Creative), Moving Picture Company London
Creative Director Michael Engleman (Syfy), Brett Foraker (4 Creative), Joseph Loskywitz (Syfy)
Director Brett Foraker (4 Creative)
Editor Adam Rudd (Final Cut)
Producer Kate Leonard (Syfy), Shananne Lane (4 Creative)
Production Company 4 Creative, Moving Picture Company London
Agency Syfy, 4 Creative, Moving Picture Company London
Client Syfy

When the Sci Fi Channel changed its name to Syfy in July of 2009, the entire identity of the network changed with it. Bigger, broader and more inclusive than ever before, Syfy faced the challenge of inviting previously hard-to-reach viewers to join in the brand's exciting new journey. The solution was a revolutionary brand film called "House of Imagination," in which incredible yet relatable feats of imagination were used to showcase the broad range of talent from all of Syfy's acclaimed original shows. Produced in collaboration with the United Kingdom's renowned 4 Creative, this groundbreaking film featured part practical, part digital environments and premium animation, and premiered to rave reviews from critics and viewers alike.

Country United States

HOUSE OF IMAGINATION IDS
SYFY

Creative Director Michael Engleman (Syfy), Brett Foraker (4 Creative), Joseph Loskywitz (Syfy)
Copywriter Brett Foraker (4 Creative), Tom Tagholm (4 Creative)
Designer Brett Foraker (4 Creative), Moving Picture Company London
Director Brett Foraker (4 Creative)
Editor Adam Rudd (Final Cut)
Producer Kate Leonard (Syfy), Shananne Lane (4 Creative)
Production Company 4 Creative, Moving Picture Company London
Agency Syfy, 4 Creative, Moving Picture Company London
Client Syfy

Country United States

MERIT | TELEVISION AND CINEMA DESIGN |
TITLE DESIGN

BROADCAT
09 TITLES
WEMAKE

Creative Director, Director, Producer Lucas Borras
Illustrator Lucas Borras, Carlota Santamaria
Audio FlowAudio
Production Company WeMake / Broadcat / ADG-FAD
Agency WeMake
Client Broadcat / ADG-FAD

Broadcat 09 titles was a very challenging project. I had one
month to prepare it.
I understood the festival credits as a movie. I was very inspired
by the sci-fi movies from the 70s and I decided to make my own
galactic broadcat world.
We made the base in CG, and then after we transformed
everything into cell animation.

It was a wonderful experience and I feel very proud of the result.

Country United States

FIND THE UNEXPECTED
WONGDOODY

TRACY WONG   **MARK WATSON**

Creative Director Tracy Wong, Mark Watson
Art Director Emily Honigsfeld
Copywriter Janelle Erickson
Designer Digital Kitchen
Editor Slavka Kolbel
Account Mananger Brianna Babb, Annie Richards
Traffic Manager Eva Doak
Producer Steph Huske
Production Company Digital Kitchen
Audio Company Clatter & Din
Agency WONGDOODY
Client Seattle International Film Festival (SIFF)

The Seattle International Film Festival, the nation's largest film festival, is a refreshing departure from formulaic and predictable multiplex fare. So to entice new filmgoers to SIFF, we invited potential audience members to "FIND the Unexpected" within the festival's 550 films. Theatrical trailers and bumpers, all inspired by Indonesian shadow puppetry, featured animated silhouettes in detail-rich scenes, created entirely in-camera, representing all that awaits discovery—new actors, new directors, fresh perspectives and never-before-seen films from over 60 countries.

Country United States

TENTH OF A CENTURY
ELASTIC

Creative Director Scott McDonald (RPA)
Designer, Director Andy Hall
Executive Producer Gary Paticoff
Production Company Elastic
Agency Elastic, RPA
Client Newport Beach Film Festival

Country United States

MERIT | BRANDING | CAMPAIGN

VINE
R/GA

**JAMES
TEMPLE**

**MARC
SHILLUM**

MERIT | BRANDING | CAMPAIGN

NOOK
R/GA

**MARC
SHILLUM**

Executive Creative Director James Temple
Creative Director Carla Echevarria
Associate Creative Director Nathalie Huni
Senior Copywriter Neil Starr
Design Director Virgilio Santos
Director of Brand Design Marc Shillum
Visual Designer Gustav Arnetz, Ennio Franco, Rasmus Knutsson
Senior Interaction Designer Kathrin Hoffmann
Flash Developer Jolyon Russ, Ben Doran, Nicolas Le Pallec, Ozay Olkan, Tomas Vorobjov
Technical Director Kevin Sutherland
Presentation Code Developer Michael Potts
Quality Assurance Engineer Neil Duggan
Managing Director, Analytics, Accountability Luane Kohnke
Planning Director, Insights, Planning Darren Savage
Group Account Director Anthony Wickham
Senior Producer Dylan Connerton
Associate Producer Krystal-Joy Williams
Agency R/GA
Client Nokia

Country United States

Director of Brand Development Marc Shillum
Executive Creative Director Andy Clark, Jay Zasa
Copywriter Jay Zasa
Senior Visual Designer Pete Golibersuch, Ronnie Ting
Visual Design Director Virgilio Santos
Group Director, Production Daniel Jurow
Senior Producer Sean Farrell
Agency R/GA
Client Barnes & Noble

Country United States

I'm in my nook　　　　　*I'm not in my nook*

MERIT | TELEVISION AND CINEMA DESIGN |
ANIMATION

TIM BURTON
THE MUSEUM OF MODERN ART

JULIA HOFFMANN

Creative Director Julia Hoffmann
Director Tim Burton
Animation Chris Tichborne
Music Danny Elfman
Puppet Joe Holman, Richard Pickersgill, Caroline Wallace, Graeme Hall, Richard Jeffers
CGI Simon Partington, Mike Whipp, John Whittington, Neil Sanderson
Director of Photography Martin Kelly
Online Editor Mark Wharton
Graphics Support Neil Sutcliffe
Production Company MacKinnon & Saunders, UK
Post Production Flix Facilities
Agency The Museum of Modern Art

Country United States

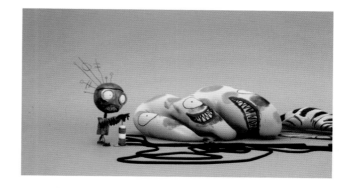

MERIT | BRANDING | CAMPAIGN |

COCA-COLA
SUMMER IDENTITY
TURNER DUCKWORTH:
LONDON & SAN FRANCISCO

**DAVID
TURNER**

**BRUCE
DUCKWORTH**

Creative Director David Turner, Bruce Duckworth
Design Director Sarah Moffat
Designer Rebecca Williams, Josh Michels
Agency Turner Duckworth: London & San Francisco
Client The Coca-Cola Company North America

The Coca-Cola Summer 2009 campaign celebrates the joy
and optimism of summer and Coke's authentic connection to
the season. The graphics, designed by Turner Duckworth, were
featured on packaging, in-store displays and select television
spots. The designs were also used for summer premiums on
everything from t-shirts and hats to beach towels. Five cans were
released overall, culminating with a special July 4th holiday can.
The designs also appeared on can packs, two liters and 20oz
bottles, all in celebration of summer's favorite beverage—Coca-
Cola.

Country United States

MERIT | BRANDING | CAMPAIGN |

EAT OUT FOR A CHANGE CAMPAIGN
FIREHOUSE

Creative Director Tripp Westbrook
Art Director Shannon Phillips
Copywriter Jason Fox
Designer Cara Stooksberry
Editor Gigi Cone Welch
Producer Julie Koellner
Production Company Fast Cuts, Boxcar Creative
Other Dave Jacobson, Shelby Miller, Ben Templeton, Hayes Smith, PK Jones
Agency Firehouse
Client Eat Out For A Change

Single-unit restaurants and chains were struggling to drive business under current economic conditions. To solve this, the industry needed a uniform push and convincing argument as to why people should choose to eat out more.

Understanding why people were holding back on restaurant spending now and in the future was imperative. Looking at consumer behavior and attitudes revealed that people were waiting for permission to eat out again. To solve this, we uncovered surprising and compelling facts that created a powerful stance for why people should feel good about eating out more.

Eat Out For A Change educates people on the impact they can have, even as individuals, by simply making the choice to eat out just one more time a week. When people see the campaign, we want them to understand that they can make a difference and help jump-start the economy.

Country United States

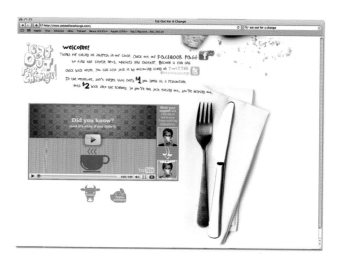

MERIT .08% of all awards given

CUBE .04% of all awards given

ADC**DESIGN SPHERE**

The awards process is always an enlightening one, with work that take you by surprise and inspires! along with the typical work that leaves a lot to be desired.

The ones that that are outstanding for their excellence and creativity set the standards for the best industry to be involved with, one that is fun, fulfilling and expecting nothing less than excellence.

This years ADC awards again produced surprises of that nature with an emphasis on media being used as a creative tool and not just as a new technology, at the end of the day work that really shines is based firmly on a great idea, and then the tools of today have been used to implement that idea purely to add excellence of presentation.

The work we picked out was all based on a foundation of a concrete idea, we need to keep the standards of our industry at its ultimate peak, otherwise anyone with a mac will be able to consider themselves a designer, which is a destination that will destroy the design industry an ADC stands proud to maintain the level of quality being submitted and awarded.

- Karen Welman
Creative partner, Pearlfischer
ADC Design Sphere Jury Chair

ADC**DESIGN SPHERE JURY**

KAREN
WELMAN
PEARLFISHER

Entrepreneur, designer and inventor, Karen Welman is passionate about the power of ideas, and uses design as a means to answer genuine human needs and desires.

In 2004, Karen developed and launched the brand 37 degrees, a clothing line for babies that regulates body temperature. 1 year later, using the same material, she launched Dick Moby's – a range of men's underwear designed to keep the the crown jewels cool.

Throughout this time, in fact since 1991, Karen has been Creative Partner of Pearlfisher. Karen still insists on pushing all the boundaries. Her mischievous and generous spirit make her a formidable presence both at work and play.

LOUISE
FILI
LOUISE FILI LTD

Louise Fili is principal of Louise Fili Ltd, specializing in food packaging and restaurant identities. She is co-author, with Steven Heller, of Italian Art Deco, Dutch Moderne, Streamline, Cover Story, British Modern, Deco Espana, German Modern, French Modern, Typology, Design Conoisseur, Counter Culture, Stylepedia, and Euro Deco. She has also written and designed A Civilized Shopper's Guide to Florence and Italianissimo. In 2004 she was inducted into the Art Directors Hall of Fame.

DAVOR
BRUKETA
BRUKETA & ZINIC

Together with Nikola Zinic, Davor Bruketa is a founder of Croatian design and advertising agency Bruketa&ZinicOM, where he works as a Creative Director.
Bruketa&ZinicOM is one of the most awarded marketing communication agencies in SE Europe with over 300 international awards such as Epica, New York Festivals, London International Awards, Art Directors Club, Cresta, Clio, Red Dot and many more. Bruketa was also judging at the D&AD, Graphis, London International Awards, Cresta Awards, NY Festivals, MIAF-Moscow etc.

WEBSITE BRUKETA-ZINIC.COM

ADC DESIGN
SPHERE | SERIES

PODRAVKA
ANNUAL REPORTS
BRUKETA & ZINIC D.O.O.

**DAVOR
BRUKETA**

**NIKOLA
ZINIC**

Creative Director Davor Bruketa, Nikola Zinic
Art Director Davor Bruketa, Nikola Zinic
Copywriter Davor Bruketa, Nikola Zinic
Designer Imelda Ramovic, Mirel Hadzijusufovic
Project Manager Drenislav Zekic
Agency Bruketa&Zinic d.o.o.
Client Podravka

Country Croatia

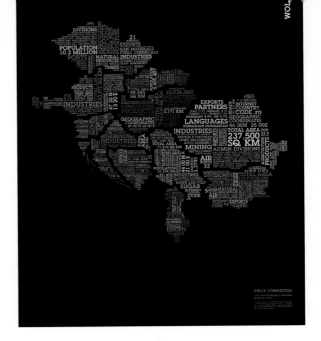

ADC DESIGN
SPHERE | SERIES

WOLF THEISS: AN UNCONVENTIONAL IDENTITY FOR AN UNCONVENTIONAL LAW FIRM.

THE PARTNERS

**MARTIN
ROWLATT**   **JACK
RENWICK**

Creative Director Jack Renwick
Copywriter Nick Asbury
Designer Tim Fishlock, Tim Brown, Bob Young, Leon Bahrani
Editor Client Director Hannah Kirkman
Producer Alex John
Strategic Consultant Martin Rowlatt
Agency The Partners
Client Wolf Theiss

Country United Kingdom

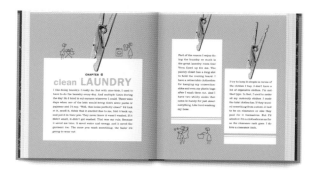

ADC DESIGN
SPHERE | SERIES

MRS. MEYER'S CLEAN DAY
WERNER DESIGN WERKS, INC.

Creative Director Werner Design Werks
Art Director Werner Design Werks
Copywriter Werner Design Werks, Clean & Co, Mono
Designer Werner Design Werks, Clean & Co, Mono
Agency Werner Design Werks, Inc.
Client Clean & Company

Mrs. Meyer's household cleaners are uncomplicated products that smell great, work hard and are inspired by the founder's mother of nine, Mrs. Thelma Meyer.
The packaging established the tone of the brand, from copy and visual vocabulary to advertising and exhibit spaces and communicates the brand story of honest hard work and establishes Thelma as an authority on clean. We consistently ask "What would Thelma do or say?" and "Does it grow in her Iowa garden?"
The brand includes four core fragrances, baby products, scent-free cleaners, seasonal fragrances, and a book chock-full of Thelma's cleaning advice. The brand presence is created by merchandising all Mrs. Meyer's products together rather than spreading them out among competitive cleaning products.
The advertising, online media, exhibit trailer and more continue to reinforce Mrs. Meyer's no-nonsense voice, spreading the word about products that clean like the dickens and smell nice too.

Country United States

ADC WINNERS BY CAMPAIGN AND COUNTRY

Follow the lines to see what country the cubes are headed to and for which pieces of work.

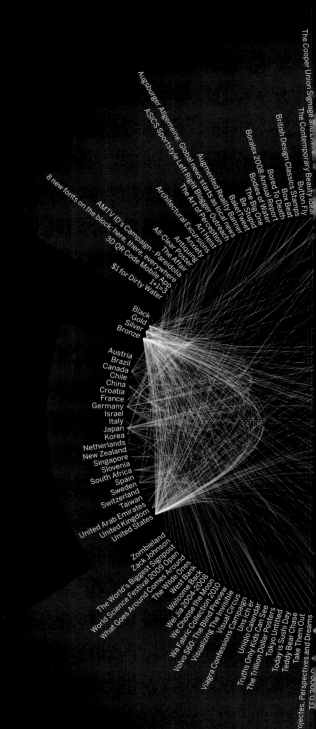

Augsburger Allgemeine. Global news starts as local news
ASICS Sportstyle Left Right Blogger Outreach
Augmented Reality Banner
The Art of Perception
Antiquing
Architectural Excursions
Anxiety
All-Clear Poster
AMTV ID's Campaign - Pareidolia
The Affair
3D QR Code Mobile App
8 new fonts on the block; here, there, everywhere
1+1=3
$1 for Dirty Water

The Cooper Union Signage and
The Contemporary Beauty Idea!
Button Fly
British Design Classics Stamps
Box Beat
Boralex 2008 Annual Report
Bored To Death
The Big One
Be Stupid
Bodies of Water
BakeTweet
BakerBanner

Black
Gold
Silver
Bronze

Austria
Brazil
Canada
Chile
China
Croatia
France
Germany
Israel
Italy
Japan
Korea
Netherlands
New Zealand
Singapore
Slovenia
South Africa
Spain
Sweden
Switzerland
Taiwan
United Arab Emirates
United Kingdom
United States

Zombieland
Zack Johnson
The World's Biggest Signpost
World Science Festival 2009 Open
What Goes Around Comes Around
The Wilde Ones
West Bank
Welcome Back
Wei Jia 2004-2008
We Choose the Moon
Volvo S60: The Blind Preview
Visualizing The Invisible
Visual Circus
Viagra Confessions Campaign
Uns ich er
Uniqlo Calendar
Truths Only Kids Can See
The Trillion Dollar Posters
Tokyo Untitled
Today is Sushi Day
Teddy Bear Chase
Take Them Out

TMB 2008 Projectes, Perspectives and Dreams

Cassette Tapes
Cause & Effect
Charles Darwin Stamps
Cheer Dark
Chinatown: Place / Space
Clocks
Comics
Congraturations ICHIRO
Corporate Identity of the 4th Biennial of Slovene Visual Communications
Congraturalize
Cowboy
Crane
Cube Film Installation
Cutter Art of OLFA
D&AD Awards Ceremony
Deadline
The Discovery
EFFP Identity
Earth in the Air
Egg
Electronic Finger Painting
Eliyah ó Planet. Planet
END THE LIES
The End
F1984T2008
Facebook Showroom
Facial Profiler
Fiat Crash Test Panda
The First Supersize Pup-up
Flyvertising - the world's first fly banner.
Furniture Messages
Freaky Robot
Game
Global Warming
Göteborgstryckeriet printing house identity
Graphic Trial 2009, Repetition on Surface
Great Performers
Hammer Throw
Happy Kid
Helicopter Boyz
IBM Smarter Planet Campaign
Icograda World Design Congress 2009 Beijing VI
Igi V Therapeutic Play Kit
Infrastructure
JAQK Cellars
Journey To South
LG FIVE
The Last Call
Le Musée Grandit (The Museum is growing)
Less and More Tokyo 01
Less and More Tokyo 02
Less and More Tokyo 03
Less Effort. More Effect!
The Life
Like a Golf
Livestrong Campaign
Logo ID
The Low Emission Hitchhiker
Lutzka Escapes
Mobilize
Monday Night Football - Interactive Storescapes
Music Concert Poster
My Best Stories
The Natural Fermentation. Homemade Bakery. Daichi no Mi.
Neenah Paper 2008 Annual Report
Nissan Cube Hostel
OIAF Signal Film
Objects of Pocket
Odyssey: Architecture & Literature
Ong Slew May Distinguished Lecture Series Book Cover
Plug into the Smart Grid
Plugs
Podravka Annual Reports
Posters
Power Leakage
Pre Organic Cotton The Day T-Shirts Project
Reading
Return of the Ornament
SVA Undergraduate Catalog 2010/11
Samsung Shakedown
The Sex Tree
Shan Shui

MERIT 2% of all awards given

BRONZE 4% of all awards given

SILVER 1% of all awards given

GOLD 3% of all awards given

INTERACTIVE

Digital awards have always been tricky, with traditional media the rules are set, here is a defined space, now who filled it with the best stuff?

Digital however is constantly inundated with new technologies, new formats and new buzzwords. It is the most exciting thing about the industry and also the worst, technologies and trends are a great camouflage for badly written ideas.

However this year at the ADC I believe we had a couple of break throughs, the industry is starting to value writing even more, it's the combination of 'old fashioned' good writing and appropriate use of technology and media that gives us the best work.

This leads us into a common phrase now ringing around agencies 'what is digital'? If it's an outdoor event but filmed and then put on youtube is that digital?

Really, in the end who cares, not the consumer. They aren't debating formats or what is digital and what is not, they just respond if it's good enough. Maybe digital is getting close to the point where we won't have to talk about digital anymore?"

- Dave Bedwood
Creative Partner, Lean Mean Fighting Machine
ADC Interactive Jury Chair

INTERACTIVE AGENCY OF THE YEAR
GOODBY SILVERSTEIN AND PARTNERS

ADC**INTERACTIVE JURY**

DAVE
BEDWOOD
LEAN MEAN
FIGHTING MACHINE

Dave Bedwood has worked with his creative partner, Sam Ball, since 1995. In 1999, they became one of the first traditional creative teams to get into digital advertising. By 2001, they were Tribal DDB's creative directors. In 2004, they launched (with Dave Cox and Tom Bazeley) Lean Mean Fighting Machine. That year, they were voted into Campaign's Top Ten Creative Directors, as well as Campaign's Faces to Watch. 2005 saw them pick up Campaign's Young Achievers of the Year Award, and they were voted by their peers to be the number one creative team in digital advertising. They have picked up awards from numerous industry competitions, including D&AD, One Show, Cannes, Clio, Creative Circle and the Webby Awards. In 2008, Dave made The Observers Future 500 list and Campaign's A-List, and he went to Cannes where his agency became the first United Kingdom agency to win Interactive Agency of the Year. In 2009, Dave was the foreman for the D&AD Awards online advertising category.

TWITTER DBEDWOOD
WEBSITE LEANMEANFIGHTINGMACHINE.CO.UK

EDU POU
WIEDEN+KENNEDY

KOSHI UCHIYAMA
GT INC

MARIO SANCHEZ
NETTHINK

I've been living a cheesy love story since 1997. It started with DoubleYou, where interactivity stole my heart. That relationship was magical. Each day I discovered something new and wonderful. Everything was perfect, but after a while I wanted to face new challenges and decided to trade Barcelona for the United States, ending up in a tiny town in the heart of the Rocky Mountains. There, with CP+B, I fell in love with advertising. Days and nights flew by so fast they were a blur. It was a very exciting period, but I missed Europe and decided to jump the Atlantic again. As soon as I landed, I lost my mind once more. For brand-building this time, and Wieden+Kennedy was to blame. This is where I am now, and so far, so awesome. Funny thing is that I've never dumped any one of my loves, so at the moment I'm part of some kind of harmonic foursome with interactivity, advertising and brand-building. Thank God Amsterdam is a very liberal city.

TWITTER EDUPOU
WEBSITE EDUPOU.COM

Throughout Koshi's 15 years in the industry, he has continuously introduced advertising that fuses media art, entertainment and cutting edge IT technology to the world. His feats have earned him wide acclaim, with substantial impacts on both the marketing and internet business industries.

I particular, Koshi is leading many innovative projects and focusing his efforts on 360 degree advertising plans and multimedia direction.

In the last couple of years, Koshi has picked up many awards from various competitions, including One Show, Clio, LIA, Adfest and the Art Directors Club. He has won three Cannes Lions Gold trophies.

TWITTER GTKOSHI

Mario Sanchez's career was offline until 1997, when he fall in love with the internet and decided to turn digital at a time when it was still new to the Spanish market. He founded his own digital agency named Triple Digital and drove it to win several and important local awards such as Ampe, Imán and Cannes (shortlisted). In 2004, he became executive creative director at Netthink, a full-service interactive agency of Isobar Group, where he was responsible of all the creative work, designing communication and online marketing strategies for a client list including Adidas, BMW Motorrad, Buenavista Internacional, Chivas, Durex, Disney, Fiat, Johnnie Walker, Kodak, MINI, Monster, Nintendo, Openbank, Saab, Schweppes, and many more. In 2008, after the international recognition of the company's creative work ("15th most awarded interactive agency of the world" Gunn Report, 2008), he became the chief creative officer of Netthink.

Throughout his career, he's been awarded in many of the most relevant national and international competitions and festivals, including Cannes (Gold Lion), One Show (Gold Pencil), LIA, Epica, Eurobest, El SOL, Fiap, Gran Prix OJO de Iberoamérica, Promax DBA, EFI, Ampe, Gran Prix Genio (Vocento), Imán, Eyeblaster Creative Awards, MSN Mouse Awards. He has been a juror at EL OJO de Iberoamérica, El SOL, Webby Awards, Cresta Awards, IAB Inspirational, MSN Mouse Awards and for the most popular advertising magazine in Spain, *Premios Anuncios*.

JULIA ROTHMAN
ALSO ONLINE

Working from New York and Chicago, ALSO is a three-headed creative team—part designer, illustrator and animator. Jenny, Julia and Matt create highly customized websites and print work for a fun and visually adventurous clientele. They have gained acclaim for the animated Charmingwall website, the redesign of Design*Sponge, and the Reform School store site. ALSO won the prestigious Young Guns Award from the Art Directors Club in 2008. Currently, they are working on authoring and curating *The Exquisite Book*, a project based on the surrealist game called The Exquisite Corpse, played by 100 contributing contemporary fine artists, illustrators, designers and comic artists. The book will be published by Chronicle Books and comes out this fall.

Aside from ALSO, Julia illustrates and creates pattern designs for companies like The New York Times, Victoria's Secret and Urban Outfitters. She also runs the daily blog that features new art books, Book-By-Its-Cover. com.

TWITTER JULIAROTHMAN
WEBSITE JULIAROTHMAN.COM

NINA BOESCH
AND PARTNERS, NEW YORK

Nina Boesch leads the interactive practice at And Partners, NY. She specializes in combining interaction design and information architecture with a deep foundation in traditional graphic design to create successful communications, both on- and off-line.

Nina's work creating websites, mobile applications, desktop applications and touch-screen kiosks has been honored by the AIGA, the IDSA, *HOW* magazine, *I.D.* magazine, and Adobe. Prior to joining And Partners, she worked for three years on Lisa Strausfeld's team at Pentagram.

A native of Bremen, Germany, Nina is a RISD graduate and an ADC Young Gun.

WEBSITE NINABOESCH.COM

LIZ SIVELL
R/GA

As creative director, R | GA London, Liz Sivell is primarily responsible for providing creative leadership and developing strong conceptual and strategic direction for global Nokia e-marketing and other core accounts.

Sivell has extensive brand knowledge and boasts more than a decade of experience in the digital industry. Her breadth of work ranges from creating retail installations and immersive campaign experiences, to managing project implementation, production and brand analysis for clients including Nike, C.O.I.-FRANK, MINI, Adidas and Unilever.

Prior to R | GA, Sivell served as creative director for Profero in London and Onedigital in Australia, where she led creative teams to build experiences that took clients beyond the traditional advertising space, transforming physical environments into powerful tools to influence behavior and attitude. She has won numerous awards over the years for her work, including a Gold World Medal, a Mouse Awards Bronze and a One Show Silver Pencil.

TWITTER MADLIZZIE
WEBSITE RGA.COM

BRENDAN
DIBONA
AKQA D.C.

JOHN
LU
BARKER / DZP

During Brendan's tenure as executive creative director, AKQA DC has consistently produced innovative, award-winning work for Volkswagen, the US Postal Service, Bethesda Softworks and the NHL, among others. Over his 13-year career, Brendan has also led design work on projects for ESPN, Discovery and vitaminwater.

Before joining AKQA, Brendan worked as a print designer in Durham, North Carolina. He earned his B.F.A. in communication arts and design from Virginia Commonwealth University in Richmond.

John Lu is the vice president, director of interactive for Barker | DZP, a full-service integrated agency based in Soho, New York. With a background in user experience design and web development, Lu heads all online and mobile work within the agency. He's worked with such clients as Estée Lauder, Crate & Barrel, Proctor & Gamble, Microsoft, American Express, Best Buy and Sesame Workshop. Prior to Barker | DZP, he was an interaction designer at Crispin Porter + Bogusky, Digitas and ESI Design. He is a graduate of Northwestern University and the Interactive Telecommunications Program from New York University.

TWITTER REALJOHNLU
WEBSITE VERHOLLYWOOD.COM
WEBSITE LABSERIES.COM
WEBSITE PEOPLESCHOICE.COM

SEAN GANANN
CAMPFIRE

As creative director, Sean is a passionate and pioneering creative with over 15 years of experience in creating and building brands. His love for doing work that is immersive, interactive and engaging has led to effective and awarded campaigns for such diverse clients as Snapple, Verizon FIOS, Discovery Channel, Lexus, Virgin Atlantic, Toyota, 3 Mobile and IBM. Sean has sat on jury panels for Cannes Lions, One Show, London International Advertising Awards, Asian Advertising Awards, Asia Pacific Adfest and many other local and regional shows. Before joining Campfire, Sean was the digital creative director at the new model agency Anomaly in New York City. Prior to that, he headed digital at Saatchi & Saatchi Australia and built the creative department and reputation of NetX, Australia's most awarded interactive agency.

TWITTER GANANN
WEBSITE GANANN.COM

LOUIE CALE
LITTLE GOLIATH

Louie Cale is a project manager and an art-based creative director who started his career with traditional advertising. He's done the rounds at different agencies, from Publicis to McCann-Erickson to TBWA, handling both local and multinational brands. His advertising work has been recognized internationally by the Asian Adfest, the New York Adfest and The One Show.

From advertising, Louie headed into the digital domain. As a product development manager of Chikka.com, creator of the first mobile instant messenger, he has worked with the core team who re-launched and created some of its applications.

Louie came back to advertising when he set up the digital arm of TBWA\SMP as its head of digital.

Today, he has relocated to New York to pursue his passion of combining creativity and technology for tech start-up ideas that use social networking, mobile technology, e-commerce and experimental approaches.

TWITTER LOUIECALE
WEBSITE LITTLEGOLIATH.COM

DAMIAN BAZADONA
SITUATION MARKETING

Damian Bazadona founded Situation Interactive (formerly, Situation Marketing) in 2001 and oversees the strategic direction for the company based in New York, Las Vegas and Los Angeles. Situation is the leading interactive agency for premier live entertainment brands worldwide, including Disney, Universal and Cirque du Soleil. Prior to forming Situation Interactive, Damian was partner and chief marketing officer of Cyber-NY Interactive where he was responsible for new business development and strategic initiatives for the firm. He is an active contributor and source for leading business publications including *The New York Times*, *Variety*, *Associated Press* and many more. In addition, he has served as a speaker and source for university research studies relating to online marketing for Yale University, New York University, Columbia University and Fordham University's graduate level programs. Damian holds a B.S. inBusiness Administration from University at Albany.

TWITTER BAZADOG

KAT STREET
CRISPIN PORTER + BOGUSKY EUROPE

In 2002, After three months as an intern, Kat Street was hired on as the youngest art director at a place known today as Crispin Porter + Bogusky. With an impressive seven years standing at the top creative shop, Kat's career includes the full spectrum of work. From traditional to digital, she started out working on guerrilla campaigns for BMW MINI Cooper, but built her roster to include integrated work for Volkswagen, Virgin Atlantic Airways, 'TRUTH' anti-tobacco effort, Guitar Hero and Burger King.

Kat has taken home awards at nearly every industry show, but just walked away with top honors at One Show and LIAA for her product innovation and development on Domino's Pizza. She most recently just made the jump across the pond to help build the new CPB Europe, in Göteborg, Sweden.

TWITTER KATSTREET
WEBSITE KATSTREET.CARBONMADE.COM

RAHUL SABNIS
EURO RSCG WORLDWIDE, NEW YORK

As executive creative director at Digital Euro RSCG Worldwide, New York, Rahul is guided by the belief that the true engine of creativity is driven by deep consumer insight, coupled with unique ideas. His experience in numerous marketing disciplines has cultivated an "authenticity" mantra, where he inspires work that reflects both the larger brand message while retaining a true, authentic flavor.

Into his third year as executive creative director at Digital at Euro RSCG, the agency has seen massive success under his leadership. They have won considerable respect and recognition from clients and the industry, including a string of integrated wins for Heineken, NYSE, Merck, in addition to AOR status for IBM's digital business.

Prior to joining Euro, Rahul served as associate creative director at Digitas, where he applied his distinct blend of creativity to multiple clients including American Express, CNN.com, Samsung and GameTap. In previous positions, Rahul worked with multiple luxury and spirit brands, including Diageo and L'Oreal. He also founded NewMantra Inc., where he repositioned internet properties for Sony Music, Lehman Brothers, TransUnion and Experian.

WEBSITE RAHULSABNIS.COM

JURY PHOTOGRAPHER: EJ CAMP - EJCAMP.COM

GOLD | INTERACTIVE ADVERTISING | BEYOND THE WEB |
PRODUCT, SERVICE or ENTERTAINMENT PROMOTION

LIVESTRONG
CAMPAIGN
WIEDEN+KENNEDY

**JAMES
MOSLANDER**

**ADAM
HEATHCOTT**

Creative Director Danielle Flagg, Tyler Whisnand
Art Director James Moslander
Copywriter Marco Kaye
Designer Adam Heathcott
Producer Deep Local
Production Company Deep Local
Agency Wieden+Kennedy
Client Nike Livestrong Foundation

Country United States

Additional Awards

◈ **ADVERTISING GOLD**
NEW MEDIA INNOVATION

⬧ **HYBRID MERIT**
CAMPAIGN

19,340ft

WE MADE IT! THANKS TO EVERYONE FOR YOUR SUPPORT.

Scroll down the site to see how we got here—and if you haven't yet, sponsor a foot of the climb to donate water. The climb is over, but the fight has just begun.

DESCENDING TO BASECAMP IN 3...

SKIP TO BASECAMP

GOLD | INTERACTIVE DESIGN | CAMPAIGN SITE | PRODUCT,
SERVICE or ENTERTAINMENT PROMOTION

SUMMIT ON
THE SUMMIT
GOODBY, SILVERSTEIN & PARTNERS

**WILL
MCGINNESS**

**JIM
ELLIOTT**

Creative Director Rich Silverstein, Steve Simpson,
Will McGinness, Jim Elliot
Art Director Stuart Brown
Copywriter Niklas Lilja
Producer Cathleen Kisich, Erin Dahlbeck, Daisy Down
Production Company @radical.media, Number9, Kurt Noble
Agency Goodby, Silverstein & Partners
Client HP

Country United States

Additional Awards

HYBRID MERIT
CAMPAIGN

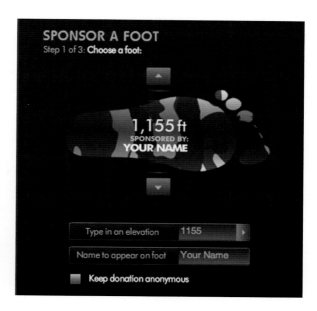

GOLD | INTERACTIVE DESIGN | WEBSITE | PRODUCT,
SERVICE or ENTERTAINMENT PROMOTION

PLUG INTO
THE SMART GRID
GOODBY, SILVERSTEIN & PARTNERS

CHRISTIAN HAAS

SHANE FLEMING

Creative Director Jeff Goodby, Christian Haas
Art Director Peter Olofsson
Copywriter Larry Corwin
Designer Shane Fleming
Producer Carey Head, Sosia Bert, Stella Wong
Broadcast Producer Brian Coate
Production Company North Kingdom
Programmer Zakowicz, Carlsson, Thyselius, Eriksson
Agency Goodby, Silverstein & Partners
Client GE

Country United States

WHAT WOULD HAPPEN IF WE ADDED MORE TURBINES?

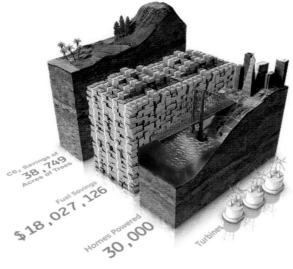

CO₂ Savings of
38,749
Acres of Trees

Fuel Savings
$18,027,126

Homes Powered
30,000

Turbines

PLUG INTO THE SMART GRID

GE imagination at work

ecomagination

My Photos – Tagga dig själv och vinn möbeln!

Photo 11 of 11 | Back to Album | My Photos · Previous · Next

Följande produkter går att tagga i bilden: TROFAST förvaringshylla med lådor, höjd 179 cm (värde 635:–), TROFAST förvaringshylla med lådor, höjd 179 cm (värde 635:–), MINNEN utdragssäng (värde 910:–), FABLER PRICKAR matta 133x133 cm (värde 249:–). OBS! Det är personen som taggar sig själv på RÄTT möbel/produkt och skriver motivering snabbast (i den ordningen) som vinner. Glöm inte att läsa "Så här tävlar du" och "Tävlingsregler" innan du tävlar, som du hittar i albumet! OBS! Du måste skriva din motivering i kommentarsfältet för att kunna vinna.

From your album:
Tagga dig själv och vinn möbeln!

In this photo: Emelie Niklasson (photos | remove tag), Tobias Herder (photos | remove tag), Cornelia Pamp (photos | remove tag), Linda Zedig (photos | remove tag), Åsa Jönsson (remove tag), Emmi Lundström (photos | remove tag), Martin Zedig (photos | remove tag), Maria Silfverberg (photos | remove tag), Caroline Brodén (photos | remove tag), Lotta Lindekrantz (remove tag), Pernilla Fyhr Marbe (photos | remove tag), Linda Cronberg (photos | remove tag), Sofie Charlie Lindberg (photos | remove tag), Katarina Olsson (remove tag), Åsa Jönsson (photos | remove tag), Therese M. Lundberg (photos | remove tag), Marika Eriksson (photos | remove tag), Mia Fredrikson (remove tag)

Henrik Hammar Will you be adding new pictures during the weekend? =) =)
31 October at 14:53 · Comment · Like · See Wall-to-Wall

 Gordon Gustavsson maybe... :)
31 October at 14:55 · Delete

Lizette Andersson Congrats to the win Henrik!
31 October at 15:10 · Delete

Write a comment...

RECENT ACTIVITY

Gordon and Annika Hedlund are now friends. · Comment · Like

Gordon and Marcus Söndergaard are now friends. · Comment · Like

2 more similar stories

GOLD | INTERACTIVE ADVERTISING | BLOGS, COMMUNITIES AND SOCIAL NET-
WORKS | PRODUCT, SERVICE or ENTERTAINMENT PROMOTION

FACEBOOK
SHOWROOM
FORSMAN & BODENFORS

**ROBERT
LUND**

**ADAM
ULVEGÄRDE**

Photographer Lennart Sjöberg
Advertiser's Supervisor Sara Zakariasson
Agency Forsman & Bodenfors
Client IKEA

Country Sweden

Additional Awards

HYBRID MERIT
CAMPAIGN

GOLD | INTERACTIVE DESIGN | ONLINE BRANDED CONTENT |
PRODUCT, SERVICE or ENTERTAINMENT PROMOTION

ZACK
JOHNSON
LEO BURNETT

**JON
WYVILLE**

**DAVE
LOEW**

Global Chief Creative Officer Mark Tutssel
Chief Creative Officer John Condon
Executive Creative Director Becky Swanson
Creative Director Dave Loew, Jon Wyville
Art Director Jon Wyville
Copywriter Dave Loew
Production Designer Jason Schuster
Director of Photography, Lighting, Cameraman Jo Willems
Video Director, Director Randy Krallman
Editor Matt Woods, Matt Walsh (The Whitehouse Chicago)
Head of Production Chris Rossiter
Executive Producer Patrick Milling Smith, Brian Carmody, Lisa Rich, Allison Kunzman
Agency Producer David L. Moore, Rob Tripas
Line Producer Cory Berg
Production Company SMUGGLER
Post Production The Filmworkers Club, Co3
Account Director Cindy Blikre
Account Supervisor Katie McClay
Original Composition Human Worldwide
Digital Shop Domani Studios
Agency Leo Burnett
Client P&G Tampax

Every woman has wished that, just once, a man could experience what she goes through every month. So Tampax built an emotionally empathetic relationship with girls by dramatizing the menstrual trials and travails of Zack Johnson, an all-American high school boy who one day wakes up more like a girl. Zack is branded content in the form of web films, a blog and social media. The program is a platform for conversation and community, and finds a fresh way to talk to young women about a not-so-fresh subject.

Country United States

ZACK.

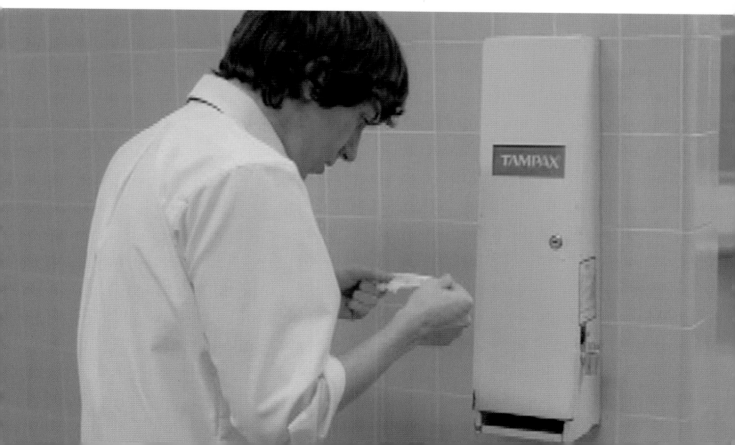

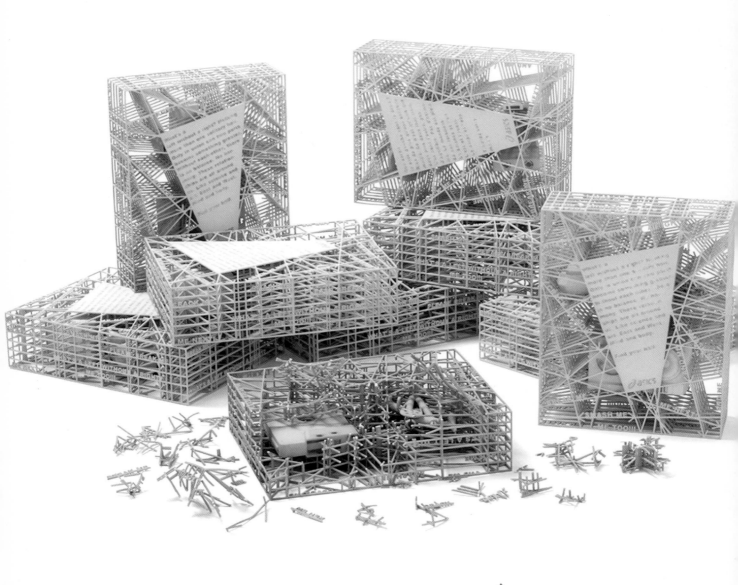

SILVER | INTERACTIVE ADVERTISING | BLOGS, COMMUNITIES AND SOCIAL NET-
WORKS | PRODUCT, SERVICE or ENTERTAINMENT PROMOTION

ASICS SPORTSTYLE LEFT RIGHT BLOGGER OUTREACH
AMSTERDAM WORLDWIDE

RICHARD GÖRODECKY

ANDREW WATSON

Executive Creative Director Richard Görodecky
Creative Director Andrew Watson
Art Director Rickard Engstrom
Copywriter Dan Göransson
3-D Designer Freedom of Creation
Business Development Director Nicolette Lazarus
Producer Samantha Koch
Planner Ben Jaffé
Agency Amsterdam Worldwide
Client ASICS Left Right Blogger Outreach

To increase awareness of the ASICS SportStyle campaign, "What's a left without a right?" we couldn't afford to shout. Instead, we whispered into the ears of those that hold the loud hailers: the bloggers. We handpicked the most influential street-style bloggers in the world and engaged them and their readers in an interactive global treasure hunt. Through blogs, Twitter and Facebook, the campaign engaged over 200,000 people. We also united and formed permanent connections between bloggers who are now writing about ASICS SportsStyle on an ongoing basis, with passion and without prompting.

Country Netherlands

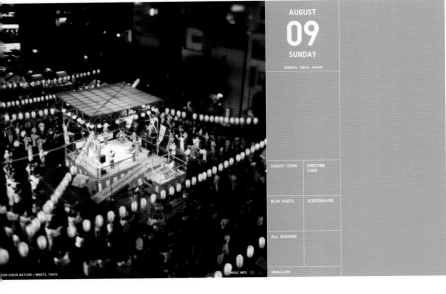

SILVER | INTERACTIVE DESIGN | WEBSITE | PRODUCT,
SERVICE or ENTERTAINMENT PROMOTION

UNIQLO
CALENDAR
PROJECTOR INC.

**KOICHIRO
TANAKA**

Creative Director, Copywriter Koichiro Tanaka
Art Director, Designer Takashi Kamada
Shooting Director Hiroyuki Kojima (TOCHKA)
Editor Shigehisa Nakao
Producer Gyosei Okada, Nozomu Naito, Shinjiro Ono
Production Company Projector Inc., puzzle inc.
Programmer Kayichi Tozaki, Yukio Sato, Susumu Arai
Agency Projector Inc.
Client UNIQLO

Country Japan

BRONZE | INTERACTIVE ADVERTISING | BEYOND THE WEB |
PRODUCT, SERVICE or ENTERTAINMENT PROMOTION

SAMSUNG
SHAKEDOWN
FROM STOCKHOLM WITH LOVE

**KRISTIN
BERGEM**

**DANIEL
WAHLGREN**

Art Director Daniel Wahlgren
Copywriter Kristin Bergem
Production Company It's Showtime, From Stockholm With Love
Agency From Stockholm With Love
Client Samsung

Samsung wanted to raise awareness of their damage-resistant
mobile phone, B2100, in an entertaining and engaging way.
Our solution was to let consumers test the phones in an online
experiment. We put 70 mobiles on a glass table, hanging high
above a concrete floor and a water tank. Each mobile had a
number. People could call any one of the mobiles and try to
vibrate it over the table edge. If your phone call made a mobile
fall, you won that mobile. This was all filmed live and streamed to
a website.

Country Sweden

BRONZE | INTERACTIVE ADVERTISING | BEYOND THE WEB |
PRODUCT, SERVICE or ENTERTAINMENT PROMOTION

MONDAY NIGHT FOOTBALL—INTERACTIVE STORESCAPE
WIEDEN+KENNEDY

ERIC STEELE   **STUART JENNINGS**

Executive Creative Director Todd Waterbury, Kevin Proudfoot
Creative Director Stuart Jennings, John Parker, Derek Barnes
Interactive Creative Director Jerome Austria
Art Director Stuart Jennings
Copywriter Eric Steele
Interactive Development Partner Monster Media
Interactive Designer Alon Zouaretz
Interactive Producer Liz Whittaker
Head of Content Production Gary Krieg
Production Company Brand New School
Agency Wieden+Kennedy
Client ESPN - Monday Night Football

ESPN's Is It Monday Yet? campaign reminds football fans that for 16 weeks a year, Monday Night Football is their light at the end of the worst day of the week.

To help make Monday a bit more bearable, we created interactive storefront games in New York, Chicago and Boston where pedestrians could let off some steam with a virtual game of catch The storefronts were outfitted with interactive touch screens and gesture-recognition technology so that passersby could try to catch the most consecutive virtual passes "thrown" at them by an NFL quarterback from an upcoming Monday night matchup. To encourage gameplay, yardage markers tracked pedestrians with call-outs hinting at their coordination and reflexes (or lack thereof), and users competed for the highest score on a national leaderboard. Play-by-play call-outs also narrated player performances until a missed catch shattered the window and ended the game.

Country United States

BRONZE | INTERACTIVE ADVERTISING | BEYOND THE WEB |
PRODUCT, SERVICE or ENTERTAINMENT PROMOTION

THE LAST
CALL
LEAN MEAN FIGHTING MACHINE

**DAVE
BEDWOOD**

**SAM
BALL**

Creative Director Sam Ball, Dave Bedwood
Art Director Sam Ball, Dave Bedwood
Copywriter Sam Ball, Dave Bedwood
Designer Mark Beacock
Director Jason Collier
Producer Annis Bailey, Emma Williamson, Dominic Waugh
Production Company Remedy Productions
Managing Partner Tom Bazeley
Account Manager Paul Vincent, Cohaesus Projects
Programmer Dave Cox, Jimmy Hay, Jeremy Willmott
Agency Lean Mean Fighting Machine
Client Samsung Mobile

The Samsung Beat DJ mobile phone, powered by Bang & Olufson
sound chip and headphones, has great acoustic credentials.
Our idea came from a single thought: When the sound is this
good, you would hate to have your music interrupted by a call
or text. It seemed interesting to sell a phone by actively telling
people not to use it.

We created a competition. On the 7th of July, 100 people from
across Europe competed in The Last Call, a 24-hour silent-disco
contest, dancing to a non-stop playlist on their Beat DJ. If they
received a call or a text, they were out of the competition. If they
stayed in, they had the chance to win €10,000. The contest was
recruited for, promoted and broadcast online for the full 24 hours.
Woven into The Last Call was an incentive for competitors to
promote it themselves (i.e. to tell people NOT to call them during
it).

Country United Kingdom

BRONZE | INTERACTIVE ADVERTISING | ONLINE | PRODUCT,
SERVICE or ENTERTAINMENT PROMOTION

AUGMENTED REALITY BANNER
CRISPIN PORTER + BOGUSKY

**MICHAEL
ACKERMANN**

**DAVID
GONSALVES**

**CHRIS
KAHLE**

Chief Creative Officer Rob Reilly
Associate Creative Officer Andrew Keller
Creative Director Bill Wright, James Dawson-Hollis
Associate Creative Director Nuno Ferreira, Ryan Wagman
Art Director Michael Ackerman, David Gonsalves, Kristian
Luoma, Elias Morales
Copywriter Chris Kahle, Zac Myrow
Designer Fabien Dodard
Producer Scott Potter, Tony Tung
Agency Crispin Porter + Bogusky
Client Burger King

Country United States

BRONZE | INTERACTIVE ADVERTISING | NEW MEDIA INNOVATION |
PRODUCT, SERVICE or ENTERTAINMENT PROMOTION

BAKERTWEET
POKE

Creative Director Nicolas Roope
Art Director Nicky Gibson
Copywriter The good people of POKE
Designer Andrew Zolty
Production Company POKE
Programmer Mattias Gunneras
Agency POKE
Client POKE, Albion Bakery

Everyone knows the best time to get your baked goods is when
they're fresh out the oven. We figured this could be a killer use of
Twitter. Let followers know that fresh goodies are ready, right now.
Bakeries don't want laptops lying around in the kitchen; flour,
eggs and technology don't mix. So we built BakerTweet.

It's a bespoke piece of hardware (with Arduino-based guts)
that allows our friends at Albion to select items that have just
been baked, and ping the relevant Twitter message out to local
customers. So you can now perfectly time your trips to Albion to
pick up the fresh goodies.

If you want to see what's coming out of the Albion's oven, you
need to follow @albionsoven.

BakerTweet has been featured in London's daily papers and *The
Times*. Biz Stone is an enthusiastic follower and has promoted it
in *Wired*, even though he's an eight-hour flight from fresh cakes
and scrumptiousness!

Country United Kingdom

BRONZE | INTERACTIVE ADVERTISING | NEW MEDIA INNOVATION |
NON-PROFIT, REFERENCE or EDUCATIONAL

$1 FOR DIRTY WATER
CASANOVA PENDRILL

**GIL
AREVALO**

**DÁMASO
CRESPO**

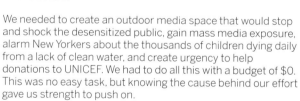

**ALEJANDRO
ORTIZ**

President, Chief Executive Officer Ingrid Otero-Smart
Creative Director Elias Weinstock, Alejandro Ortiz
Art Director Dámaso Crespo, Gil Arevalo
Copywriter Gil Arevalo, Dámaso Crespo
Editor James Long "Proton"
Post Production Supervisor Keith Olwell
Production Company Proton
Agency Casanova Pendrill
Client UNICEF

We needed to create an outdoor media space that would stop
and shock the desensitized public, gain mass media exposure,
alarm New Yorkers about the thousands of children dying daily
from a lack of clean water, and create urgency to help
donations to UNICEF. We had to do all this with a budget of $0.
This was no easy task, but knowing the cause behind our effort
gave us strength to push on.

Country United States

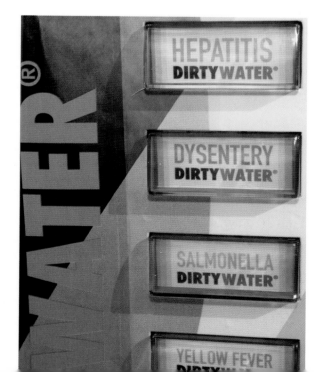

BRONZE | INTERACTIVE ADVERTISING | WEBSITE |
PRODUCT, SERVICE or ENTERTAINMENT PROMOTION

THE WORLD'S BIGGEST SIGNPOST
FARFAR

**TOMAS
JONSSON**

**CARL FREDRIK
JANNERFELDT**

Creative President Matias Palm Jensen
Creative Director Jon Dranger, Erik Norin
Art Director Tomas Jonsson
Copywriter Carl Fredrik Jannerfeldt
Programmer David Looberger
Head of Strategy Niku Banaie
Account Director Marten Forslund, Christian Nord
Account Manager Marie Persson, Ulrika Hojgard,
Louise Stenborg
Flash Mikael Ring, Robert Jarvi, Bjorn Uppeke
Agency Farfar
Client Nokia

Nokia offers a range of navigation services both online and on
their mobile devices. But awareness about these services is low.
Our challenge was to raise awareness and increase use of Nokia's
navigation service. Both on handsets and online.
We started out with one of the simplest navigation tools around,
the signpost. And turned that into a giant interactive
installation. A 50 meter tall, fully automated remote controlled
beast. People could text their favourite spot to the signpost and
within moments the giant turned and displayed the distance to
that location.

Country Sweden

Additional Awards

HYBRID MERIT
CAMPAIGN

BRONZE | INTERACTIVE ADVERTISING | ONLINE BRANDED CONTENT |
PRODUCT, SERVICE or ENTERTAINMENT PROMOTION

VOLVO S60: THE BLIND PREVIEW
EURO RSCG 4D AMSTERDAM

MARCO ANTONIO MORALES   **NIELS ARNBAK**

Creative Director Bram de Rooij
Art Director Marco Antonio Morales
Copywriter Niels Arnbak
Account Jeff Dunlap, Katrin Buckert
Producer Nicole Siers
Production Company Great Guns London
Agency Euro RSCG 4D Amsterdam
Client Volvo Car Corporation

Our challenge was to create buzz about the all-new Volvo S60 before its official release in early 2010, while keeping its design secret. We came up with an abstract way to provide the public with a vision of the car. Esref Armagnan, a Turkish painter who was born blind, taught himself to draw in perspective. We invited him to experience the S60 by touch and then recreate what he felt on canvas. Over seven days, he reproduced his interpretation of the S60 to show the public what they cannot see. A five-minute documentary narrates this fascinating creative journey at the Volvo Design Centre in Gothenburg.

Country Netherlands

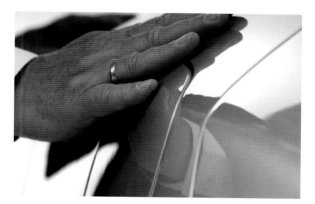

BRONZE | INTERACTIVE ADVERTISING | ONLINE BRANDED CONTENT |
PRODUCT, SERVICE or ENTERTAINMENT PROMOTION

HELICOPTER BOYZ
DDB JAPAN INC.

**NAOKI
ITO**

**TOHRU
TANAKA**

Creative Director Tohru Tanaka, Naoki Ito
Art Director, Copywriter Naoki Ito
Director Hideyuki Tanaka
Editor Masaya Yoshida
Producer Atsuki Yukawa
Production Company GT Inc., ROCK'N ROLL JAPAN
Choreography Kaoruko
Music DJ TASAKA
Agency DDB Japan Inc.
Client Nikon Corporation

Helicopter Boyz was introduced to support the launch of Nikon
Coolpix S1000pj, the world's first compact digital camera with
a built-in projector. This viral film campaign features two young
boys entertaining the audience by projecting photos from the
S1000pj onto a screen.

Helicopter Boyz is designed to combat the more traditional
image of the Nikon brand. This is not the high end function
camera but the personal, fun communications device. The
blogosphere and social media networks were targeted as a way
to drive engagement and awareness. Helicopter Boyz is really
meant to be a brand experience and to be shared, as "sharing" is
at the core of the S1000pj product proposition.

Helicopter Boyz achieved 20,000+ views in the first 10 days and
more than 150,000 views in less than two months. It was viewed
in more than 120 countries and featured in 20,000+ blogs in
multiple languages.

Country Japan

BRONZE | INTERACTIVE ADVERTISING | ONLINE BRANDED CONTENT |
PRODUCT, SERVICE or ENTERTAINMENT PROMOTION

FACIAL PROFILER
CRISPIN PORTER + BOGUSKY

JUSTIN SMITH　　　　**CHAD LYNCH**

Executive Creative Director Andrew Keller, Rob Reilly
Creative Director Dave Schiff, Alex Burnard
Associate Creative Director Patrick Maravilla, Dayoung Ewart
Art Director Justin Smith, Nuno Ferreira
Copywriter Chad Lynch, Jason Marks
Designer Christian Layugan, Dustin Tomes
Editor Wayde Samuel
Producer Paul Aaron, Idalia Deshon, Suzanne Chambers, Andrea Krichevsky
Agency Crispin Porter + Bogusky
Client Coke Zero

Country United States

Additional Awards

HYBRID MERIT
CAMPAIGN

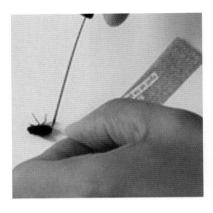

BRONZE | INTERACTIVE ADVERTISING | ONLINE BRANDED CONTENT | SELF-PROMOTION

FLYVERTISING—THE WORLD'S FIRST FLY BANNER.
JUNG VON MATT AG

JACQUES PENSE   **NORMAN SCHOLL**

Creative Director Jacques Pense, Michael Ohanian
Art Director Thomas Lupo, Benjamin Beck
Copywriter Norman Scholl, Lennart Frank
Editor Alfonso Arribas
Director of Photography Jochen Keitel
Account Supervisor Christine Seelig
Producer Gun Aydemir
Production Company emenes
Client Eichborn
Agency Jung von Matt AG

Eichborn is the publisher with the fly. Humorous, brave and unconventional. To strengthen the publisher's positioning at the Frankfurt Book Fair 2009 and to bring an audience to their exhibition stand, we used the Eichborn logo (the fly) to invent a new form of advertising: FLYVERTISING—The World's First Fly Banner. We equipped 200 real flies with an ultralight banner and released them at the Eichborn exhibition stand. To maximize the effect and spread FLYVERTISING further, we documented the event and uploaded a 90 second viral video to YouTube.

Country Germany

MERIT | INTERACTIVE ADVERTISING | ONLINE | PRODUCT, SERVICE, or ENTERTAINMENT PROMOTION

MINI IS LOADING
PLAN.NET/SERVICEPLAN

**MIKE HILZINGER &
CHRISTIAN AUSSEM**

**TOBIAS PECHSTEIN
& JÜRGEN RIEGER**

Chief Creative Officer Alex Schill
Creative Director Markus Maczey, Cornelia Blasy-Steiner
Art Director Tobias Pechstein, Mike Hilzinger, Jürgen Rieger
Copywriter Christian Aussem
Designer Tobias Pechstein, Mike Hilzinger, Jürgen Rieger
Chief Development Officer Friedrich von Zitzewitz
Programmer Jürgen Rieger
Agency PLAN.NET, Serviceplan
Client MINI AG

If you place the MINI and the MINI Clubman side by side and behold both from above, you will recognize one thing: The MINI Clubman looks like a stretched MINI. Or rather, like a MINI that is packed with suitcases. The idea was born. Based on the arcade game Snake, users were able to collect suitcases with a MINI in a rich media banner. The suitcases were placed between the Yahoo! content, and the users had to navigate the MINI through it. With each bag collected, the trunk extended. The users dealt playfully with the brand and tried to beat their own highest score over and over again.

Country Germany

MERIT | INTERACTIVE ADVERTISING | BLOGS, COMMUNITIES AND SOCIAL NETWORKS | PRODUCT, SERVICE or ENTERTAINMENT PROMOTION

TWELPFORCE
CRISPIN PORTER + BOGUSKY

**DJ
PIERCE**

**JUSTIN
EBERT**

Chief Creative Officer Andrew Keller, Rob Reilly
Associate Creative Director DJ Pierce, Justin Ebert
Creative Director Evan Fry
Art Director DJ Pierce, David Brown, Kat Street
Copywriter Justin Ebert, David Littlejohn, Tom Pettus
Designer Daisy Chavoshi, Christian Behrendt, Slava Morshch, Leif Abraham
Editor Lucas Spaulding
Producer Pam Scheideler, Paul Gunnarson, Brenda Fogg
Production Company Smuggler Productions
Agency Crispin Porter + Bogusky
Client Best Buy

Country United States

MERIT | INTERACTIVE DESIGN | WEBSITE |
SELF-PROMOTION

THE NEW FB.SE
FORSMAN & BODENFORS

Production Company Thomson Interactive Media
Sound Morningdew Media
Agency Forsman & Bodenfors

Country Sweden

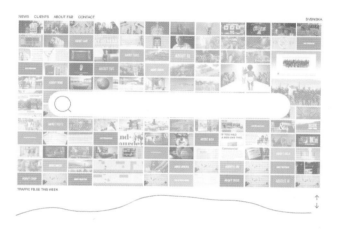

2008 Grandmasters

2009 Grandmasters

ADC**GRANDMASTERS**

The disciplines of Advertising and Design are only as good as the young talent that fuels their flames; and young talent is only as good as the educators who embrace students as they enter art school, college or university. The GrandMasters Award was established in 2008 by The Art Directors Club to applaud outstanding educators in our field and raise the bar on arts education.

Educators are more than teachers in classrooms - they are the catalysts of students' careers and drive for success. They propel students to develop skills, goals, and stomachs for a competitive industry and a career of success and failure. ADC GrandMasters are educators who embrace the practical, technical and emotional needs of their students – those who challenge students to tap into the talent they hope they possess. With ten+ years experience, ADC GrandMasters have demonstrated the ability to drive generations of industry greats and a sphere of cultural influence as seen through their graduates in advertising, design and new media.

The ADC GrandMaster Selection Committee includes prominent leaders from the visual communications industry and fellow educators who nominate and select recipients for this honor. Alumni endow scholarships for current students, further supporting students in their studies.

In the overcrowded category of awards shows, GrandMasters is unique in its focus on teachers and education. The GrandMasters program opens with an awards presentation, followed by a three-week exhibition at the ADC. The 3rd induction of GrandMasters will be held Fall 2011.

- Bill Oberlander
Director of ADC GrandMasters
Former President of Art Directors Club

ADC**GRANDMASTERS**

2009

Deborah Morrison
University of Oregon

Tom Ockerse
Rhode Island School of Design

Hank Richardson
The Portfolio Center

Ron Seichrist
Miami Ad School

2008

Mark Fenske
VCU Brandcenter

Ray Nichols
University of Delaware

Carin Goldberg
School of Visual Arts

Sheila Levrant de Bretteville
Yale University

Jeffrey Metzner

2009**SELECTION COMMITTEE**

Bill Oberlander
Committee Chair, executive vice president, chief operating officer, Cossette New York and ADC past-president

Bob Barrie
Partner, Executive Creative Director, Barrie D'Rozario Murphy

Wayne Best
Executive Creative Director, JWT New York

Julian Bittiner
Lecturer, Yale School of Art

Rick Boyko
Director, VCU Brandcenter

Kathleen Creighton
Chairperson, Arts Communications Design, Pratt Institute

Ann Lemon
Professor, University of Delaware

Kurt Souder
Partner, Executive Creative Director, GMMB

Richard Wilde
Chairman, Advertising/Graphic Design Departments, School of Visual Arts

Laetitia E. Wolff
Founding Director, FutureFlair

Deborah Morrison, PhD is the Chambers Distinguished Professor of Advertising at the University of Oregon. For two decades (maybe a little more), she's worked with students in Oregon and at The University of Texas at Austin, where she and colleagues built Texas Creative, one of the best university-based portfolio programs in the country. Deborah has been at the University of Oregon since 2005. She and her colleagues developed the successful Creative Strategist Model, wherein all advertising specialties are grounded in creativity and strategic thinking, aapplied with honesty and sustainability expertise.

DEBORAH**MORRISON**

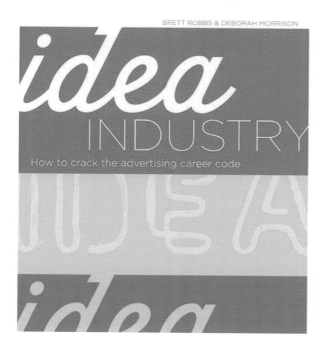

Morrison served on The One Club for Art & Copy's board of directors for two terms (and is the only university educator to do so). She's judged regional, national and international shows for students and professionals. She's honored to have won the University of Oregon School of Journalism and Communication's Marshall Award for Innovative Teaching in 2008 and 2009, the only two-time winner. She was awarded the Blunk Professorship for teaching at The University of Texas and recognized as GrandMaster in Education by The Art Directors Club.

In 2010, she and co-author Glenn Griffin wrote *The Creative Process Illustrated: How Advertising's Big Ideas are Born*, an homage to how writers and art directors see the creative process. She and co-author Brett Robbs wrote *Idea Industry: How to Crack the Advertising Career Code* in 2008. Along with Kim Sheehan, she partnered with Enviromedia to develp the Greenwashing Index, an aid to spotting greenwashing in advertising and design. She's had the good fortune of visiting, studying and thinking about hundreds of agencies while learning from thousands of students, to whom she owes so much. She lives in Eugene, Oregon with her dashing photojournalist husband Dan, and three wonderful sons, all growing up to be astounding men.

Head Cowboy of Design at Portfolio Center, a nationally renowned brand communications school in Atlanta, Richardson is everywhere and knows everyone; he is the ubiquitous, amiable presence at business talks, industry seminars, guild conferences, portfolio reviews, board meetings and creative clubs.

Richardson believes the best education pushes the boundaries of traditional instruction, and he has spent the last 17 years educating young designers, charging them with the responsibility of creating culture. He believes his job is to put the students off balance, test their sense of reality, help them realize the effects of their perceptions on their sense of reality, and then, ultimately, change their reality altogether—proving, once again, McLuhan's premise that "we become what we behold."

HANK**RICHARDSON**

As a result of this philosophy, Portfolio Center graduates inhabit the most respected design and advertising firms in the world, living testaments to Richardson's ability to nudge (an understatement) each student to their personal threshold, that existential edge where their best work is conceived.

It is only fitting that his personal design hero and friend, Milton Glaser, is an educator himself, and one whose stance on teaching nestles close to Richardson's heart: "I suspect you teach for yourself, in a sense, for your own fulfillment. Teaching is useful for defining and testing one's own ideas. It is inspirational, and it points out how other generations are responding to events in their own lifetime."

Richardson inspires his students to observe, to grow and to interpret the truth. He pushes them to take risks and to collaborate. To exercise their own voices in a safe yet spontaneous environment, and to infuse their projects with personal resonance, all while successfully solving the inherent problems presented by each project. If design is a plan to create something, then that something is a story. Once Richardson's students learn to tell a story (or to sing it), there's nothing they can't do; they have the ability to change their world.

Above all, Richardson encourages his students to do what they love and to love what they do, because, as all good cowboys and hotrods should know, "Aren't we finally our best selves when we find and follow our passion?"

Tom's involvement in graphic design education began at Indiana University, from 1967 to 1971. In 1971 he came to Rhode Island School of Design, where he is a professor of graphic design. He was Head of the Graphic Design Department for twenty years (1973-93), and was Dean of the Division of Design from 1978 to 1989. He instituted and directed RISD's Summer Institute for Graphic Design Studies (SIGDS). He initiated the Graduate Program of Graphic Design in 1976, and was its Program Head until 2004. He continues to teach full time in both the graduate and undergraduate studies.

TOM**OCKERSE**

Ockerse is known for his development of theory in semiotics as this applies to the visual communication, design practice and design education. He has authored articles on this theory such as "Semiotics and Design Education," "De-Sign/Super-Sign" and "The Semiosis of Design." His theories are also present in his work with concrete poetry and bookworks in which he explores visual/linguistic systems.

From 1993 to 1997, he was a regular adjunct faculty member at the Jan van Eyck Akademie (Holland) for post-graduate studies in Fine Arts, Design and Theory. He has served as educational consultant to UCLA, Virginia Commonwealth University, University of the Arts, Universidad de las Americas (Mexico), Hull College and Sheffield Polytechnic in England, University of Texas, and for Jan van Eyck's graduate Design program. In 1986, he was the United Nations' UNIDO consultant to the the National Institute of Design in Ahmedabad, India, to "acquaint visual communication faculty and students with contemporary trends and technology in the field of graphic design and to help the Institute in the planning of its program." From 1981 through 1985, he served as vice president of the AIGA Board of Directors, established the AIGA Education Committee as a standing committee, and initiated the AIGA publication Graphic Design Education that describes what a graphic design education should encompass. He also served on the Board of the Graphic Design Education Association. The American Center for Design presented Ockerse with their 1991 Education Award.

Soccer - I learned to play the game on a hardscrabble field outside a German prisoner of war camp in Norfolk, Virginia. My father, born in Germany, was daily recruited by the marine guards to come to the camp and translate for them; I became a kind of mascot to the POWs. We lived only two blocks away, and nearly every day we were in the camp. Once the prisoners were allowed to scrape out a field outside the camp, I was there afternoons after school and on weekends to play with them. When the war was over, I continued to play on the field with all the foreign sailors who docked nearby. In high school I played American football; I was a quarterback, but soccer was my true love.

MIAMI AD SCHOOL FUTBOL POSTERS

or~another way to teach typography, design & concept to aspiring art directors and designers

RON**SEICHRIST**

I spent many years later as I moved from one ad agency to another, from one city to another, seeking out a soccer team to play with on the weekends. One of those teams I played on for several years had an extraordinary coach, an old German man who I must admit, looked a great deal like I look today. Same white messy hair, same too-big nose, almost the same face. He believed football was life and he reduced every single coaching comment to its counterpoint in daily living. He had a profound effect on me and the rest of my life.

I discovered that he was absolutely right. And once I began to follow his philosphy, I let that insight become the cornerstone of my own philosophical approach to life. It's no accident that soccer is a fundamental part of Miami Ad School, along with the dogs that roam our galleries and classrooms. In fact, students, faculty, graduates and visiting Heroes from the creative community play a very long soccer game every Sunday afternoon. It is required. And if a student doesn't show up on Sunday, when the time comes for that student to go on our Quarter Away program to such places as London, New York, Amsterdam, Madrid, Beijing, etc., the Absentee-from-Sunday-Soccer may find his only choice is Miami Ad School Kabul or Miami Ad School Siberia.

I inject my football fundamentalism into every story, every lecture and every critique. Here you will see some of the soccer posters my students have done.

MERIT 5% of all awards given

BRONZE 5% of all awards given

GOLD 2% of all awards given

SILVER 4% of all awards given

STUDENT
This year 39 student awards were given in the categories of graphic design, photography, illustration, advertising and interactive. 7 Gold, 9 Silver, 11 Bronze and 12 were Merit.

SCHOOLS OF THE YEAR
SCHOOL OF VISUAL ARTS
MIAMI AD SCHOOL

GOLD | ILLUSTRATION |
CARTOON or COMIC BOOK

TODAY IS
SUSHI DAY
SCHOOL OF VISUAL ARTS

JUNGYEON
ROH

Illustrator Jungyeon Roh
Instructor David Sandlin
School School of Visual Arts

Sisters who are sushi masters went to a rotating sushi restaurant
and taught American people how to be a master sushi eaters.

Country United States

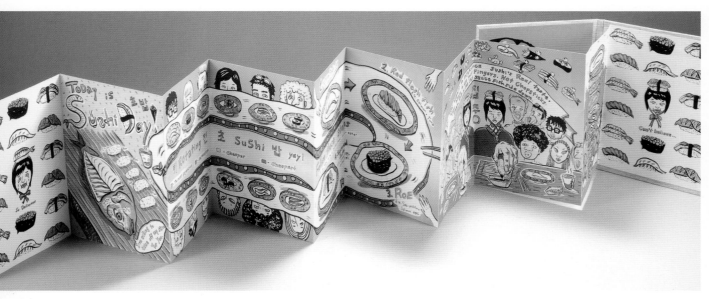

311 WEST 34TH STREET, NEW YORK, NY 10001

KRAFTWERK/
MOZART

Hammerstein
Ballroom

THURSDAY, DECEMBER 20. 2010

Piano Sonata No. 9 in D major, K. 311
Symphony in D major "No. 44"

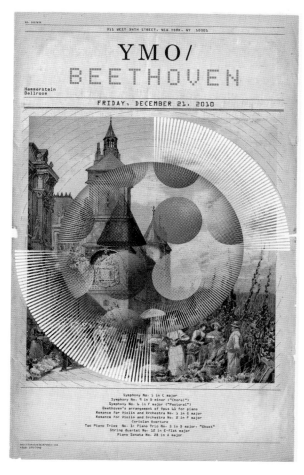

MUSIC CONCERT POSTER
ART CENTER COLLEGE OF DESIGN

**HYEJUNG
BAE**

Designer Hyejung Bae
Instructor Clive Piercy
School Art Center College of Design

Poster series for a concert of electronic musicians playing classical music with digital instruments. Newspaper illustrations from the 1800s combine with contemporary optical patterns to represent the timeless value of classical music and its digital interpretation.

Country United States

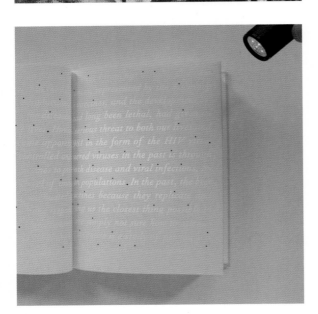

GOLD | EDITORIAL DESIGN | LIMITED
EDITION or PRIVATE PRESS

MUSIC CONCERT POSTER
ART CENTER COLLEGE OF DESIGN

MATHIEU STEMMELEN

Art Director, Designer, Illustrator, Photographer Mathieu Stemmelen
Instructor Dennis Crowe, Michael Vanderby
Production Company Ilathieu
School California College of the Arts

Visualizing the Invisible is a conceptual and interactive book that invites its audience to visualize the Invisible. A first read of the book exposes my personal interpretation of the Invisible, while a second read renders the previously Invisible, Visible under a new light.

The book's content revolves around my own definition of the Invisible: things we blindly accept. It illustrates my existential theory—specifically, that the human condition drives us to visualize the invisible forms as a pretext for visualizing ourselves. Thus, the three chapters of the book are a direct reference to human life:

I. The Origin: our physical world through microscopic life.
II. The Present: our environment and cultures through borders.
III. The Future: our metaphysical and spiritual world through religion.

Ultimately, *Visualizing the Invisible* is a portrait of what we are, where we are, and where we're going.

Country United States

GOLD | ADVERTISING | BROADCAST MEDIA |
CRAFT AND DIGITAL TECHNIQUE | ANIMATION

DEADLINE
SAVANNAH COLLEGE OF ART AND DESIGN

BANG-YAO LIU

Art Director, Copywriter, Director, Editor Bang-yao Liu
School Savannah College of Art and Design

3 months of planning, 4 days of shooting, and more than 6,000 post-it notes. If you ask me how to make a post-it stop motion, I will say, "passion and patience."

Country United States

GOLD | ADVERTISING | CONSUMER MAGAZINE |
PRODUCT or SERVICE PROMOTION

TAKE
THEM OUT
MIAMI AD
SCHOOL—EUROPE

**BEN
HOLDER**

**ALPHONS
CONZEN**

Art Director Alphons Conzen
Copywriter Ben Holder
School Miami Ad School—Europe
Client Colgate

Country Germany

SILVER | EDITORIAL DESIGN | LIMITED EDITION,
PRIVATE PRESS or SPECIAL FORMAT BOOK

F1984T2008
SAVANNAH COLLEGE OF ART AND DESIGN

**NAMOO
KIM**

Art Director, Copywriter, Designer Namoo Kim
Photographer Hyun Min Lee
School Rhode Island School of Design
Client RISD Alumni Association

F1984T2008 has been published on the occasion of the RISD
Annual Graduate Exhibition of 2009. This book examines the
relationship between privacy and technology. In formal response to
this research subject, the design (technology) is crafted to
systematically reveal all of the contents (private matter). The book
is composed of six sections (or districts) ranging from A to F. Each
section has its own pointer and a section marker. Additionally, all of
the photos and illustrations are laid out on the basis of this pointer
according to X, Y coordinates of the map of the book. Through the
pointers, section markers and numbers, readers become aware
of where they are, what they are reading and how each section
is correlated. This system is reflective of the editor/designer's
thoughts and inquiry into this particular subject and relationship.

Country Republic of Korea

F1984T2008
The Relationship between Privacy & Technology

eight new fonts on the block: here, there, everywhere.
typeface development using the grids of seoul pavement.

SILVER | DESIGN | BRANDING |
CAMPAIGN

8 NEW FONTS ON THE BLOCK;
HERE, THERE, EVERYWHERE
EWHA WOMENS
UNIVERSITY

JIWON
PARK

Creative Director Jiwon Park
Font Developer Jaedeok Yun
School Ewha Womans University

Designing new typefaces using the grids and modules of Seoul pavement. With the repetition of their simple periodic arrangement, the bricks and paving stones of pavements create patterns on the ground of a city. From a current collection including examples of different pavement designs, eight patterns were selected as representative of the city of Seoul. When the modules and patterns of the blocks are combined, the urban space of Seoul can be regarded as a symbolic typeface that transmits meaning. The project's goal was to express the city's regional culture, which is conveyed in the form of eight new fonts.

Country Republic of Korea

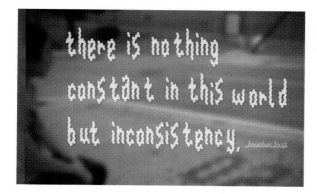

SILVER | ADVERTISING | PRINT | POSTERS AND BILLBOARDS | OUTDDOR or BILLBOARD

CRANE
SCHOOL OF VISUAL ARTS

SARA
RODERICK

JYN
YI

Art Director, Copywriter Sara Roderick, Jyn Yi
Instructor Frank Anselmo
School School of Visual Arts
Client Caterpillar

Actual Caterpillar cranes holding billboards are positioned off highways.

Country United States

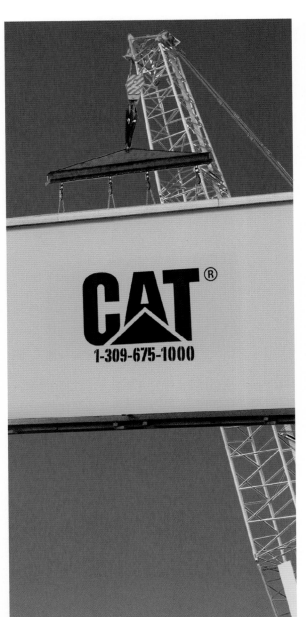

The Art of Perception.

The streets of Berlin – interpreted live by the new E-Class.

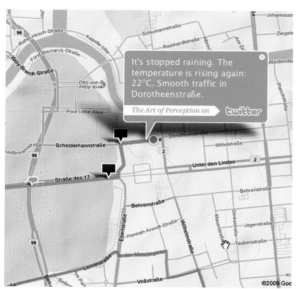

SILVER | NEW MEDIA INNOVATION | PRODUCT, SERVICE or ENTERTAINMENT

THE ART OF PERCEPTION
UNIVERSITY OF APPLIED SCIENCES SALZBURG

MAX BRANDL

Creative Director Bernd Krämer (Jung von Matt/AG)
Designer Max Brandl
Idea, Implementation Max Brandl
Music David Philipp
School University of Applied Sciences Salzburg, Austria
Client Mercedes-Benz

For my final year project, I joined the online team of Jung von Matt in Hamburg, racked my head for a while and finally came up with The Art of Perception.

Employing more than 80 sensors, the new Mercedes-Benz E-Class is even more finely attuned to its environment than the human body—making every ride more comfortable and safe. In order to demonstrate this advantage in an innovative manner, one E-Class sedan, which is available for test drives, is equipped in a way that allows the data from every sensor to be transmitted to the internet while driving. This information is converted into text and pictures and published live on the social web platforms Twitter and Flickr, and one can watch the complete creative journey on a GoogleMaps-based website in real time.

Country Germany

SILVER | INTERACTIVE ADVERTISING | BLOGS, COMMUNITIES AND SOCIAL NETWORKS | PRODUCT, SERVICE or ENTERTAINMENT PROMOTION

THE
SEX TREE
MIAMI AD SCHOOL—EUROPE

**HENRIK
DÜFKE**

**THIBAULT
GERARD**

Art Director Thibault Gerard, Bjorn Borstelmann
Copywriter Henrik Dufke
School Miami Ad School—Europe
Client Durex

To demonstrate the importance of using a condom to teenagers, we use the most simple function of Facebook. Just mark your previous sex partners on your friends list, and the application will instantly track the connections to let you know how many indirect sex partners you've had.

Country Germany

SexTree
durex

Through your **6** sexual relations,
you've been sexually linked to:

692 persons

durex
Order condoms

◉   Yes, I want this live counter to appear on my profile page

◉   Yes, I allow my friends to see if we are sexually connected

THE PROJECT   THE CREW

GIANT FREAKING ROBOT

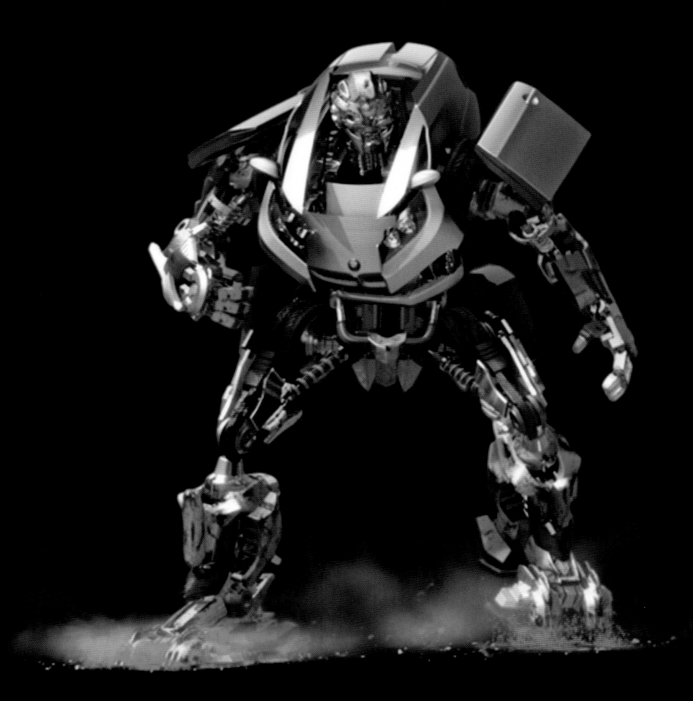

SILVER | INTERACTIVE | BLOGS. COMMUNITIES AND SOCIAL NETWORKS | PRODUCT, SERVICE or ENTERTAINMENT PROMOTION

FREAKY ROBOT
SAVANNAH COLLEGE OF ART AND DESIGN

ALDRICH TORRES

Director Aldrich Torres
Editor Shaun Galinak
Producer Bum Joon Kim
Compositer Adam Flynn
School Savannah College of Art and Design

This is my first student project for studio 2 at Savannah College of Art and Design. It was a collaborative project involving several people, months of hard work and plenty of challenges. My job consisted of Lighting, shaders, modeling (maya+MR) Bum Joon Kim:modeling, animation, rigging (maya) 'Neon' Shaun Galinak: Effects, supporting animation, textures (houdini) Adam Flynn: Compositing (shake). The whole breakdown was created using houdini's compositing side. Freaky Robot also won best 2009 VFX collaborate project at SCAD.

Country United States

SILVER | ADVERTISING BROADCAST MEDIA |
CRAFT AND DIGITAL TECHNIQUE | DIRECTION

EARTH IN
THE AIR
SAVANNAH COLLEGE
OF ART AND DESIGN

**JARED
HOGAN**

Designer, Director, Editor Jared Hogan
Copywriter Michael Bailey
Producer Samuel Eidson, Matthew J. Kern, Jared Hogan
Production Company Savannah College of Art and Design
Music Clint Snow, Houston Snyder
Sound Craig Dunlavey, Houston Snyder
School Savannah College of Art and Design

This film was a chance for me to explore visual storytelling in a
strictly visual manner. I wanted to convey raw humanity in its most
vulnerable and barbaric forms, and pit that against a more positive
perspective. The film is split into two acts. The first conveys the
optimism that perhaps there is beauty and life to be found and
discovered. The second act stands as a testament that life is rarely
like that. Instead, optimism is overcome by the reality that each
individual is out for what is best for themselves.

Country United States

BRONZE | DESIGN |
BRANDING

ELECTRONIC FINGER PAINTING
ART CENTER COLLEGE OF DESIGN

JIYUN HA

Designer Jiyun Ha
Instructor Brad Bartlett
School Art Center College of Design

I designed a promotional package for an exhibition, Electronic Finger Painting. EFP is a group show created in the spirit of Nam June Paik. Paik is an author of video works and interactive installations who introduced electronic media into contemporary art. There are five components in the exhibition: paintings, installation art, media art, performances and audience participation workshops. Five rectangles in the logo are highlighted to imply those five parts, and yet also refer to five fingers. As for the applications, a pattern of stripes is used throughout, referring to graphic representations of electronic media.

Country United States

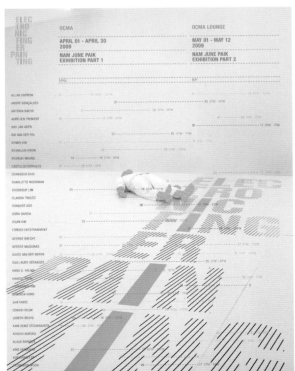

BRONZE | ADVERTISING | BROADCAST MEDIA |
CRAFT AND DIGITAL TECHNIQUE
TECHNIQUE DIRECTION | SINGLE

1+1=3

BECKMANS
COLLEGE OF DESIGN

Creative Director, Art Director, Director Petter Prinz,
John Falk Rodèn, Kalle Hagman, Linn Mork, Samuel Nilsson,
Martin Wâgnert, Andreas Lewandowski
Editor Petter Prinz, Andreas Lewandowski, Martin Wâgnert,
Linn Mork
School Beckmans College of Design
Client Stockholm Furniture Fair

Why do things look like they do? We were asked to make an
exhibition for 12 furniture designers. We started to question why
the furniture looked as it did. All work is created from things and
memories of our lives that we mix together to make something
new. Therefore we took all of the furniture and the stuff from
the designers homes to make our piece of art. The exhibition
became a visualization of why things look like they do. The name
symbolizes that a meeting between two equals something new.

Country Sweden

BRONZE | ADVERTISING |
INTEGRATED

THE LOW EMISSION HITCHHIKER
MIAMI AD SCHOOL—EUROPE

HENRIK DÜFKE

THIBAULT GERARD

Art Director Thibault Gerard, Bjorn Borstelmann
Copywriter Henrik Dufke
School Miami Ad School—Europe
Client Toyota

People hardly trust hybrid cars. In order to prove to the masses that some people have taken the leap to buy a Prius, we challenged Kako to hitchhike from Madrid to COP15 in Copenhagen only accepting rides from Toyota Prius owners.

Country Germany

BRONZE | PRINT | COLLATERAL ADVERTISING |
UNCONVENTIONAL or GUERRILLA

CASSETTE TAPES
SCHOOL OF VISUAL ARTS

JULISSA ORTIZ   **ALEX SUNYOUNG KOO**

Art Director Alex Sunyoung Koo, Julissa Ortiz
Copywriter Julissa Ortiz, Alex Sunyoung Koo
Instructor Frank Anselmo
Agency School of Visual Arts
Client XM 80S RADIO

Posters designed as audio cassette labels are affixed to construction barriers, which resemble audio cassette tapes, to promote the XM Satellite Radio station, The 80s.

Country United States

BRONZE | ADVERTISING | PRINT | CONSUMER MAGAZINE |
PRODUCT or SERVICE PROMOTION

CANON POWERSHOT D10 WATERPROOF CAMERA
THE UNIVERSITY OF TEXAS AT AUSTIN—TEXAS CREATIVE

JOSE JORGE NETTO

DANIEL VALLE

Art Director Daniel Valle
Copywriter, Photographer Jose Jorge Netto
School The University of Texas at Austin—Texas Creative
Client Canon

Country United States

BRONZE | ADVERTISING | BROADCAST MEDIA |
CRAFT AND DIGITAL TECHNIQUE | ANIMATION

THE DISCOVERY
SAVANNAH COLLEGE OF ART AND DESIGN

RODGERS DAMERON

Designer, Director, Editor, Rodgers Dameron
School Savannah College of Art and Design

Vanye and Natalia Ivanov, two children in rural Russia, walk through a meadow one day in the cold of winter and discover a mysterious lump in the snow. The thing veiled underneath the snow changes the outlook of their young lives.

Country United States

BRONZE | EDITORIAL DESIGN | TRADE MAGAZINE |
PUBLIC SERVICE or NON-PROFIT

VIEWPOINT
ART CENTER
COLLEGE OF DESIGN

**YOUN HEE
LEE**

**EUN JOO
KIM**

Art Director Eun Joo (Annie) Kim, Youn Hee Lee
Designer Eun Joo (Annie) Kim, Youn Hee Lee
Director Annie Huang Luck, Hannah Huang
Editor Annalisa Swank
School Art Center College of Design

Viewpoint is an Art Center student-produced publication that
highlights the cultural diversity within the Art Center community
on campus and abroad. The goal is to promote understanding
and dialogue, and to encourage global exchange.

Country United States

BRONZE | EDITORIAL DESIGN |
GENERAL TRADE BOOK

ARCHITECTURAL
EXCURSIONS
JENNIFER STERLING DESIGN

**DANIEL
TRAN** **JENNIFER
STERLING**

Art Director Jennifer Sterling
Copywriter Donald Langmead, Donald Leslie Johnson
Designer Daniel Tran, Jennifer Sterling
Agency Jennifer Sterling Design, San Francisco
Client Donald Langmead and Donald Leslie Johnson

We wanted the text to drive the book, and so used blocks of texts
that created an architectural feel through the typography. There
are several pages that are vivid and bold, much like the Architect's
work as well. Those we kept to a minimum, while using the
architectural plans for the foundation of the graphics.

Country United States

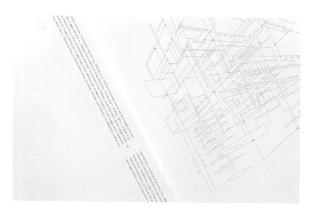

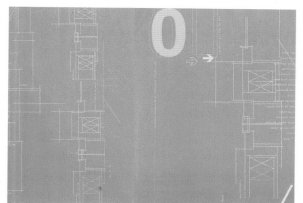

BRONZE | EDITORIAL DESIGN | LIMITED EDITION,
PRIVATE PRESS or SPECIAL FORMAT BOOK

CHINATOWN: PLACE | SPACE
UNIVERSITY OF HAWAII

YONGHAO YAN

Art Director, Designer Yonghao Yan
Instructor Anne Bush
School University of Hawaii at Manoa

Considering an area of Honolulu as both place (the public perception of a site) and space (the private use of the same site), this book project is an investigation into Honolulu's Chinatown, and the intersection between two types of adaptation (immigrant to local, and local to immigrant). It is indexed using the juxtaposition of metric and imperial (inch) measurement systems within the book, as well as the book-within-a-book.

Country United States

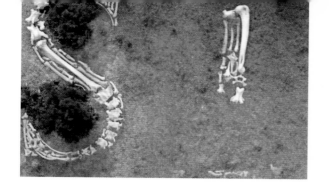

BRONZE | TELEVISION AND CINEMA
DESIGN | TYPOGRAPHY

MY BEST STORIES
SCHOOL OF VISUAL ARTS

WESLEY GOTT

Designer Wesley Gott
School School of Visual Arts

Failures are not something we usually savor, but they embody what makes us human. This stop motion animation attempts to excavate the personal truism, "my best stories always involve a failure." The bone typography alludes to the frailty of memory and the ways stories are reconstructed each time we retell them. The project was created for Stefan Sagmeister's class at the School of Visual Design, where we were tasked with finding and illustrating our own maxims.

Country United States

MERIT | INTERACTIVE ADVERTISING | WIRELESS DEVICE APPLICATIONS | NON-PROFIT, REFERENCE, EDUCATIONAL

MALE INSTINCT
MIAMI AD SCHOOL—EUROPE

BEN HOLDER

BOB HAARMANS

Art Director Bob Haarmans
Copywriter Ben Holder
Agency Miami Ad School—Europe
Client Pink Ribbon Breast Cancer Awareness

Using male instinct, Pink Ribbon encourages men to persuade their wives and girlfriends to be tested.

Country Germany

MERIT | INTERACTIVE ADVERTISING |NEW MEDIA INNOVATION | PRODUCT, SERVICE or ENTERTAINMENT PROMOTION

GLOBAL CURRENT
MIAMI AD SCHOOL—EUROPE

NINA MANTHEY

Art Director, Nina Manthey, JP Schwartz, Chris Vimini
Copywriter Nina Manthey, JP Schwartz, Chris Vimini
School Miami Ad School—Europe
Client Mastercard

Mastercard is one of the leading credit card companies in the world. Last year, they processed 21 billion transactions in 28 million locations. However, people place value on their credit card, not on Mastercard. So how can Mastercard be more of a resource to its customers on a personal level? Global Current is a real time data visualization based on Mastercard swipes worldwide that instantly shows where Mastercard users are making purchases. This gives people a whole new way to view brands, like viewing the most popular brands or the top retailers in the world at a current point in time. Global Current enables Mastercard to be the spending authority for purchasing trends.

Country Germany

MERIT | INTERACTIVE NEW MEDIA INNOVATION PRODUCT | SERVICE | ENTERTAINMENT PROMOTION | CAMPAIGN

THE MIXTAPE
MIAMI AD SCHOOL—EUROPE

DINA RUWE   **ODDBJORN STENSRUD**

Creative Director Stefan Haverkamp, Jan Rexhausen
Art Director Samuel Huber, Dina Ruwe
Copywriter Oddbjorn Stensrud
Agency Miami Ad School—Europe
Client Fred Perry Subculture

Country Germany

MERIT | DESIGN | BRANDING | NON-PROFIT

CITY HARVEST
SCHOOL OF VISUAL ARTS

Art Director Wade Convay, Carla A Echevarria
Designer Eunjung Yoo
School School of Visual Arts

City Harvest is a non-profit organization that rescues food for New York's hungry. The goal of this campaign is to raise awareness for City Harvest, and to encourage more people to donate. This is achieved by introducing the real stories of the donation recipients, making the donation process transparent and human. Once a consumer makes a donation, she receives a unique number that allows her to track her donation online and see the story of the particular individuals she has assisted. Donations can be made via mobile phone and internet, or at supermarket checkouts and MTA ticketing machines.

Country United States

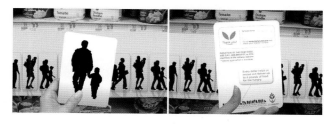

MERIT | POSTER DESIGN |PUBLIC
SERVICE or NON-PROFIT

MUSEUM OF
MAKING MUSIC
ART CENTER
COLLEGE OF DESIGN

JULIANNE
KIM

Designer Julianne Kim
Instructor Brad Bartlett
School Art Center College of Design

Identity for the Museum of Making Music that is inspired by the
flow of music: The name also represents the silence in music,
which is as important as the music itself.

A series of three posters for Glenn Gould, Exhibition at Museum
of Making Music: They capture Glenn Gould's emotions and the
unique characteristics of his performances. The series is posted
vertically to create a representation of his whole body.

Country United States

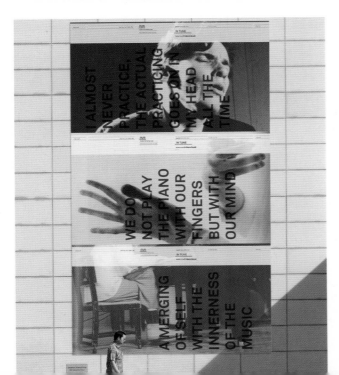

MERIT | ADVERTISING | PRINT | POSTERS AND
BILLBOARDS | OUTDOOR or BILLBOARD

TOOLS
SCHOOL OF VISUAL ARTS

MARIANNA D'ANNUNZIO

Art Director, Copywriter Marianna D'Annunzio
Instructor Frank Anselmo
School School of Visual Arts
Client DEWALT

DEWALT tools play off billboard support poles, creating the illusion that the tools are at work.

Country United States

MERIT | ADVERTISING | PRINT | POSTERS AND
BILLBOARDS | OUTDOOR or BILLBOARD
BILLBOARD
LIGHT
SCHOOL OF VISUAL ARTS

Designer Jang Cho
Instructor Jack Mariucci
School School of Visual Arts
Client Colgate

Country United States

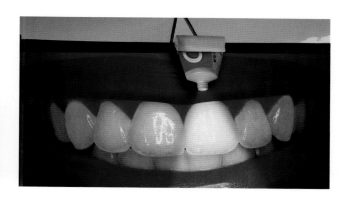

MERIT | ADVERTISING | PRINT | CONSUMER MAGAZINE |
PRODUCT or SERVICE PROMOTION

NATURE
SCHOOL OF VISUAL ARTS

SUNGKWON HA

Art Director, Copywriter Sungkwon Ha
Instructor Frank Anselmo
School School of Visual Arts
Client National Geographic

It all begins with nature.

Country United States

MERIT | ILLUSTRATION |
BOOK

GOOD DREAMS, BAD DREAMS
PARSONS THE NEW SCHOOL FOR DESIGN

Copywriter, Designer, Editor, Illustrator Haejeon Lee
School Parsons the New School for Design

This project is an effort to visually explore the mechanism and deep structure of common dreams by understanding their images and archetypes. I categorized images and patterns found in traditional Asian dream analysis and represented them visually through my own illustrations and writing in a two-volume set of books. I attempted to convey the principle that dreams are universally disguised representations of our deepest needs, desires, wishes and fears. They can be interpreted by deciphering the recurrent images and symbols, in addition to story patterns. By interpreting and knowing the proper messages of these good and bad dreams, we can use them as guidance in our everyday lives. In viewing this book, I would like you to experience a moment of epiphany in which you realize that personal dreams both hide and reveal the universal human truth.

Country United States

Being Chased

MERIT | ILLUSTRATION |
BOOK

CHILDREN OVERHEARD
IN NEW YORK
PARSONS THE NEW
SCHOOL FOR DESIGN

Copywriter, Designer, Editor, Illustrator Haejeon Lee
School Parsons the New School for Design

This project is a graphic novel with illustrations and designs
based on quotes from the website Overheard in New York, where
people post funny quotes they hear all over the city. I selected
the humorous, yet incredibly inappropriate comments made
by children in New York City, and illustrated them using line
drawing and hand lettering. The monotonous colors represent
the sarcasm and dark humor found in the rude remarks made by
children.

Country United States

NISSAN**STUDENT BRIEF**

ADC JURY CHAIR
CHRIS LYNCH
TBWA\CHIAT\DAY

Chris has been with TBWA\CHIAT\DAY since 1997 and is currently the creative director/ art director. As an award winning art director, he's helped develop work for Nissan, The Principal Financial Group, Visa, Pepsi and Mars. Chris is also a published illustrator. He's provided cartoon illustrations for two college textbooks. A fourth generation Californian, Chris was born and raised in the Los Angeles suburb known as the Valley, which is probably why he starts every sentence with, "dude..."

JULIA
NEUMANN
Y&R NEW YORK

Julia Neumann joined Y&R New York in the fall of 2009. She started her career as a copywriter at Saatchi & Saatchi New York in 2006, after graduating from the Miami Ad School Europe in Hamburg. As a student she was named Austrian Student of the Year, and while she was still interning at Saatchi & Saatchi, she helped them become the third most awarded agency at Cannes, winning one third of their total awards. Her team partner is Michael Schachtner, who tries hard every day to bring some German order into her chaotic life.

MICHAEL
SCHACHTNER
Y&R NEW YORK

Michael joined Y&R New York in August 2009. He is currently creating work for global brands such as Dell, LG, Virgin Atlantic and MTV.

Michael began his advertising career at Saatchi & Saatchi New York, where he won a Cannes Lion for P&G's Tide—the brand's very first Lion.

Since then, Michael has won awards from several major advertising festivals, including Cannes, Art Directors Club NY, Clio Awards and The One Show. Michael was also part of the Saatchi team that earned the Agency of the Year title at the Cannes Festival as well as at the Clio Awards in 2007.

One of Michael's proudest accomplishments is his Stuffit Deluxe "Pregnancy" commercial, which was selected to be part of the permanent collection in the Museum of Modern Art in New York.

Some interesting facts about Michael that you probably wouldn't expect from someone in advertising: He originally comes from the field of computer engineering. And he once was a Bavarian weightlifting champion.

DAN
SORMANI
LIFELONG FRIENDSHIP

In 2007, LFS welcomed Dan Sormani as executive producer/partner to help tie together the past with the future. Born in New York, he grew up in Washington, DC and lived in Los Angeles while attending Art Center College of Design prior to joining the world of advertising. His background spans top design shops, advertising agencies and production companies such as Crispin Porter + Bogusky LA, Lowe NY, RSA, Brand New School and Stardust where he has worked with international advertising clients, broadcast and music video clients. He has received awards from the MVPA, BDA and a nomination for an MTV video Music Award in 2005. He currently lives in the South Street Seaport in Manhattan with his girlfriend and dog, Leroy.

GOLD | INTEGRATED ADVERTISING |
OUTSIDE THE BOX

NISSAN CUBE
HOSTEL
PARSONS THE NEW
SCHOOL FOR DESIGN

**PETER
MEGLER**

**MÁRTON
JEDLICSKA**

Art Director Márton Jedlicska
Copywriter Peter Megler
School Miami Ad School
Client Nissan Cube

The Nissan Cube is an automobile, mobile lounge and mobile device wrapped in one. The Cube Hostel truly captures the essence of what the Cube was designed for: fun and friendship.

Book online, pick up your key at reception and head to your room. Restrooms and showers are located downstairs. We only ask that you sign in via Facebook Connect to spread the word.

Rules? You must be a student with a valid ID and cannot stay for more than one week. That's it.

Placing the Cube Hostel in major cities and in high profile locations puts us in a position to capture the college and backpacking crowd. It is also an attraction that will generate plenty of PR.

What better way to make something a part of your life than to live in it? Especially, when it's FREE.

Country United States

MOBILIZE
ON 10.10.10
WWW.MOBILIZE.COM
Fidelity
DO NOT ENTER
Fidelity

GOLD | INTEGRATED ADVERTISING |
OUTSIDE THE BOX

MOBILIZE
ACADEMY OF ART UNIVERSITY

**MICHAEL
WALDMAN**

**SHAVRAN
HEGDE**

Art Director, Copywriter Shravan Hegde, Michael Waldman
School Academy of Art University
Client Nissan Cube

We created an innovative campaign for the Nissan Cube to reach a target whose lives revolve around their digital devices. To them, it's not technology; it's life. The challenge was to direct the target away from their computers and at the same time get them to expand their social network. So, how do we make the Cube mobile device a natural extension of their digital lives? The answer was an interactive first-person shooter game that bridges the gaps between traditional social media, gaming and face to face interaction. To do this we developed an event and a mobile gaming platform around the Cube that takes advantage of the best attributes of the targets, physical and digital lives. To promote the event we created a microsite, deep linking viral videos and interactive wild postings, all focused on getting people together around one idea: Mobilize.

Country United States

SILVER | ADVERTISING | INTEGRATED

BOX.BEAT
MIAMI AD SCHOOL—MINNEAPOLIS

JESSICA KATHLEEN STEWART

ZACHARY GOREN SLOVIN

Art Director Jessica Kathleen Stewart
Copywriter Zachary Goren Slovin
School Miami Ad School—Minneapolis
Client Nissan Cube

Country United States

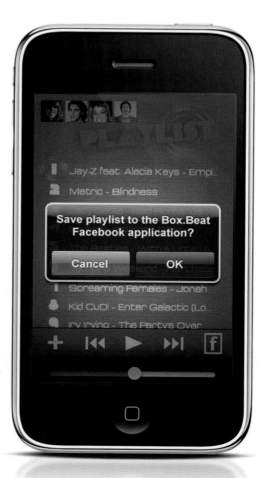

JACK TOOK 357 LESSONS, SPENT 91 HOURS ON SONG , GOT BACK ACHE FROM CARRYING HIS (WHICH HAS CAUSED PRETTY SEVERE DAMAGE TO HIS EARS OVER THE YEARS) HAD 219 BAND REHEARSALS, DRANK TOO MANY BOTTLES OF TO KEEP HIS VOICE ROUGH AND SPENT 11 SESSIONS Á 3 HOURS AT HIS FAVOURITE TATTOOIST.

ALL TO IMPRESS HIS FANS.

JOHN INSTEAD:

LESS EFFORT, MORE EFFECT!

LISA STRAIGHTENED HER  FOR 37 MINUTES, GOT HER FINGERNAILS DONE AND SQUEEZED HER PERFECTLY PEDICURED FEET INTO HER BRANDNEW 4 INCH , GOT BADLY CUT TWICE WHILE SHAVING HER LEGS, NEARLY POKED HER 👁 OUT WHILE TWEEZING HER BROWS AND IT TOOK HER ANOTHER 65 MINUTES TO PICK THE RIGHT 👗. ALL TO IMPRESS HER DATE.

LUCY INSTEAD:

LESS EFFORT, MORE EFFECT!

⬡NISSAN **cube** MOBILE DEVICE

BEN ORGANIZED A ROMANTIC NIGHT AT A ★★★★ HOTEL, AT DINNER HE TIPPED THE VIOLINIST TO PLAY HER FAVOURITE SONG, BOUGT A  FOR 149 💵, GOT HIS SUIT DRYCLEANED, PREORDEREŠ 2 BOTTLES OF 🍾, POLISHED HIS SHOES, GOT A HAIRCUT AND AFTER 1 HAND CRAMP AND 2 ANGRY OUTBURSTS HE FINALLY ASKED HIS GRANDMOTHER HOW TO TO TIE A 👔. ALL TO IMPRESS HIS GIRLFRIEND.

BILL INSTEAD:

LESS EFFORT, MORE EFFECT!

⬡NISSAN **cube** MOBILE DEVICE

SILVER | ADVERTISING | NEWSPAPER | MAGAZINE

LESS EFFORT. MORE EFFECT!
HTL1 BAU UND DESIGN

DANIELA SOBITSCHKA

Art Director, Copywriter, Designer Daniela Sobitschka
School HTL1 Bau und Design, Department for Art and Design
Client Nissan Cube

The main goal of this campaign is to exemplify how a person who owns a Nissan Cube can achieve the same result as someone without a Nissan Cube without expending nearly as much effort. The subjects, who represent the target consumers, describe various situations in young people's lives. While the subject without a Nissan Cube has to go through a rigorous routine of hard work, the other gains the exact same result with almost no effort at all. Basically, owning a Nissan Cube brings the same outcome without the hassle. Less effort, more effect.

In today's world it is necessary for a brand tells a story that reflects the product's purpose and image. This is what I was trying to implement with this concept.

Country Austria

CONNATURALIZE
BRINGHAM YOUNG UNIVERSITY

**ELIZABETH
TERAN**

**RYAN
MOORE**

**HANG
LEE**

Art Director Hang Lee, Ryan Moore
Creative Director Adrian Pulfer
Copywriter Elizabeth Teran
Designer Hang Lee
Editor Ryan Moore
School Brigham Young University
Client Nissan Cube

In our integrated advertising campaign, the idea of tangible socialization and a necessary connection between the organic and technological is represented by a single word: Connaturalize. The campaign's look and feel focuses on iconic symbol images and animations. These animations will be printed into actual collectable flipbooks. Animations will be re-created in frames along the walls of a train tunnel providing the same flipbook experience on a train or subway. A virtual version of these flipbooks will be created for the touch screen devices where users can use their fingers to animate the story and interact with the art. The images themselves will be sold as posters and used as guerilla art. All of these elements work together to create brand awareness through positive iconic images and animations relatable to the Nissan Cube.

Country United States

MERIT | ADVERTISING | PRINT |
NEWSPAPER | MAGAZINE PRINT

CUBE OUTLINES
SCHOOL OF VISUAL ARTS

**JAE
SUNG JUNG**   **HANSO
LEE**

Art Director, Copywriter Jae Sung Jung, Hanso Lee
School School of Visual Arts
Client Nissan Cube

Country United States

MERIT | CORPORATE AND PROMOTIONAL DESIGN |
IDENTITY PROGRAM

CUBE
SCHOOL OF VISUAL ARTS

**JAMES
KYUNGMO YANG**

Art Director, Designer James Kyungmo Yang
School School of Visual Arts
Client Nissan Cube

I made a customized logotype where each letter represents
one color of the Nissan Cube. Each letter are also forms the
components of one side of the cube, and creates different
variations of that cube. There are 24 different versions of the
cube, all of which create beautiful patterns and capture the design
sensibility of the target audience.

Country United States

ADC WINNERS BY FLAG

Cube winning work came from 24 countries. Here are the combined colors of the flags of the countries that won.

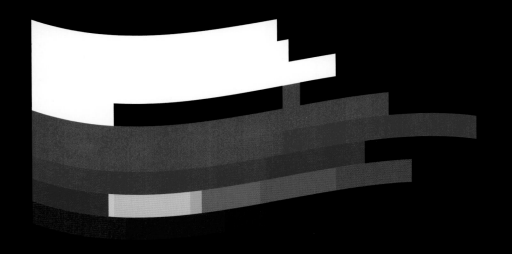

BLACK CUBE

South Africa

SILVER CUBE

Austria, Canada, China, Germany, Italy, Japan, Netherlands, South Africa, South Korea, Taiwan, United Arab Emirates, United States.

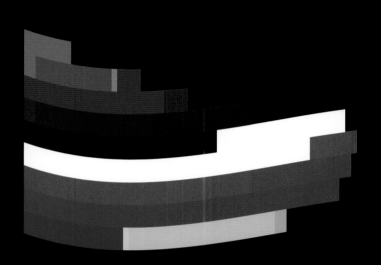

GOLD CUBE

Chile, China, Croatia, Germany, South Africa, Sweden, United Arab Emirates,
United Kingdom, United States.

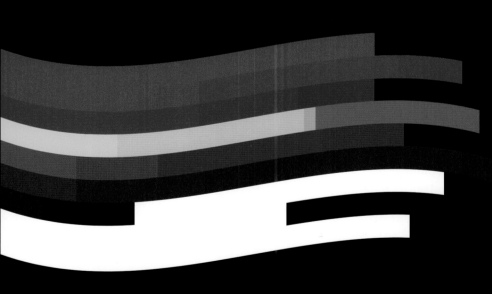

BRONZE CUBE

Brazil, Canada, China, France, Germany, Israel, Japan, Netherlands, New Zealand, Singapore,
Slovenia, South Africa, Spain, Sweden, Switzerland, United Kingdom, United States.

BRONZE 7% of all awards given

MERIT 8% of all awards given

ADVERTISING

Chairing the Advertising Jury of the Art Directors' Club judging has not only been a great honor and a privilege for me, it was a fun and fulfilling experience. I'm thankful and I feel energized by the fact that we were the first jury to award a Black Cube to a campaign that truly celebrates our craft and freedom of speech. Cheers!

- Luis Miguel Messianu
President/CCO ALMA DDB
ADC Advertising Jury Chair

AGENCY OF THE YEAR
BBDO NEW YORK

NETWORK OF THE YEAR
YOUNG & RUBICAM

ADC**ADVERTISING JURY**

LUIS MIGUEL MESSIANU
ALMA DDB

From copywriter to president/chief creative officer, Luis Miguel Messianu's career has spanned more than 20 years. Having worked with notable clients such as Coca-Cola, General Motors, L'Oreal, Levi's and Unilever while working as creative director at some of the top ad agencies: Scali, McCabe, Sloves; McCann-Erickson; Mendoza-Dillon; GSD&M and Lintas, Luis Miguel now heads his own creative agency, Alma DDB, based in Miami, Florida.

As one of the top Hispanic ad agencies in the United States, Alma DDB creates advertising for McDonald's, State Farm Insurance, H&R Block and Perdue and Clorox, to name a few. Alma DDB has won more than 500 advertising awards globally over the last few years, and Luis Miguel has been called to lecture and act as juror for many of them. Aside from Alma's roster of big name clients and industry awards and recognition, what is most noteworthy is the longstanding relationships that Alma DDB is capable of cultivating. Both McDonald's and State Farm have been with Alma DDB for more than 12 years. It is no wonder Luis Miguel Messianu was recognized as "The Most Influential Leader of the Hispanic Advertising Industry in the Last 20 Years" by *P&C Hispanic* magazine, and was recently inducted into the Hall of Fame of FIAP (Festival Iberoamericano de la Publicidad).

Luis Miguel was a founding member and the first president of the Creative Circle of the Latin Market. Currently, he sits on the Board at Miami Ad School and the Clorox Advisory Board.

Luis Miguel was born and raised in Mexico City, Mexico by Rumanian parents. In his free time, he enjoys music, independent films, contemporary art, playing tennis, cycling and all things soccer.

TWITTER LUISMIQUIJOTE

LAUREN
PUGLIA
UNDERCURRENT

Lauren is the development director at Undercurrent (undercurrent.com), a strategy firm in New York City that applies a digital worldview to the challenges and ambitions of complex organizations like PepsiCo, GE and Ford Motor Co. Prior to joining the advertising world, she worked in creative development for the Blue Man Group, figuring out where the worlds of art and commerce meld, but mostly figuring out new ways to toss buckets of paint around.

Lauren hails from New Orleans and is a shaker and a stirrer. She loves ideas, art, people and is a total technophile. She likes to split her time exploring the globe via the internet and using her feet. Thoughts and adventures can be found at: fortheartofit.wordpress.com.

TWITTER FORTHEARTOFIT
WEBSITE LAURENPUGLIA.COM

LAURENCE
KLINGER
LAPIZ

Senior vice president and chief creative officer Lápiz Laurence Klinger was born in São Paulo, Brazil.

He started in advertising in 1972, as a copywriter. Since then, he has worked in agencies in Brazil, Spain and the United States.

Since joining Lápiz in 1999, the agency has won awards in the most important competitions of the industry, including Cannes Lions, Art Directors Club, The One Show, Clios, Fiap, Addys, ANA, Ojo de Iberoamerica and El Sol.

Lápiz was also elected AAAA's Multicultural Agency of the Year in 2004 and 2006, and is the recipient of more Effie awards than any other United States Hispanic agency. In 2009, it won Best of Show at Ad Age's Hispanic Creative Advertising Awards.

Laurence is also a fiction writer, with two short-story books published in the United States.

WEBSITE LAPIZUSA.COM

SCOTT
MCAFEE
SANDERS\WINGO

Scott brings blue-chip brand experience and an eye for bold, creative work to our clients. His hallmarks are simple, vibrant concepts based on honest strategy. A consummate team player, Scott enjoys encouraging Sanders\Wingo talent in all departments.

A graduate of the Portfolio Center, Scott worked at Earle Palmer Brown in Atlanta and Bethesda, Maryland, before joining GSD&M in 1992. In 1998, he was named vice president/creative director. Scott joined Sanders\Wingo as executive creative director in 2002.

Scott's work has been showcased in the Austin Addys, the District Addys, the PRINT Regional Design Annual, The One Show and the Communication Arts Advertising Annual and Design Annual. His portfolio includes work with AT&T, Pennzoil, Shell, State Farm, Chevrolet, YMCA and Goodwill Industries.

Scott is a guest lecturer on advertising creative at the University of Texas at Austin. He also serves on the board of directors for the Austin Advertising Federation and the Gazelle Foundation.

Scott lives in Austin with his wife, Kathryn, and their daughter, Amelia.

TWITTER SCOTTMCAFEE

KASH
SREE
PEREIRA & O'DELL

Kash came to Pereira & O'Dell most recently from JWT where he was executive creative director. Kash's talents have been applied to global brands including Axe, British Airways, DeBeers, Kleenex, Nike, Nintendo, Purell, Scott Toilet Tissues, Sunsilk Haircare, Vaseline and Visine. Prior to JWT, he served as group creative director at BBH, with award-winning work for Leo Burnett, Wieden+Kennedy and DDB.

Over the course of his career in advertising he has amassed over 300 awards from the industry's most important competitions: Grand Prixs at Cannes, London International, Singapore CCA, National Addys and Best of Show at the Portland Rosey's. He has talked at Miami Ad School, The Wolfsonian Museum, The One Club's Ad-versity group, Singapore Adclub. He is no stranger to awards juries, having judged for The One Show, ADCNY, the Andys, Clios, AICP, Young Guns, Hong Kong AAA Awards, London Festival and Singapore CCA Awards among others.

TWITTER DODGBOY
WEBSITE KASH-SREE.COM

MENNO
KLUIN
Y&R NEW YORK

An up-and-coming talent in the industry, Menno Kluin joined Y&R in October 2008. He oversees the international intern program and functions in head of art capacity while working across brands, including Bacardi, Dell, Virgin Atlantic, LG, Colgate, MTV, VH1 and Land Rover.

Kluin started his career at Saatchi & Saatchi NY, where he won every top international award for his creative work.

Within his first two years in the business, Kluin had already collected eight Cannes Lions, and was named 2007's "Most Awarded Art Director," according *Creativity Magazine*. That same year, Kluin contributed to Saatchi NY winning the coveted Agency of the Year at Cannes and Clios. Last year he was ranked one of the Top 50 Young Creatives in the world by Art Directors Club.

As a student, he was named Dutch Talent of the Year, German Student of the Year, International Student Young Gun of the Year, International Student of the Year by Luerzers Archive, and a Top-Five Graduate by Adweek.

WEBSITE MENNOKLUIN.COM

CHUCK
TSO
DDB NEW YORK

Chuck is a creative director at DDB New York, where he works on NY Lottery, Hertz and a host of Unilever brands.

Prior to DDB, he spent five years at crosstown BBDO, where his work on FedEx, BBC World, Monster, Havaianas and eBay helped contribute to the successful reboot of the New York office. He has brought home gold from all the big ad shows. Last year, The Won Report ranked him second most-awarded art director globally.

He has a preference for short bios and is stubbornly rooted in New York City.

JAMES CLUNIE
BBDO NEW YORK

James is senior vice president/creative director at BBDO New York. Over the past three years, he has led the award-winning launches of both the Brazilian flip-flops, Havaianas and *The Economist* magazine in the United States. In addition to these accounts, he has contributed to campaigns for HBO (Big Love), FedEx, eBay, AT&T, Smart Car, Special Olympics and a few ugly ones he'd rather just forget.

His work has won Gold at Cannes, The One Show, Clios, New York Art Directors Club, and The Andys. He lives in New York City with his sweet wife, Lisa, and their son, Jimmy.

WEBSITE JAMESCLUNIE.COM

BETRAND SUCHET
DDB PARIS

1978: Bertrand is 18 years old. His rock group opens for the The Cramps. He gets his first job at the St. Tropez nightclub, The Voom Voom, owned by Charlie Marcantoni.

1982-95: Along with a gang of friends, he organizes the Nioulargue, the international regatta of St. Tropez, as well as the offshore world championships and the International Yacht Club of Pampelonne.

1983-90: Bertrand goes to Paris and works at ECOM, where he wins two Cannes Lions. He collaborates with his friend Voutch. Together, they transfer to TBWA.

1992: Creative director at Léo Burnett.

1993: Launch of Louis XIV with his friend, Jean-Luc Bravi. The agency starts with six people, increasing to a staff of 70 after three years. The agency regularly creates award-winning campaigns for clients such as Audi, Nike, Leclerc and Neutrogena.

1999-2000: While still president of Louis XIV and heading Création, he organizes three archeological expeditions in the Indian Ocean. He works on an excavation exhibition at the Maritime Museum of Zanzibar.

2001: Louis XIV and DDB join forces. After seven magnificent years, Bertrand becomes president of the new entity. The agency is comprised of just over 300 people.

2005-06: Co-president of the group DDB France. President of the French Art Directors Club.

End of 2009: His agency takes on a new associate—Matthieu de Lesseux, the founder of the digital agency, Duke.

TWITTER DDBPARIS
WEBSITE DDBPARIS.COM

SPENCER WONG
McCANN HONG KONG

Spencer is now the head of McCann Hong Kong and the chief creative officer of McCann Worldgroup China.

Spencer has been working in advertising creative for more than 22 years, with Leo Burnett, Ogilvy & Mather, M&C Saatchi and Euro & Bates. His experience also includes being a TVC director, directing more than 50 TVCs for Hong Kong, China and Singapore markets.

Spencer has been responsible for numerous advertising accolades and multiple Grand Prize and gold awards in most of the local and regional creative competitions. He has made McCann the top creative agency of Hong Kong since 2006, and the fifth most creative agency in Asia.

Spencer's personal honors also include the "Creative Person of the Year" by Media, the Design Grand Prize winner at Cannes and Spike Asia in 2009.

He is now 46, yet looks like he's 33, acts like he's 21, and dreams like he's 10.

NIKLAS FRINGS-RUPP
MIAMI AD SCHOOL

Niklas Frings-Rupp started his career as an account manager working for agencies like DDB London, TBWA Germany, Springer & Jacoby and Jung von Matt. Over the years he worked for a large number of clients like BMW, Mini, Apple, Media Markt, GlaxoWelcome, Weihenstephan, Der Spiegel, UNICEF and many more.

In 2003, he founded Miami Ad School Europe together with Oliver Voss, one of Germany's leading creatives. The school started in an old hospital in Hamburg with only 12 students. The school grew rapidly, and now has over 70 students from about 30 different countries. Recently Niklas and Oliver expanded the school by opening part-time locations in Stockholm, Vienna, Amsterdam and Brussels. They are currently planning a school in Shanghai. In the summer of 2009, he opened the MAS Berlin.

After the second year, the school was already the most awarded school in the world, collecting the top prizes at all major student award shows. Titles won by the students so far include; German Student of the Year, Dutch Student of the Year, the first ever Lüerzers Archive International Student of the Year, and last year's Student Young Gun of the Year. The school is the only advertising school outside of the United States to be mentioned consistently in The Gunn Report's list of the best advertising schools worldwide. Work done by students interning have resulted in seven Lions at Cannes, five Pencils at The One Show, additional awards from the Andy's and Clios, nominations and six Yellow Pencils at D&AD, and a couple accolades from the German Art Directors Club.

In his spare time, Niklas likes to race his dusty, somewhat old Porsche on the German Autobahn and professional race tracks.

MARC LINEVEIDT
SAATCHI & SAATCHI

Marc Lineveldt is executive creative director of Saatchi & Saatchi Dubai and regional creative director of Saatchi & Saatchi Middle East & North Africa. Marc is also currently chairman of the Creative Club of Dubai. Marc began his career at TBWA Hunt Lascaris, where he spent ten years, the first three in Johannesburg as an art director, the rest at TBWA Hunt Lascaris Cape Town as co-creative director. Marc has also worked at Ogilvy Cape Town, Y&R Dubai and FP7 Dubai. Marc has won awards at Cannes Lions, Clio Awards, D&AD, The One Show, Art Directors Club, The Loerie Awards and, since working in Dubai, he's won three Grands Prix, four Gold, five Silver and 13 Bronze Dubai Lynx Awards. Marc has participated as a jury member at award shows, including The Loerie Awards, Meribel Ad Festival, Campaign, Clio Awards and Cannes Lions Festival.

TWITTER MARCLINEVEDIDT

MARCOS KOTLHAR
ALMAPBBDO

I was born in Porto Alegre, Brazil and studied fine arts at The Cooper Union in New York. At graduation time, I was a recipient of The ADC William Taubin Scholarship. I started my career as a designer at the on-air-graphics department at MTV Networks in New York City. I worked with fashion labels, book publishers, motion graphics studios and branding companies before getting into advertising at AlmapBBDO in São Paulo. Here, I have been an art director for the past five years and I've developed work for several clients, including several worldwide campaigns for Havaianas. My work has been recognized and awarded by international festivals and competitions, including: Cannes Lions, ADC, Clio, AD&D, One show, LIA, El Sol and FIAP. I was also chosen as one of the ADC Young Guns 5.

WEBSITE EMCASA.TO

GRAHAM
CLIFFORD
GRAHAM CLIFFORD DESIGN

STEVE
SIMPSON
GOODBY, SILVERSTEIN & PARTNERS

Graham Clifford is a second-generation type/design director. He was trained by his father before working for some of London's best advertising agencies, including Collett Dickenson Pearce and Gold Greenlees Trott. He relocated to New York City and plied his craft at Chiat/Day and Ogilvy.

In the '90s he opened his own design consultancy, collaborating with ad agencies and directly with clients on various projects, including advertising, logo design, brand identity and packaging. Clients range from Fortune 500 companies to start-ups.

Awards include: One Show Pencils, Communication Arts, Type Directors Club and Art Directors Club appearances as well as a Silver Pencil at D&AD.

He is currently the secretary/treasurer of the Type Directors Club.

Steve began his advertising career in Chicago with a now-defunct agency (you make the connection). He afterwards spent six years at Hal Riney & Partners in San Francisco, before joining Goodby, Silverstein & Partners in 1990. At GS&P, Steve worked on such diverse accounts as HP, the Commonwealth Bank of Australia, Emerald Nuts, *The Wall Street Journal, The New Yorker*, Porsche, the NBA, Norwegian Cruise Line and Chevys Mexican Restaurants. In 1995, Steve was made partner and creative director.

His work has won every major award in the industry—Gold at Cannes, The One Show, The Art Director's Club of New York, the Clios, Addys and ANDYs. He has won the MPA Kelly Award and its Copywriting award twice. Two of his campaigns were judged by The One Club of New York to be among the Ten Best of the 1990s, and in 2003, his Fresh TV campaign for Chevys was inducted into the Clio Hall of Fame. As Creative Director on HP, he has taken pleasure in winning "Campaign of the Year" honors three times from three different magazines: *Campaign* (United Kingdom) in 2001, *Adweek* in 2004, and *Ad Age* in 2007. Steve has been named to *Adweek*'s "Creative All Star Team," both as copywriter and as creative director, and has been named to *Creativity* magazine's list of Top 50 Creatives from Media and Tech Companies three times.

He rides some kind of bike nearly every day of the week—a passion continued from his glory days as "Newspaper Carrier of the Year" in his hometown of Shelbyville, Indiana.

IT'S **HBO**.

CUBE
FILM INSTALLATION
BBDO NEW YORK

ADAM   **BRANDON**
REEVES   **MUGAR**

Executive Creative Director Greg Hahn, Mike Smith
Chief Creative Officer David Lubars, Bill Bruce
Art Director Brandon Mugar
Copywriter Adam Reeves
Director Noam Murro
Director of Integrated Production Brian DiLorenzo
Producer Nicholas Gaul
Production Company Biscuit Filmworks
Digital Agency The Barbarian Group
Client HBO

Country United States

Additional Awards:

DESIGN GOLD
ENVIRONMENTAL DESIGN | ENVIRONMENT

GOLD | BROADCAST MEDIA | INNOVATION |
TELEVISION AND CINEMA DESIGN

THE
AFFAIR
BBDO NEW YORK

**ADAM
REEVES**

**BRANDON
MUGAR**

Executive Creative Director Greg Hahn, Mike Smith
Chief Creative Officer David Lubars, Bill Bruce
Art Director Brandon Mugar
Copywriter Adam Reeves
Director Noam Murro
Director of Integrated Production Brian DiLorenzo
Producer Nicholas Gaul
Production Company Biscuit Filmworks
Digital Agency The Barbarian Group
Client HBO

Country United States

Additional Awards:

DESIGN BRONZE
TELEVISION AND CINEMA DESIGN | ART DIRECTION

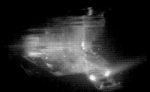

MERIT | BROADCAST MEDIA | CRAFT AND DIGITAL
TECHNIQUE | CINEMATOGRAPHY
IMAGINE
TV CAMPAIGN

BRONZE | BROADCAST MEDIA | CRAFT AND DIGITAL
TECHNIQUE | CINEMATOGRAPHY
TEDDY
BEAR CHASE

BRONZE | TELEVISION AND CINEMA
DESIGN | ART DIRECTION
HAPPY
KID

It's more than you imagined.

MERIT | INTERACTIVE ADVERTISING | BEYOND THE WEB |
PRODUCT, SERVICE or ENTERTAINMENT PROMOTION
HBO IMAGINE
INTERGRATED CAMPAIGN

GOLD | PRINT | POSTERS AND BILLBOARDS
OUTDOOR or BILLBOARD

CAUSE
& EFFECT
Y&R DUBAI

SHAHIR
ZAG

KOMAL
BEDI SOHAL

Executive Creative Director Shahir Zag
Creative Director Shahir Zag, Komal Bedi Sohal
Art Director Komal Bedi Sohal, Dash Gaude, Sajesh Pudussery
Copywriter, Designer Shahir Zag
Photographer Tejal Patni
Account Planner Nadine Ghossoub
Agency Y&R Dubai
Client Harvey Nichols

Harvey Nichols Dubai wanted to promote its Spring/Summer collection with the theme of sensuality, magnetism and overt sexiness—in short, everything you can't talk about in the Middle East. Our solution was to use extremely suggestive and yet very subtle visual metaphors to tell that story. We propped an item from the collection in the center of each ad (cause) and surrounded it with a metaphor for the overwhelming response you would receive (effect). We wanted the ads to look flat and under-designed so that they would be a truly popping antithesis to other high-end fashion advertising. The entire collection was sold out in just three weeks. A first for Harvey Nichols.

Country United Arab Emirates

Additional Awards:

● **ADVERTISING SILVER**
MAGAZINE, CONSUMER

Title: Industrial Pollution
Headline Translation: Let the hills be hills and the rivers be rivers.

GOLD | PRINT | POSTERS AND BILLBOARDS |
OUTDOOR or BILLBOARD

SHAN
SHUI
JWT SHANGHAI

**LILLIE
ZHONG**

**RAFAEL
FREIRE**

**YANG
YEO**

Creative Director SheungYan Lo, Yang Yeo
Art Director Lillie Zhong, Yang Yong Liang
Copywriter Jacqueline Ye, Rafael Freire
Designer Sean Tang
Illustrator, Photographer Yang Yong Liang
Print Production Liza Law, Joseph Yu, Tao Shen
Account Service Betty Tsai
Agency JWT Shanghai
Client Critical Ecosystem Partnership Fund

Country China

全球气温

GOLD | PRINT | POSTERS AND BILLBOARDS |
OUTDOOR or BILLBOARD

SHAN
SHUI
JWT SHANGHAI

Title: Automotive Pollution
Headline Translation: Leave nature alone.

Title: Global Warming
Headline Translation: Don't let nature come to an end.

Additional Awards:

⬡ **DESIGN SILVER**
TELEVISION AND CINEMA DESIGN
|ANIMATION

⬡ **DESIGN BRONZE**
PHOTO, ILLUSTRATION

⬡ **ADVERTISING BRONZE**
MAGAZINE, CONSUMER

⬡ **ADVERTISING MERIT**
CRAFT | DIGITAL TECHNIQUE

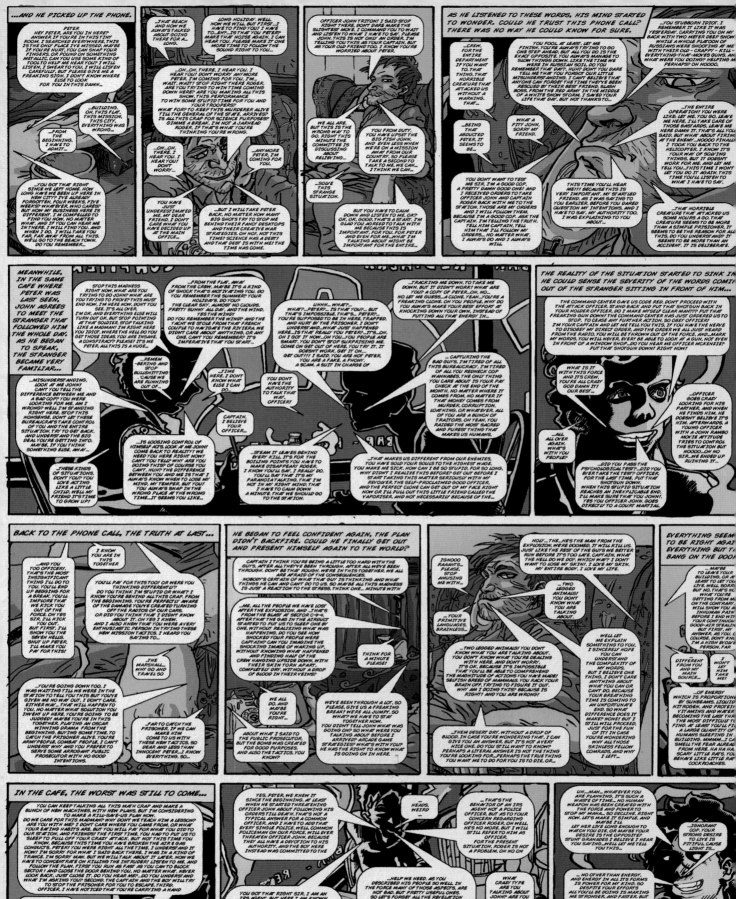
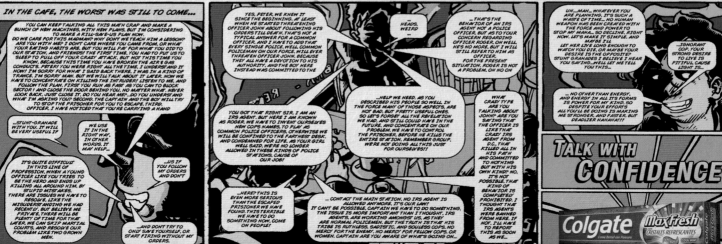

GOLD | PRINT | CONSUMER MAGAZINE |
PRODUCT or SERVICE PROMOTION

COMICS
PROLAM Y&R

**FABRIZIO
CAPRARO**

**MIHAIL
ALEKSANDROW**

**FRANCISCO
CAVADA**

**ALVARO
BECKER**

**JORGE
MUÑOZ**

Creative Director Tony Sarroca, Guillermo Vega, Alvaro Becker
Art Director Fabrizio Capraro, Mihail Aleksandrow
Copywriter Max Konig
Illustrator Raul Pardo
Agency Prolam Y&R
Client Colgate

Country Chile

SILVER | PRINT | COLLATERAL ADVERTISING |
UNCONVENTIONAL or GUERRILLA

THE CONTEMPORARY BEAUTY IDEAL
OGILVY & MATHER WERBEAGENTUR GMBH

DR. STEPHAN VOGEL

ALBERT S. CHAN

SABINA HESSE

REMUS GRECU

Creative Director Dr. Stephan Vogel, Christian Mommertz
Art Director Sabina Hesse, Albert S. Chan
Copywriter Sabina Hesse, Albert S. Chan
Painter Remus Grecu
Photographer Jo Bacherl
Account Management Veronika Sikvölgyi
Art Buyer Valerie Opitz
Agency Ogilvy & Mather Werbeagentur GmbH
Client ANAD (National Association of Anorexia Nervosa and Associated)

The Brief:
ANAD is a pro bono organization that educates the public about the dangers of anorexia. The challenge was to find an innovative way to raise money and awareness.

The Solution:
To demonstrate the unhealthy beauty ideals promoted by the media and fashion industry, we went for a completely new approach: We re-painted world famous masterpieces, but replaced healthy women with anorexic subjects. These paintings were then displayed in fine art museums—exactly where visitors would expect to see manifestations of true beauty.

Country Germany

Additional Awards:

◆ **DESIGN BRONZE**
ILLUSTRATION MAGAZINE ADVERTISMENT

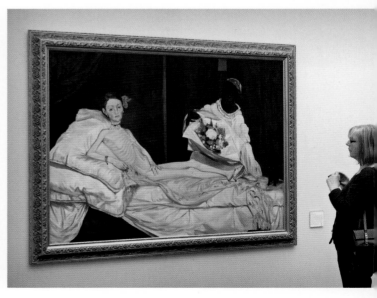

BEAUTY IDEALS CHANGE.
HELP THE VICTIMS TO SURVIVE:
WWW.**ANTIANOREXIA**.NET

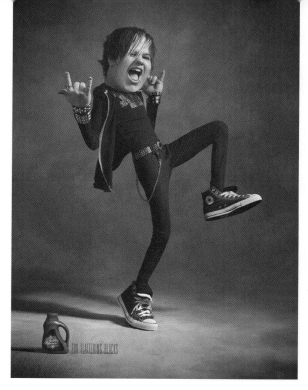

SILVER | PRINT | CONSUMER NEWSPAPER |
PRODUCT SERVICE or NON-PROFIT
CHEER
DARK
LEO BURNETT TORONTO

ANTHONY
CHELVANATHAN

STEVE
PERSICO

Chief Creative Officer Judy John
Creative Director Heather Chambers, Israel Diaz
Art Director Anthony Chelvanathan, Israel Diaz
Copywriter Steve Persico
Photographer Ishi
Producer Anne Peck
Art Buyer Heather Morton
Agency Leo Burnett Toronto
Client Procter & Gamble

Country Canada

Additional Awards:

◆ **ADVERTISING SILVER**
CHEER DARK: COWBOY NEWSPAPER, SINGLE

SILVER | BROADCAST MEDIA |TELEVISION
PRODUCT or SERVICE PROMOTION

ANTIQUING
TAXI CANADA INC.

**NATHAN
MONTEITH**

**STEFAN
WEGNER**

Executive Creative Director Darren Clarke
Creative Director Steve Mykolyn
Art Director, Copywriter Nathan Monteith, Stefan Wegner
Cinematographer Marten Tedin
Director The Perlorian Brothers
Editor Brian Wells
Assistant Editor Mark Lutterman
Vice President Integrated Production Cynthia Heyd
Agency Producer Eugene Marchio
Production Company Soft Citizen, Furlined
Agency TAXI Canada Inc.
Client Pfizer Canada Inc.

Country Canada

Additional Awards:

 ADVERTISING SILVER
BROADCAST MEDIA TELEVISION CAMPAIGN

Video: Open on a man outside on his front porch.
He speaks to camera. Porcelain figurines...oil
lamps...those tiny spoons.

Man: My wife and I couldn't control our antiquing.

Flashback: The couple are antique shopping at
a flea market

Man: Antiquing took over our lives. So I tried
Viagra.

Man: And now my antiquing is pretty much gone

Super: (Viagra pill) Talk to your doctor. Viagra.ca

Talk to your doctor

VIAGRA™

viagra.ca

Talk to your doctor

viagra.ca

SILVER | BROADCAST MEDIA | TELEVISION
PRODUCT or SERVICE PROMOTION

STROLLING
TAXI CANADA INC.

**NATHAN
MONTEITH**

**STEFAN
WEGNER**

Executive Creative Director Darren Clarke
Creative Director Steve Mykolyn
Art Director Nathan Monteith, Stefan Wegner
Copywriter Stefan Wegner, Nathan Monteith
Director The Perlorian Brothers
Editor Brian Wells
Assistant Editor Mark Lutterman
Agency Producer Eugene Marchio
Production Company Soft Citizen, Furlined
Cinematographer Marten Tedin
Vice President Integrated Production Cynthia Heyd
Agency TAXI Canada Inc.
Client Pfizer Canada Inc.

Country Canada

Additional Awards:

◆ **ADVERTISING SILVER**
BROADCAST MEDIA TELEVISION CAMPAIGN

Video: Open on a man in his kitchen. He speaks to the camera.

Man: My wife and I got hooked on strolling. We'd stroll anywhere.

Flashback: The couple walk down a suburban sidewalk.

Man: Our little strolls were turning into full outings. So I tried Viagra. And my strolling, sort of, stopped.

Super: (Viagra pill) Talk to your doctor. Viagra.ca

SILVER | BROADCAST MEDIA | TELEVISION
PRODUCT or SERVICE PROMOTION

READING
TAXI CANADA INC.

**NATHAN
MONTEITH**

**STEFAN
WEGNER**

Executive Creative Director Darren Clarke
Creative Director Steve Mykolyn
Art Director Nathan Monteith, Stefan Wegner
Copywriter Stefan Wegner, Nathan Monteith
Director The Perlorian Brothers
Editor Brian Wells
Assistant Editor Mark Lutterman
Agency Producer Eugene Marchio
Production Company Soft Citizen, Furlined
Cinematographer Marten Tedin
Vice President Integrated Production Cynthia Heyd
Agency TAXI Canada Inc.
Client Pfizer Canada Inc.

Country Canada

Additional Awards:

⬡ **ADVERTISING SILVER**
BROADCAST MEDIA TELEVISION CAMPAIGN

Video: Open on a man sitting in a living room.
He speaks to camera.

Man: Our reading was out of control. My wife
and I read every night.

Flashback: The couple are sitting on a park
bench. The woman is reading to her husband.

Man: We even started reading to each other.
So I tried Viagra and my reading kinda went
away.

Super: (Viagra pill) Talk to your doctor. Viagra.ca

Talk to your doctor

viagra.ca

CONGRATULATIONS
ICHIRO
200
HITS!
2001-2009 EVERY SEASON

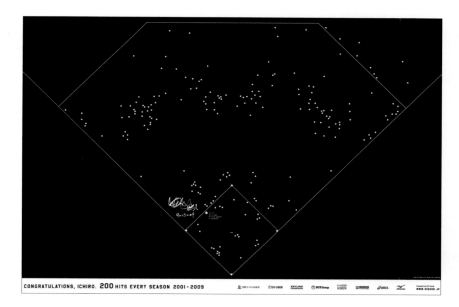

CONGRATULATIONS, ICHIRO. **200** HITS EVERY SEASON 2001-2009

SILVER | PRINT | CONSUMER NEWSPAPER |
PRODUCT or SERVICE PROMOTION

CONGRATULATIONS
ICHIRO
HAKUHODO INC

KAZUKI   **SHINICHI**
OKAMOTO   **TAKIZAWA**

Creative Director Go Koshiyama
Art Director, Designer Kazuki Okamoto
Copywriter Shinichi Takizawa
Producer Yozo Itonaga , Tomohiko Sato ,Tsutomu Goto
Agency Hakuhodo Inc.
Client Hakuhodo DY Media Partners

Country Japan

SILVER | PRINT | CONSUMER MAGAZINE |
PRODUCT or SERVICE PROMOTION

WELCOME BACK
DDB

ALESSANDRO MIAN

RICARD VALERO

Creative Director Vicky Gitto
Art Director Ricard Valero
Copywriter Alessandro Mian
Photographer Andrea Melcangi
Post Production The Scope
Agency DDB
Client Henkel Italia - Super Attak

Country Italy

SILVER | PRINT | COLLATERAL ADVERTISING |
PRODUCT or SERVICE PROMOTION

POWER
LEAKAGE
JUNG VON MATT AG

Executive Creative Director Sascha Hanke, Wolf Heumann
Creative Director Tobias Grimm, Jens Pfau
Art Director Arne Weitkaemper
Copywriter Rudolf Ruessmann
Designer Benjamin Busse, Julia Stoffer
Director Markus Hofer
Agency Jung von Matt AG
Client RWE AG

Country Germany

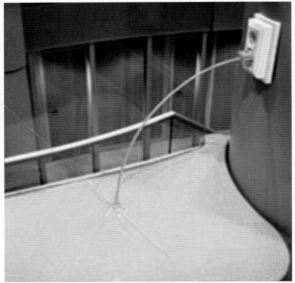

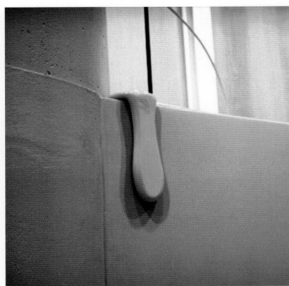

SILVER | COLLATERAL ADVERTISING |
UNCONVENTIONAL or GUERRILLA

TRUTH ONLY
KIDS CAN SEE
DENTSU INC.

**HIDETOSHI
KURANARI**

**TETSUYA
TSUKAMOTO**

Creative Director Akira Kagami, Yuya Furukawa, Yoshimitsu
Art Director Tetsuya Tsukamoto
Copywriter Hidetoshi Kuranari, Nadya Kirillova Sawamoto
Producer Koji Wada
Agency Dentsu Inc. Tokyo
Client Kadokawa Shoten Publishing Co., Ltd

Country Japan

"THE LIFE"
HUMAN

Creative Director Scott Duchon, John Patroulis
Art Director Aramis Israel
Copywriter Rick Herrera
Designer Simon Cassels, Aaron Benoit
Director Rupert Sanders
Editor Eric Zumbrunnen
Editorial Final Cut LA
Producer Eric Stern
Production Company MJZ, Los Angeles
Visual Effects Asylum
Music Company, Agency Human
Client Microsoft XBOX 360 Halo 3 ODST

We wanted the music to convey the ceremony and honor of the
film without being brash and heroic. The hero's journey wasn't
supposed to feel desperate or helpless. His needed to be a
story of honor, told in an unconventional way. We also needed to
emphasize the cyclical structure of the story—it ends as it began.
The three-part instrumentation is very simple; a drone, a vocal
and bagpipes during the two funeral scenes, and in the middle it's
very primitive hand percussion and one person howling, repeated
over and over.

The lyrics to the song contain many hidden references to different
aspects of the game—hidden only because we translated the
lyrics from English to a combination of Modern Welsh and Old
Welsh. This dialect gives the whole piece a more timeless feeling,
like what you are seeing has happened many times before.

Country United States

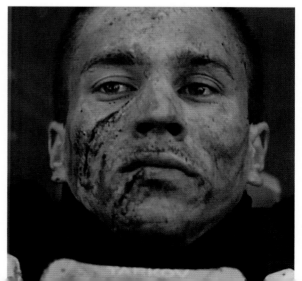

BRONZE | PRINT | POSTERS AND BILLBOARDS |
POINT-OF-PURCHASE

SMART CAR
POSTER CAMPAIGN
BBDO NEW YORK

**JAMES
CLUNIE**

**PIERRE
LIPTON**

Chief Creative Officer David Lubars, Bill Bruce
Creative Director James Clunie, Pierre Lipton
Art Director James Clunie
Copywriter Pierre Lipton
Computer Generated Imagery Artist Nicolas Rieben
Agency BBDO New York
Client Chrysler/Smart Car

Country United States

Additional Awards:

ADVERTISING BRONZE
PRINT | POSTERS AND BILLBOARDS |
POINT-OF-PURCHASE

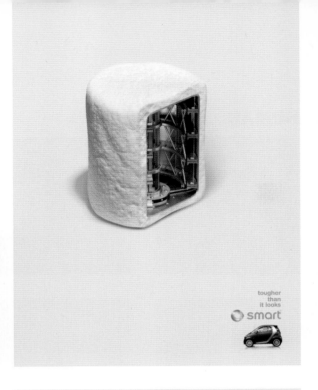

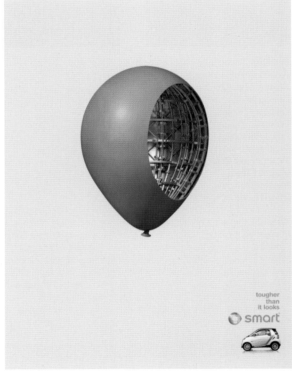

tougher
than
it looks

BRONZE | BROADCAST MEDIA |
TELEVISION SMALL BUDGET

WEST
BANK
DDB NEW ZEALAND

**ADAM
KANZER**

**SCOTT
KAPLAN**

**CHUCK
TSO**

Group Executive Creative Director Toby Talbot
Creative Director Adam Kanzer
Art Director Chuck Tso
Copywriter Adam Kanzer, Scott Kaplan
Director Cole Webley
Editor Kim Bica
Producer Jared Harris
Production Company Uber Content
Agency DDB New Zealand
Client SKY Television

The objective of this spot was to make people aware that SKY offers five channels of unbiased news coverage. So we came up with the idea of showing news subjects actually delivering the news themselves, as the news was happening...using the style and mannerisms of a traditional news reporter. We ended with the line, "Let the news speak for itself," as a way to wrap up that concept. Hopefully, it worked.

Country New Zealand

BRONZE | BROADCAST MEDIA | TELEVISION
PRODUCT or SERVICE PROMOTION

GAME
BBDO NEW YORK

**PETER
KAIN**

**GIANFRANCO
ARENA**

Chief Creative Officer David Lubars
Creative Director Peter Kain, Gianfranco Arena
Art Director Gianfranco Arena
Copywriter Peter Kain
Director Craig Gillespie
Editor Ian Mackenzie
Producer Amy Wertheimer
Production Company MJZ
Agency BBDO New York
Client Mars Snack Food US/Snickers

Country United States

BRONZE | BROADCAST MEDIA | TELEVISION
PRODUCT or SERVICE PROMOTION

LIKE A
GOLF
DDB UK

Creative Director Jeremy Craigen
Art Director Feargal Ballance, Dylan Harrison
Copywriter Feargal Ballance, Dylan Harrison
Agency DDB UK
Client Volkswagen

Country United Kingdom

BRONZE | BROADCAST MEDIA | TELEVISION
PRODUCT or SERVICE PROMOTION

HAMMER
THROW
DENTSU INC.

Creative Director, Art Director Norifumi Adachi
Copywriter Akira Yao, Hiroshi Akinaga, Kazuhide Adachi
Director Shinya Kawakami
Producer Masami Hirotsuka
Production Company Pict Inc.
Agency Dentsu Inc. Tokyo
Client Toyota Motor Corporation

The Toyota iQ is an ultra compact hatchback, less than three meters in length. We thought the best way to demonstrate the iQ's functionality and powerful 1.3L engine was to show a passenger performing a hammer throw from the car.

Country Japan

BRONZE | BROADCAST MEDIA | TELEVISION
PRODUCT or SERVICE PROMOTION

CAR PARK
SHOPPING
H

Creative Director Gilbert Scher
Art Director Luca Cinquepalmi
Copywriter Marco Venturelli
Director ACNE
TV Producer Christopher Thiery, Martine Dechaume
Production Company Wanda Production
Agency H
Client CITROEN

Country France

BRONZE | BROADCAST MEDIA | TELEVISION
PRODUCT or SERVICE PROMOTION

FIAT CRASH
TEST PANDA
MARCEL PARIS

Creative Director Frederic Temin, Anne de Maupeou
Director Rémi Devouassoud
Editor Jérôme Lozano
Producer François Brun
Production Company WIZZdesign
Agency Marcel Paris
Client Fiat

Country France

BRONZE | PRINT | CONSUMER NEWSPAPER |
PRODUCT or SERVICE PROMOTION

OBJECTS OF POCKET
ALMAPBBDO

SUZANA HADDAD

RENAN TOMMASO

Creative Director Luiz Sanches, Dulcídio Caldeira
Art Director Suzana Haddad
Copywriter Renan Tommaso
Illustrator 6B Studio
Photographer Latin Stock
Account Supervisor Yoshico Saito
Advertiser's Supervisor Joana Fernandes
Agency AlmapBBDO
Client Cia das Letras

Country Brazil

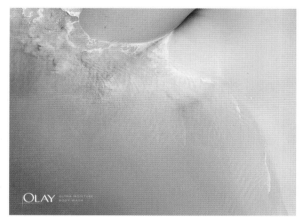

BRONZE | PRINT | CONSUMER NEWSPAPER |
PRODUCT or SERVICE PROMOTION
BODIES OF
WATER
SAATCHI & SAATCHI NY
Chief Creative Officer Gerry Graf
Creative Director Ralph Watson, Beverly Okada
Art Director Ralph Watson
Photographer Ric Frazier
Retoucher Yan Apostolides
Art Buyer Maggie Sumner
Agency Saatchi & Saatchi New York
Client Olay

Country United States

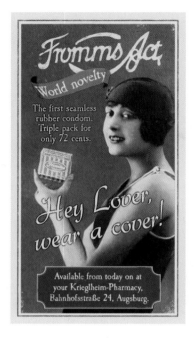

BRONZE | PRINT | CONSUMER NEWSPAPER |
PRODUCT or SERVICE PROMOTION

AUGSBURGER ALLGEMEINE: GLOBAL NEWS STARTS AS LOCAL NEWS

SCHOLZ & FRIENDS GMBH

Executive Director Martin Pross, Matthias Spaetgens
Creative Director Oliver Handlos, Mathias Rebmann
Art Director Felix Roy, Erik Dagnell
Copywriter Roman Senkl, Jens-Petter Waernes
Graphic Designer Yifeng Wang
Account Manager Michael Schulze, Salvatore Amato
Agency Scholz & Friends Berlin GmbH
Client Augsburger Allgemeine

Country Germany

We know you wouldn't read a long text about the features of the new Passat. So, here's the short one.

Blue, sky blue, green and metallic white. Nope, these aren't the colors the Passat comes in. They are the colors passengers turn when you accelerate this 250 horsepower car.

The Passat offers two engine choices: 2.0 FSI Turbo or 3.2 V6 FSI, both powered by gasoline. The 2.0 FSI Turbo, standard with the Comfortline Turbo model, has been named in England the best engine in the world for four consecutive years. And it generates a top speed of 230 km/h.

The 3.2 250HP V6 engine attains speeds of up to 210 km/h. It goes from zero to a fainted passenger in just 6.9 seconds. That's mind-boggling acceleration. You should be as responsible when driving as we were when making this car.

But you don't have to open the Passat's hood to see the perfectionism of German engineering. The Passat's every detail is perfection itself. And there are not just a few details. The car is fully loaded. With one more standard feature, the driver's manual would have to go from the glove compartment to the trunk.

In terms of comfort, we mustn't forget to mention the Climatronic air conditioning. It features dual-zone temperature controls: left and right. This means that in the same Passat, a bikini-clad blonde and a brunette wearing a fur coat can travel comfortably together. That is, if the driver's a bachelor and really lucky, of course. But since the Germans are so proper, that's not what they had in mind when they decided to equip the Passat with Climatronic. They were just focused on passenger comfort, considering that even members of the same family can have different reactions to a given temperature. What's warm for someone might be freezing cold for someone else. With Climatronic, problem solved.

So, at just the right temperature, you can enjoy all the superior quality of a CD / MP3 player with integrated CD changer. Obviously, nobody expected an awesome car like this to come with a cheap radio. That's why a very high quality audio system will, perhaps, not come as such a big surprise, right? Wrong. The Passat's excellent acoustics, paired with the quality of ten strategically positioned speakers turn the simple act of listening to music into a special experience. We suggest, when you drive out of the dealership for the first time, Beethoven's 9th Symphony with the Berlin Philharmonic Orchestra, directed by Herbert von Karajan. You'll be hearing some wonderful music while paying a deserved tribute to German engineers.

Now, let's switch from music to literature. The Passat comes with four reading lights. Two in the front and two in the back, with dimming. If you happen to fall asleep reading a book, for example, the lights could suddenly go off and you'd wake up. But that doesn't happen in the Passat. Naturally, this example doesn't apply to the driver. We recommend the driver not read anything, except the road signs, even if the road is deserted and the car's on cruise control. If you have the privilege of driving the Passat, please make sure you only use the reading light when you want to consult a map, after parking properly on the side of the road.

In addition to the reading lights, the Passat features two object holders on the dashboard. You know, those little frills we love when we first get a new car, and then end up using much more than we thought. And the superfluous becomes a real necessity. That explains, at least partially, why so many people trade in their old Passats for new Passats over the years. When you get used to a car like this, it's hard to drive anything else. After all, luxury, comfort and pleasure are so lovely they easily become addictions.

We already mentioned how impressively the Passat accelerates. But it's also impressive when it comes to braking. All models are equipped with disc brakes for all 4 wheels and an electronic stability system plus assisted steering. This system includes ABS with ASR, EDS and MSR. You'll understand exactly what these acronyms mean when an absent-minded dreamer decides to cross the street right ahead of you when you've got a green light.

But obviously the braking system is not the only safety feature. The Passat received 5 stars in vehicular safety from the Euro NCAP, the most respected automotive safety board in the world. Volkswagen works more or less like this: for each valiant engineer, we hire six scaredy-cats. That's why the Passat has 250 HP and six airbags: front, with dual-stage deployment, side and rear head curtain, guaranteeing the safety of the driver and all occupants. And since we're talking about safety, the Passat also comes with Servotronic engine-speed sensitive, variable-assist power steering. Exterior rearview mirrors with LED illumination of peripheral field. Power adjustable headlight beams. Fog lights. And, in the Comfortline model, xenon adaptive headlights. The Passat 3.2 V6 also comes with the 4Motion system, which provides handling never before seen in a sedan. You'll be taking the most perfect curves of your life.

The 6-speed Tiptronic automatic transmission can also be considered a safety feature. You can choose between a comfortable and a sportive ride. When you choose the latter, the six speeds with DSG transmission and dual clutching can be changed on the wheel in the V6 model. After all, you'd better have your hands on the wheel when you accelerate a 250 HP car. The fact is, there are many standard features in the Passat that are either directly or indirectly related to safety. Because there are lots of crazies out there on the road and none at Volkswagen.

And since you're probably already picturing yourself sitting at the wheel of a Passat, let's talk about the seats. The front seats feature power adjustments, including height, plus lumbar support and temperature control. The driver's seat also features a massage function on the back. And, in case you're crazy enough to loan this car to someone else, the V6 model keeps your personal seat and mirror adjustments in its memory. With so much comfort, you're never going to want to get out of the Passat, no matter what.

That must be why the fuel cap and the trunk can be controlled from inside the car. On the central console, the Passat has a cup holder with lid. And this keeps your soda from refreshing the Tiptronic handle in case of sudden braking, which, incidentally, frequently happens in cars not designed by German engineers.

The dual-folding visors feature illuminated mirrors. Both for the driver and the passenger. And, when you look at your face in the mirror, you'll see that it really is true what many Passat owners say: "It's amazing how much better I look in this car."

Both front and rear windows are power controlled. And the V6 model even has power blinds on the rear window and the rear door windows. The interior is entirely upholstered in leather. Even the gearshift handle. The floor mats are made of fabric. That's right: the floor mats for you to put your feet on are made of fabric. And the same criteria used for the internal finish was applied to the exterior, which features chrome frames around the side windows plus a chrome front grille. This is a car built with standards higher than those many architects use when building houses. That's why we say that, when you have a Passat, you don't give a ride. You receive friends.

If you've read the text this far, you must already be impressed with the quality of the Passat and, above all, with the extensive list of standard features. By now you're probably thinking your present car left the factory totally stripped down. And, you'll probably agree, it's embarrassing to drive around in a stripped car, don't you think? We better not talk about that, right? Let's go back to talking about the comfort features of this impressive German sedan.

Park distance control system. Even this is a comfort feature. When you use it, you no longer have to worry when parking your Passat in a small space. An audible signal is emitted at small intervals, which diminish as you approach an obstacle. So you don't have to worry about denting or scratching your car. Of course, lots of machos will say that the park distance control system was designed just for the ladies. Or for the peace of mind of those guys who, when not thinking clearly, make the unspeakable mistake of loaning their car to their wife. That's nonsense. First of all, because this thing about women being bad drivers is totally unjustified. Or at least, not justifiable anymore. After all, whether you're a man or a woman, you will be slightly nervous when parking your car. Especially if the car is a beautiful Passat you just drove out of the dealership.

Anti-theft alarm with siren. Ok, Ok, this is not really a comfort feature. But you'll probably feel more comfortable at a party knowing that the car you parked on the street is equipped with an alarm like this.

The advanced technology used in the Passat makes it hard to separate the purpose of each standard feature. In other words, the same feature that apparently was designed for comfort, is also a powerful ally in terms of safety. This is truly impressive in the Passat. With so much technology and so many features, it gives you the impression that the car was designed by a thousand German engineers. But when we realize how harmoniously everything works, we then think it could only be the creation of one person alone. And despite the ample number of accessories that are standard, after we've studied the car a little more closely, we end up feeling that there's not one unnecessary feature. And that everything should be exactly the way it is. Definitely, it's the perfect car.

And the perfect car comes with cruise control. An extremely useful feature for our roads with radar everywhere. You adjust to the desired speed and you can take your foot off the gas pedal. Whether going uphill or downhill, the Passat will maintain the predefined speed with minimal variations. And all you have to do is brake and the cruise control is immediately disengaged. Once again, Passat engineers thought of comfort without overlooking safety.

The multi-functional display has more than forty functions and adjustments. Whenever you want, you can check mileage traveled, instant consumption, remaining fuel as well as much more data. All this guarantees a much safer trip and, of course, the ability to satisfy your curiosity about many things. Such as, for example, what was the average speed of the trip from home to the beach?

And here's an extremely cool feature: tire pressure can be monitored on the dashboard via a system that alerts you when the pressure is low. Yes, you got it right. From inside the car, you can monitor tire pressure. It might seem almost supernatural that a car can do this. But this is not just a car. We're talking about a Passat.

Now let's suppose you're in your Passat on the road and it starts to rain. All you have to do is to slightly reduce the pressure on the gas pedal and be more alert. As for the windshield wiper, fear not. It will automatically turn on and then will turn off as soon as it stops raining. The same thing will happen if somebody drools on your windshield when you're parked.

As you must have realized, the space for this ad is running out and many qualities of the Passat, unfortunately, cannot be mentioned. Incidentally, problems with space is another thing you won't have when you've got your Passat. In addition to comfortably seating 5 people, the trunk has a capacity of more than 500 liters of cargo.

We suggest that you go to a Volkswagen dealer this very day and see up close your next and ultimate car. In short, that's all.

The new Passat.

BRONZE | PRINT | CONSUMER NEWSPAPER | PRODUCT or SERVICE PROMCTION

PASSAT LONG TEXT **ALMAPBBDO**

RYNALDO GONDIM

ANDRÉ NASSAR

Creative Director Luiz Sanches, Dulcídio Caldeira
Art Director André Nassar
Copywriter Rynaldo Gondim
Illustrator Volkswagen Images
Director Marcello Serpa
Typographer José Roberto Bezerra
Agency AlmapBBDO
Client Volkswagen

Country Brazil

THE FIRST
SUPERSIZE POP-UP
JUNG VON MATT AG

**OLIVER
FLOHRS**

**NICOLE
GROEZINGER**

Creative Director Michael Ohanian, Jacques Pense
Art Director Nicole Groezinger
Copywriter Oliver Flohrs
Designer Sarah Illenberger
Photographer Attila Hartwig
Account Supervisor Kristin Schombel
Post Production Recom
Agency Jung von Matt AG
Client Sara Lee Household, Body Care Germany

To grab attention for the new AmbiPur Pink Flower Room Spray
and its amazingly fresh fragrance in an innovative and unseen
way, we not only sprayed the fragrance Pink Flower into the air—
we also visualized its effect with a supersize pop-up.

The pop-ups were installed behind doors. So as soon as someone
opened and closed the door, the pop-up flowered out, just like the
fragrance itself.

Together with a professional artist we did a number of sketches to
find the perfect set up. Afterwards, we defined the materials that
worked best, visually and practically.

After a test series with dummies, we finally came up with this
amazing artwork of beautifully handmade paper flowers.

Country Germany

BRONZE | PRINT | TRADE MAGAZINE |
PRODUCT or SERVICE PROMOTION
POSTERS
CLM BBDO

**VINCENT
PEDROCCHI**

**CEDRIC
MOUTAUD**

Chief Creative Officer Gilles Fichteberg, Jean-Francois Sacco
Creative Director Jean-Francois Sacco, Gilles Fichteberg, Eric Pierre
Art Director Cedric Moutaud
Copywriter Vincent Pedrocchi
Photographer Jean-Yves Lemoigne
Producer Sylvie Etchemaite
Agency CLM BBDO
Client HP

"The new power of print": that's what this campaign is all about and that's what Hewlett Packard's communication strategy is all about. Meanings are multiple. Because beyond communicating superior printing quality and a truer-than-life impression, what matters here is what you do with the output, what the printed page triggers and reveals about you. Simply ask a little girl to talk to you about her favorite pony poster. The one that's on her bedroom wall. And prepare for a long story.

Country France

BRONZE | PRINT | INNOVATION |
POSTER, BILLBOARD, OUTDOOR

CLOCKS
BETC EURO RSCG

**ARNAUD
ASSOULINE**

**BENJAMIN
LE BRETON**

Creative Director Stèphane Xiberras
Art Director Benjamin Le Breton
Copywriter Arnaud Assouline
Artist Nadine Grenier
Agency BETC Euro RSCG
Client Solidarité Sida

In Africa, 1.6 million children and adults die from AIDS each year; some 4,380 people every day. Faced with this health disaster, in February 2006, Solidarité Sida (AIDS Solidarity) created a dedicated fund, the Fonds Solidarité Sida Afrique (AIDS Africa Solidarity Fund).

To emphasize these shocking statistics, we came up with a creative idea that highlights how every minute counts in the fight against AIDS.

At a set time, twice a day, the hands of 321 clock mechanisms come together and align to deliver the following message:

Every 12 hours in Africa, over 2,000 people die from AIDS because they have no access to care. Every minute counts. www.solidarite-sida.org

Country France

MERIT | PRINT | COLLATERAL ADVERTISING |
PRODUCT or SERVICE PROMOTION

HOUSE OF CARDS— PACK OF CARDS
LEO BURNETT LONDON

Creative Director Jonathan Burley
Art Director Richard Brim
Copywriter Daniel Fisher
Designer Domenic Lippa, Jeremy Kunze
Agency Leo Burnett London
Client Shelter

Country United Kingdom

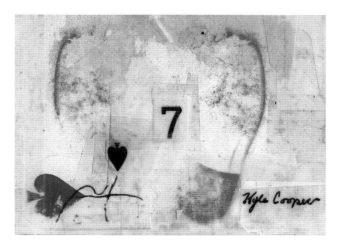

MERIT | BROADCAST MEDIA | TELEVISION
PRODUCT or SERVICE PROMOTION

PLANT
TBWA\CHIAT\DAY, NEW YORK

KRIS WIXOM   **ALISA SENGEL WIXOM**

Chairman, Chief Creative Officer Mark Figliulo
Creative Director Rob Baird, Jens Gehlhaar (Brand New School)
Art Director Kris Wixom
Copywriter Alisa Sengel Wixom
Graphic Designer Brand New School
Director of Photography Mott Hupfel
Animator Robin Kim, Peter Murphy
Director Guy Shelmerdine
Director of Broadcast Production Ozzie Spenningsby
Editor Jon Grover, Steve Gandolfini
Assistant Editor Zach Neumeyer, Isaac Chen
Editorial Company Cut + Run
Executive Producer Patrick Milling Smith, Brian Carmody, Lisa Rich, Ned Brown (Brand New School), James Razzall (Cut + Run)
Executive Producer of Media Arts Matt Bijarchi
Senior Agency Producer Jason Souter
Producer Kathy Rhodes (SMUGGLER), Josh Wakefield (Brand New School), Ashely Carrier (Cut + Run), Carr Schilling (Cut + Run)
Production Company SMUGGLER
Special Effects Company Framestore
Audio Mix Sound Lounge
Mixer Philip Loeb
Colorist Tim Masick
Telecine Company 3
Senior Flame Artist Marryanne Butler
Flame Artist Miyuki Shimamoto
Cast Beth Grant, Todd Bosley, Larry Kenney
Agency TBWA\Chiat\Day, New York
Client Wrigley/Skittles

Country United States

MERIT | BROADCAST MEDIA | TELEVISION
PUBLIC SERVICE or NON-PROFIT

GIVE IT
A PONDER
YOUNG & RUBICAM

Executive Creative Director Ian Reichenthal, Scott Vitrone
Creative Director Darren Moran
Art Director Jeff Blouin, Evan Benedetto, Jan Jaworski
Copywriter John Battle, Tara Lawall
Director Ulf Johnansson
Editor Carlos Arias
Producer Alex Gianni, Lora Schulson, Nathy Aviram
Production Company Smith & Sons
Agency Young & Rubicam
Client LG Electronics

Country United States

MERIT | BROADCAST MEDIA | TELEVISION
PRODUCT or SERVICE PROMOTION

FINALLY
FORSMAN & BODENFORS

Director Joachim Back
Producer Ulrica Seehausen
Production Company Road Map Institute
Post Production Sto.pp
Music George Keller
Advertiser's Supervisor Bengt Junemo
Media Agency Mindshare
Agency Forsman & Bondenfors
Client Volvo

Country Sweden

MERIT | BROADCAST MEDIA | CRAFT AND DIGITAL
TECHNIQUE | ART DIRECTION

LOCAL
RADIO
RKCR/Y&R

Creative Director Damon Collins
Art Director Jules Chalkley, Nick Simons
Copywriter Jules Chalkley, Nick Simons
Director Vince Squibb
Producer Joanna Yeldham
Production Company Red Bee Media
Agency RKCR/Y&R
Client BBC

Country United Kingdom

MERIT | BROADCAST MEDIA | INNOVATION |
TELEVISION or CINEMA

HALF SECOND
CINEMA
ZIG

MICHAEL   **NIALL**
CLOWATER   **KELLY**

Creative Director Martin Beauvais, Aaron Starkman
Art Director Niall Kelly
Copywriter Michael Clowater
Director Lisa Mann
Editor Mark Paiva
Editing House School
Producer Sheri Hachey
Production Company Revolver Films, Imaginary Forces
Post Facility Tantrum
Agency zig
Client Corus Entertainment (DUSK TV)

To launch DUSK TV (a horror and suspense channel in Canada)
we created multiple-second ads that were designed to scare
people during cinema previews. They ran in between the
commercials and paid off with a slightly longer ad that claimed
responsibility.

Country Canada

MERIT | PRINT | COLLATERAL ADVERTISING |
INSTITUTIONAL PROMOTION

CONCERT FOR
THE PEOPLE
JUNG VON MATT AG

Creative Director Goetz Ulmer, Fabian Frese
Art Director Simon Hiebl, Julia Ziegler
Copywriter Dr. S. Fockenberg, F. Bill, J.F. Ege
Designer Tobias Fritschen
Public Relations J. Kortlepel, Lutz Nebelin
Agency Jung von Matt AG
Client Philharmonic Orchestra of Hamburg

Country Germany

MERIT | PRINT | TRADE MAGAZINE |
PRODUCT or SERVICE PROMOTION

VOLKSWAGEN TRUCKS (BOXES)
ALMAPBBDO

**MARCUS
KAWAMURA**

**EDUARDO
ANDRIETTA**

Creative Director Luiz Sanches, Dulcídio Caldeira
Art Director Marcus Kawamura, Ary Nogueira
Copywriter Eduardo Andrietta
Photographer Hugo Treu
Account Supervisor Fernao Cosi
Advertiser's Supervisor Ana Maria Oliveira
Agency AlmapBBDO
Client Volkswagen Trucks

Country Brazil

Additional Awards:

ADVERTISING MERIT
MAGAZINE, TRADE

MERIT | PRINT | CONSUMER MAGAZINE |
PRODUCT or SERVICE PROMOTION

BAD FOOD
BAD DOG
PROLAM Y&R

**ANDRÉS
ECHEVERRÍA**

**FRANCISCO
CAVADA**

Creative Director Tony Sarroca
Art Director Fabrizio Capraro, Andrés Echeverría
Copywriter Francisco Cavada
Photographer Patricio Pescetto
Agency Prolam Y&R
Client Nutripro

Country Chile

MERIT | PRINT | CONSUMER MAGAZINE |
PRODUCT or SERVICE PROMOTION

BAD
MOOD
PROLAM Y&R

**JORGE
MUÑOZ**

**FRANCISCO
CAVADA**

Creative Director Tony Sarroca, Francisco Cavada
Art Director Jorge Muñoz, Carlos Carrasco
Copywriter Fabrizio Baracco, Cristian Martinez
Agency Prolam Y&R
Client Laboratorios Chile

Country Chile

MERIT | PRINT | POSTERS AND BILLBOARDS |
PUBLIC SERVICE or NON-PROFIT

YOKOHAMA COCKTAIL COMPETITION 2009
SAGA INC.

KOTA SAGAE

Art Director, Copywriter Kota Sagae
Designer Kota Sagae, Yohei Miyagawa
Agency SAGA Inc.
Client Nippon Bartenders Association

These are advertisement posters for a cocktail competition event commemorating the 150th anniversary of the Port of Yokohama.

The designs were based on the fact that Commander Matthew C. Perry, who played a vital role in opening the Port, was a huge fan of alcohol; that the letter "Y" in "Yokohama" looked like a cocktail glass; and that Mr. Matsubara, the client of this project, respected the discovery.

Country Japan

MERIT | PRINT | TRADE MAGAZINE |
PRODUCT or SERVICE PROMOTION

SHOUTS
EURO RSCG SPAIN

Creative Director Germán Silva
Art Director Jacobo Concejo
Copywriter Luis Munné, Daniel Balbás
Photographer Grupo Rafael
Director Germán Silva
Agency Euro RSCG Spain
Client Strepsils

Country Spain

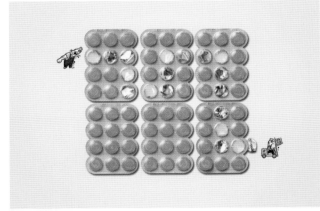

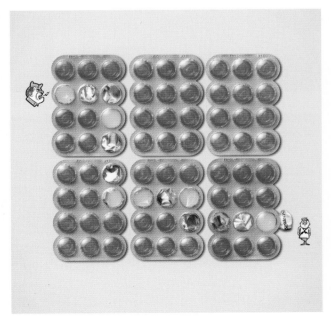

MERIT | PRINT | POSTERS AND BILLBOARDS |
POINT-OF-PURCHASE DISPLAY

BUKATSU IN-STORE CAMPAIGN 200

BEACON COMMUNICATIONS K.K.

SEIYA MASUMOTO

YUSUKE MOROTOMI

Creative Director Kazz Ishihara
Art Director Yusuke Morotomi, Yasuo Matsubara, Daisuke Suzuki
Copywriter Seiya Matsumoto
Designer Yusuke Morotomi, Osamu Abiko
Illustrator Nobuki Kato
Producer Ryohei Ando, Hiroko Okushima
Production Company orb-it
Agency beacon communications k.k.
Client Nike Japan

Country Japan

MERIT | PRINT | COLLATERAL ADVERTISING |
PRODUCT or SERVICE PROMOTION

LEIBNIZ ORIGINALS
KOLLE REBBE

**TOBIAS
FRITSCHEN**

**FABIAN
BILL**

Creative Director Sven Klohk, Lorenz Ritter
Art Director Tobias Fritschen
Copywriter Fabian Bill
Illustrator Tobias Fritschen
Agency Producer Martin Luehe
Production Company Paperlux
Account Manager Katharina Voss
Agency Kolle Rebbe
Client Bahlsen GmbH & Co. KG

Communications Task:
Develop a campaign to thank deserving employees, supporters and companions of the brand, and strengthen their personal relationship with Leibniz.

Solution:
Leibniz gave friends, supporters and employees an extra-special present for their birthday:

The first Leibniz Cookie Portrait.

Utilising laser technology, the birthday boy or girl's portrait and personal greetings were laser-cut into a Leibniz cookie. Each cookie was uniquely manufactured for the receiver.

Leibniz Butterkeks: The Original for an Original.

Country Germany

MERIT | PRINT | POSTERS AND BILLBOARDS |
OUTDOOR or BILLBOARD

THE LEGO
CODES
LUKAS LINDEMANN ROSINSKI

Creative Director, Copywriter Tom Hauser
Art Director, Illustrator Dennis Mensching
Designer Moritz Schmidt, Chris Mizutani
Director Arno Lindemann, Bernhard Lukas
Editor Sarita Timmermann
Producer Dominik Meis
Production Company Markenfilm GmbH & Co. KG, Hamburg
Cross Marketing Production GmbH,
Sound Engineer Hannes Hoenemann
Media Agency Jost von Brandis
Agency Lukas Lindemann Rosinski GmbH
Client myToys.de

Country Germany

MERIT | PRINT | COLLATERAL ADVERTISING |
PRODUCT or SERVICE PROMOTION

ONION
CALENDAR
SERVICEPLAN GRUPPE GMBH

Executive Creative Director Matthias Harbeck
Chief Creative Officer Alex Schill
Creative Director Helmut Huber, Florian Drahorad
Art Director Christian Sommer, Ivo Hlavac, Sören Porst
Copywriter Nicolas Becker, Tom Hauser
Photographer Layoutsatz 2000
Production Company Pinsker Druck und Medien GmbH
Agency Serviceplan Gruppe GmbH & Co. KG
Client Wüsthof

Country Germany

MERIT 8% of all awards given

HYBRID 2.3% of all awards given

HYBRID

The hybrid category is ever evolving. This year, we tried to define it by using criteria that forced us to look at each entry through a slightly different lens. The entry had to not only change our industry, but also change culture. In the end, the more we celebrate ideas that win hybrid, the better off we will be in the long run. That does not mean the crafts of writing and art direction are not important anymore. It just means that things like technology and product innovation are becoming areas we should play in if we want to remain relevant to our clients.

- Rob Reilly
Partner – Chief Creative Officer, Crispin Porter + Bogusky
ADC Hybrid Jury Chair

ADC**HYBRID JURY**

ROB
REILLY
CRISPIN PORTER + BOGUSKY

Rob Reilly (partner and chief creative officer) joined Crispin Porter + Bogusky (CP+B) in 2003, after spending a decade at a number of New York ad agencies. He began as a copywriter, creating some of the most awarded campaigns in history, and then went on to serve as the global creative director on Burger King, helping to transform the burger chain into one of the most culturally relevant companies in the world. (Yes, he can be partially blamed for the creepy King.)

In his current role, he and his partners oversee all of CP+B's clients. In addition to Burger King, this includes category-leading brands such as Microsoft, Microsoft Windows Phone, Coke Zero, Old Navy, Best Buy, Domino's Pizza, American Express OPEN, Jose Cuervo and Kraft Macaroni & Cheese. CP+B has been named Agency of the Year by multiple publications and, recently, Interactive Agency of the Year at the 2010 Cannes Lions International Advertising Festival, and Agency of the Decade by Advertising Age.

Rob lives in Colorado with his lovely wife, Laura. In his spare time, he can be found trying to keep up with the younger employees on the company soccer team.

The Hybrid category is ever-evolving. This year, we tried to define it by using criteria that forced us to look at each entry through a slightly different lens. The entry had to not only change our industry, but also change culture. In the end, the more we celebrate ideas that win Hybrid, the better off we will be in the long run. That does not mean the crafts of writing and art direction are not important anymore. It just means that things like technology and product innovation are becoming new areas to play in if we want to remain relevant to our clients.

WAYNE
BEST
JWT NEW YORK

Wayne started his creative career at one of the least creative agencies in the country: N.W. Ayer. After less then six months on the job, he learned he was going to be laid off while urinating in the men's room. It was nowhere but uphill from there.

He is currently an executive creative director at JWT New York. Prior to that, he was at TAXI NY, where, under his leadership, the AAAA's voted Taxi the best small agency in America two years in a row. He has also worked at Fallon, Wieden+Kennedy, KBP and Cliff Freeman and Partners. Notable accounts have included Fox Sports, JetBlue, ESPN, Starbucks, Pepsi, Time Magazine, Virgin Mobile, Staples and Coca-Cola.

He has won awards in print, radio, television, interactive and branded entertainment.

TWITTER WAYNEITUP
WEBSITE WAYNEBEST.COM

KEITH
CARTWRIGHT
WIEDEN + KENNEDY

Keith Cartwright's work life began in 1997 after receiving a B.F.A. in Communication Design from Syracuse University. After graduating, he spent the early part of his career as a graphic designer working at a number of award-winning design firms. His advertising career began at Tracy Locke in Dallas, from there he moved on to Ogilvy & Mather, where he spent most of his time working on Miller Lite and American Express. After six years with Ogilvy he moved on to become associate creative director at TBWA/Chiat/Day in San Francisco on Adidas and Motorola. Keith currently is creative director at Wieden+Kennedy in New York, where he is responsible for management of all creative development for Jordan Brand, Nike Canada and Nike New York.

Keith has been awarded and recognized by almost every awards organization in his field including; The One Show, Clio's, AICP, AIGA, Addis, Art Directors Club, The London and New York Festivals and D&AD.

MASASHI KAWAMURA
BBH NEW YORK

Masashi was born in Tokyo and raised in San Francisco.

He currently works at BBH New York as a senior art director.

Masashi attended Keio University where he studied computer science. After becoming a member of Masahiko Sato Laboratory, it wasn't long before he was lured into the world of design. There he worked on a variety of projects, such as the flipbook collection, *Ugoke Enzan*, the 3-D book, *Arbitrary Point P*, and the children's television show, *Pythagora Switch*.

From there, Masashi moved on to advertising agencies Hakuhodo, BBH Tokyo, 180 Amsterdam and BBH New York, creating global campaigns for brands such as Nissan, PlayStation, Levi's, Google and AXE.

Outside of advertising, Masashi continues to explore with design experiments ranging from music videos to product designs to publications. These work have won numerous international awards, such as The One Show Design, ADC Young Guns, D&AD, Clio, Webby People's Choice, Cannes Cyber Lion and more.

TWITTER MASAKAWA
WEBSITE MASA-KA.COM

PIERRE LIPTON
BBDO NEW YORK

Pierre Lipton is senior vice president and creative director at BBDO-NY. Since joining, he has been recognized by the Art Directors Club, The One Show, Cannes and The Clio Awards (amongst others) for work on HBO's Big Love, Smart Car, *The Economist*, AT&T and the Special Olympics.

He previously worked at TBWA\Chiat\Day New York, Fallon New York and kbpand DeVito/Verdi. He has helped create a number of notable multimedia campaigns for brands such as Absolut, Snickers, Starbucks, Virgin Mobile, Time and the A.C.L.U. His rabbis include David Lubars, Gerry Graf, Ari Merkin, Wayne Best and the one and only Sal DeVito. He lives in New York with his lovely wife, Julie, and their wonder boy, Lucian.

KIRK SOUDER
GMMB

Kirk is currently brand director for the University of Santa Monica, where he is helping bring the Spiritual Psychology Program (Kirk is a master's graduate) into a global online offering. Prior to USM, Kirk was partner and executive creative director of GMMB, the world's foremost cause and advocacy communications agency (lead agency for Obama For America) where Kirk is still a strategic and creative consultant. Before GMMB, Kirk was president and executive creative director of Hal Riney in San Francisco, which had followed his tenure as co-founder and creative partner of Ground Zero Advertising in Los Angeles. *Art & Copy*, a film about creativity that Kirk co-concepted and co-executive produced, was one of 15 documentaries selected as a finalist in Sundance 2009, and had its theatrical release in Fall 2009.

TWITTER KIRKSOUDER
WEBSITE KIRKSOUDER.COM

ADC
HYBRID

WE CHOOSE
THE MOON
THE MARTIN AGENCY
& DOMANI STUDIOS

**BRIAN
WILLIAMS**

**WADE
ALGER**

Executive Creative Director Jon Hills
Creative Director Ben Tricklebank, Joe Alexander
Art Director Brian Williams, Saulo Rodrigues
Copywriter Wade Alger
Technology Director Oscar Trelles
Motion Graphics Designer Justin Young
Animator Petter Safwenberg
Senior Developer Mark Llobrera
Flash Developer Chris Wise
Editor Rick Lawley, Jim Vaile
Assistant Editor Shang Gao
Editorial Company Running With Scissors, The White House
Agency Producer Darbi Fretwell, Norma Kwée
Art Producer Cindy Hicks
Senior Interactive Producer Steven Hubert
Interactive Production Domani Studios
Composer Chip Jenkins
Music Company HUM Music
Account Supervisor Carrie Bird
Director of Accounts Jarrod Bull
Project Manager Sandra Snead
Agency The Martin Agency
Client The John F. Kennedy Presidential Library and Museum

Country United States

Additional Awards:

INTERACTIVE GOLD
WEBSITE

INTERACTIVE SILVER
WEBSITE DESIGN

WE **THE MOON**
CHOOSE
CELEBRATE THE 40 YEAR ANNIVERSARY OF THE
APOLLO 11 LUNAR LANDING

July 16, 1969. 9:32 AM ET.
Three men head to the Moon. Four days later,
they make history.

Now it's your turn. On July 16, 2009 you are
invited to climb aboard Apollo 11 and travel to
the moon. The experience will be a real time
visual and audio recreation of the historic
mission and will last for four days. Sign up
now to go back and witness it all again. See
you onboard.

Powered by: **AOL**

MERIT | INTERACTIVE ADVERTISING | CAMPAIGN SITE |
PRODUCT, SERVICE or ENTERTAINMENT PROMOTION

SUMMIT ON
THE SUMMIT
GOODBY, SILVER-
STEIN & PARTNERS

Creative Director Rich Silverstein, Steve Simpson,
Will McGinness, Jim Elliot
Art Director Stuart Brown
Copywriter Niklas Lilja
Producer Cathleen Kisich, Erin Dahlbeck, Daisy Down
Production Company @radical.media, Number9, Kurt Noble
Agency Goodby, Silverstein & Partners
Client HP

Country United States

Additional Awards:

INTERACTIVE GOLD
WEBSITE

IMERIT | INTERACTIVE ADVERTISING | BLOGS, COMMUNITIES AND SOCIAL
NETWORKS | PRODUCT, SERVICE or ENTERTAINMENT PROMOTION

FACEBOOK
SHOWROOM
FORSMAN & BODENFORS

Photographer Lennart Sjöberg
Advertiser's Supervisor Sara Zakariasson
Agency Forsman & Bodenfors
Client IKEA

Country Sweden

Additional Awards:

INTERACTIVE GOLD
BLOGS, COMMUNITIES AND SOCIAL NETWORKS

MERIT | INTERACTIVE ADVERTISING | WEBSITE |
PRODUCT, SERVICE or ENTERTAINMENT PROMOTION

THE WORLD'S BIGGEST SIGNPOST
FARFAR

Creative President Matias Palm Jensen
Creative Director Jon Dranger, Erik Norin
Art Director Tomas Jonsson
Copywriter Carl Fredrik Jannerfeldt
Flash Designer Mikael Ring, Robert Jarvi, Bjorn Uppeke
Head of Strategy Niku Banaie
Account Director Marten Forslund, Christian Nord
Account Manager Marie Persson, Ulrika Hojgard, Louise Stenborg
Programmer David Looberger
Agency Farfar
Client Nokia

Nokia offers a range of navigation services, both online and on their mobile devices. But awareness about these services is low.

Our challenge was to raise awareness and increase use of Nokia's navigation service. Both on handsets and online.

We started out with one of the simplest navigation tools around, the signpost. We then turned it into a giant interactive installation. A 50 meter tall, fully automated remote-controlled beast. People could text their favorite spot to the signpost and within moments the giant turned and displayed the distance to that location.

Country Sweden

Additional Awards:

◆ **INTERACTIVE BRONZE**
WEBSITE

MERIT | INTERACTIVE ADVERTISING | BLOGS, COMMUNITIES AND SOCIAL NETWORKS | PRODUCT, SERVICE or ENTERTAINMENT PROMOTION

FACIAL PROFILER
CRISPIN PORTER + BOGUSKY

Executive Creative Director Andrew Keller, Rob Reilly
Associate Creative Director Patrick Maravilla, Dayoung Ewart
Creative Director Dave Schiff, Alex Burnard
Art Director Justin Smith, Nuno Ferreira
Copywriter Chad Lynch, Jason Marks
Designer Christian Layugan, Dustin Tomes
Editor Wayde Samuel
Producer Paul Aaron, Idalia Deshon, Suzanne Chambers, Andrea Krichevsky
Agency Crispin Porter + Bogusky
Client Coke Zero

Country United States

Additional Awards:

◆ **INTERACTIVE BRONZE**
WEBSITE

1 CUBE .04% of all awards given

ADC**BLACK CUBE**

This year marked the first time ADC has ever bestowed an ADC Black Cube, which was established for last year's 88th Annual Awards but had no winner, and the first time in 12 years the club has recognized a best-in-show.

BEST IN SHOW | PRINT | INNOVATION
POSTER, BILLBOARD, OUTDOOR

TRILLION
DOLLAR POSTER
TBWA\HUNT\LASCARIS

**RAPHAEL
BASCKIN**

**NADJA
LOSSGOTT**

**SHELLY
SMOLER**

**NICHOLAS
HULLEY**

Creative Director Damon Stapleton
Art Director Nadja Lossgott, Shelley Smoler
Copywriter Nicholas Hulley, Raphael Basckin
Photographer Chloe Coetsee, Des Ellis, Michael Meyersfeld, Rob Wilson
Director Chloe Coetsee
Account Manager Bridget Langley
Agency TBWA\Hunt\Lascaris Johannesburg
Client The Zimbabwean

The Zimbabwean newspaper has been driven into exile for reporting on how the Mugabe regime has ruined the country, and has also been slapped with a 55% luxury import duty (as if freedom of speech is a luxury) that makes it unaffordable for Zimbabweans.The paper therefore needs to be subsidised, and our client can only do that by raising awareness and driving sales outside Zimbabwe.

The most eloquent symbol of Zimbabwe's collapse is the Z$ trillion note. This useless currency cannot buy any advertising. But it can become the advertising. We turned the money into the medium by making posters entirely out of the money. Overnight, Zimbabwean banknotes achieved what they'd never been able to buy—worldwide media coverage, two million visits to The Zimbabwean website and an 85% increase in revenue. We used Mugabe's own creation against him.

Country South Africa

Additional Awards:

⬢ **ADVERTISING GOLD**
POSTER/BILLBOARD | OUTDOOR

⬢ **ADVERTISING SILVER**
INTEGRATED ADVERTISING

⬢ **DESIGN BRONZE**
POSTER DESIGN

Z$250 000 000 CANNOT BUY THE PAPER TO PRINT THIS POSTER ON

A VOICE FOR THE VOICELESS

TheZimbabwean

The Trillion Dol

SOUR 'Hibi No Neiro' (Tone of Everyday

The Cooper Union Signage and Enviro

Campaign | Great Performers | Podravk

Livestrong Campaign | Summit on the S

the Moon | Plug into the Smart Grid | Zac

Today is Sushi Day | Deadline | Take The

Sushi Day | The Affair | Comics | Shan Sh

paign | Cube Film Installation | We Choos

The Big One | Bored To Death | Shan Shui | Zombieland | AMTV ID

made Bakery, Daichi no Mi. | Cascades 2008 Report on Sustainab

End | Le Musée Grandit (The Museum is growing) | Furniture Me

Graphic Trial 2009, Repetition on Surface | Global Warming | ASIC

The Moon | F1984T2008 | 8 new fonts on the block; here, there,

tion. | Less Effort. More Effect! | Box Beat | Earth in the Air | Freak

Reading | "The Life" | Welcome Back | Cause & Effect | Congratura

Leakage | The Contemporary Beauty Ideal | The Trillion Dollar Cam

Happy Kid | The Affair | OIAF Signal Film | The Wilde Ones | Logo ID | TED 2009 Conferen

jectes, Perspectives and Dreams | END THE LIES | Göteborgstryckeriet printing house iden

Play Kit | Charles Darwin Stamps | British Design Classics Stamps | Icograda World Design

Distinguished Lecture Series Book Cover | Small Studios | Uns ich er | SVA Undergraduate

sual Circus | The Contemporary Beauty Ideal | Lutzka Escapes | Shan Shui | Wa Fabric Coll

Day T-Shirts Project | Return of the Ornament | Button Fly | Less and More Tokyo 01 | Less

The Last Call | Monday Night Football - Interactive Storescapes | Augmented Reality Banner

ality Banner | Helicopter Boyz | Volvo S60: The Blind Preview | Flyvertising - the world's firs

Space | My Best Stories | Connaturalize | 3D QR Code Mobile App | Canon PowerShot D10 V

West Bank | Like a Golf | Hammer Throw | Car Park Shopping | Fiat Crash Test Panda | Tedd

Bodies of Water | Augsburger Allgemeine: Global news starts as local news. | Egg | Smart Car F

Tenth of a Century" | Fukutake House 2009 | Network IDs | Brand ID | Tim Burton | Broadcat 09 Titles | Find The Unexpect

| Let's start | The Cooper Union | ROSE | Earth Hour 2009 | 20th Macao Arts Festival | Handle with Care. Wine Bags | HANA

sung Profile 2009 | Walk Up Press Logo | Futuretainment | Dororo | Things We Didn't See Coming | 3 | 4 POLAR Collection

Free Europe | Radio Liberty Sculpture Sign | Voestalpine Stahlwelt | The Official NYC Information Center | Grey Group Signa

Change Campaign | nook | viNe | House On The Hill | Coca-Cola Summer Identity | I Am the World | The Other Half of the S

Bookmark Promotion | Panda Series | Opposite Earth | DEW Action Sports Tour | Gut Oggau Wine Bottles & Wine Box | Drag

pig's meat) | Acupuncture needles | Mrs. Meyer's Clean Day | Wolf Theiss: An unexpected society for unconventional

Good Dreams, Bad Dreams | Male Instinct | Museum of Making Music | The Mixtape | Global Current | Cube Outlines | Cube | Tod

Food Bad Dog | Bad Mood | Bukatsu In-Store Campaign 2009 | What Goes Around Comes Around | Welcome Back | The LEGO Ce

Volkswagen Trucks (boxes) | Shouts | Facebook Showroom | Summit on the Summit | Livestrong Campaign | The World's Biggest

EFFP Identity | Cube Film Installation |
nental Graphics | IBM Smarter Planet
Annual Reports | Facebook Showroom |
mit | Livestrong Campaign | We Choose
Johnson | Mobilize | Nissan Cube Hostel |
Out | Visualizing The Invisible | Today is
| Cause & Effect | The Trillion Dollar Cam-
he Moon |
mpaign - Pareidolia | Be Stupid. | The Natural Fermentation, Home-
velopment | Boralex 2008 Annual Report | Journey To South | The
es | Infrastructure | Elyjah ó Planet, Planet | Cutter Art of OLFA |
rtstyle Left Right Blogger Outreach | Uniqlo Calendar | We Choose
ywhere | Music Concert Poster | The Sex Tree | The Art of Percep-
bot | Crane | Viagra Confessions Campaign | Antiquing | Strolling |
s ICHIRO | Cowboy | Cheer Dark | Truths Only Kids Can See | Power
n |
n | World Science Festival 2009 Open | Neenah Paper 2008 Annual Report | TMB 2008 Pro-
Corporate Identity of the 4th Biennial of Slovene Visual Communications | Igi V Therapeutic
ss 2009 Beijing VI | Odyssey: Architecture & Literature | Wei Jia 2004-2008 | Ong Siew May
2010 | 11 | LG FIVE | JAQK Cellars | D&AD Awards Ceremony | Tokyo Untitled | Anxiety | Vi-
2010 | Plugs | What Goes Around Comes Around | All-Clear Poster | Pre Organic Cotton The
re Tokyo 02 | Less and More Tokyo 03 | The Trillion Dollar Campaign | Samsung Shakedown |
r Dirty Water | BaketTweet | Facial | Profiler | The World's Biggest Signpost | Augmented Re-
nner. | Electronic Finger Painting | Viewpoint | Architectural Excursions | Chinatown: Place |
oof Camera | 1+1=3 | The Discovery | Cassette Tapes | The Low Emission Hitchhiker | Game |
Chase | Art Heist | SOUR 'Hibi No Neiro' (Tone of Everyday) | Shan Shui | Objects of Pocket |
ampaign | Clocks | The First Supersize Pup-up | Posters |
her Letterpress and Engraving 2010 Promotional | We Make Light | Ellery's Theory of Neoconservative Creationism Catalogue
no-hi Weekly Calendar | Cass Art Kids | Wedding invitation | Seeds of the Cities | X Exhibition | Big Business | 26&26 | Sam
k of Penguin | Abstract 07 | 08 | Chocolate Research Facility - Wheelock Place | BMW EfficientDynamics - Joy is BMW | Radio
vironmental Graphics | Harley-Davidson Museum Signage and Environmental Graphics | The Library Initiative | Eat Out For A
erine Ledner 2009 Promo | The Unseen | Chinua Achebe Books | Red Riding Hood Redux | The Patterns Found In Space | The
e | Sea signals | railroad crossings | street lights | parking lots | SANSAN FARM Co Poster (Poster of company that sells
Twelpforce | HBO Imagine Integrated Campaign | MINI IS LOADING | The new fb.se | City Harvest | Children go in New York
ard Light | Nature | Finally | Plant | Give It A Ponder | Imagine TV Campaign | Shan Shui | Local Radio | Half Second Cinema | Bac
ohama Cocktail Competition 2009 | Concert for the People | Leibniz Originals | House of Cards - Pack of Cards | Onion Calendar |
Facial Profiler |

ADC**NOW**

ADC**EXHIBITIONS**

The Art Directors Club is one of the most concentrated groups of creative talent in the world, and is a gathering place for leaders in visual communication. ADC Members share the vision of our founder, Louis Pedlar, who brought his colleagues in advertising together in 1920 to dignify their profession and judge advertising art by the same stringent standards as fine art. For 89 years ADC members have taken up Pedlar's challenge by funding programs to Connect, Provoke and Elevate creative professionals around the world. Each year ADC brings together the best minds in the creative industries to celebrate the winners of our Annual Awards and Young Guns competitions, help a new generation of creative leaders rise up through the National Student Portfolio Reviews and Saturday Career Workshops, and celebrate the achievements of Hall of Fame inductees and GrandMasters recipients.

The Art Directors Club is a self-funded non-profit working on behalf of its members. The events and programs detailed in this timeline are the result of the collective energy of nearly 1500 creative professionals worldwide, led by our President and Board of Directors. For 89 years the ADC has enjoyed bringing together the most interesting creatives in Advertising, Design, Interactive Media and Communications - we invite you to join us as we continue on our mission to Connect, Provoke and Elevate.

ERIC MEOLA INDIA EXHIBITION
SEPTEMBER 14TH, 2009

SPECTACULAR, SPECTACULAR
AUGUST 10TH - 14TH, 2009

"Spectacular, Spectacular" opened two of Lucas Stoffel's newest projects. Stoffel's pop meditation, explored India's deep religious and cultural themes, and in juxtaposition the work ventured into a nuanced look at Japanese culture on the islands of Hawai'i entitled "Little Japan".

ADC was the setting for a swirl of color at the opening party for the exhibition, INDIA: In Word and Image, featuring Eric Meola's dazzling color photography drawn from his stunning book India: In Word and Image.

TALKING BACK EXHIBITION
OCTOBER 5TH - 9TH, 2009

CORBIS STORIED
SEPTEMBER 21ST - 31ST

With more than 100 million editorial, creative, entertainment, and historical images, the Corbis collection is a vital archive of personalities, global events, and the natural world. Corbis celebrated its 20th anniversary with an exhibition of renowned photography paired with insider commentary. The insights of thinkers, writers, artists, heroes, celebrities, photographers, and people who were there when the shutter snapped uncovered the hidden truths in the images and illuminate the events, places, and personalities they captured.

Talking Back: A Presentation of T-shirt Messages and the Bodies Who Wear Them by photographer Leslie Lyons aimed to elucidate the dynamics of personal expression across the landscape of pop culture in America with a fashion monograph celebrating the unique personal essence of t-shirt culture and its power to convey the essential passions of its wearer.

ADC**EXHIBITIONS**

DECEMBER EDITIONS
DECEMBER 7TH - 13TH, 2009

THE STORYTELLER'S ART
NOVEMBER 5TH, 2009

Sappi Fine Paper hosted an entertaining look at 40 years of narrative design, through the eyes of Kit Hinrichs, Principal of Studio Hinrichs, San Francisco. The presentation featured a series of case studies demonstrating the power of visual storytelling. Hinrichs also spoke about the importance of forming relationships with printers and having the opportunity to work on Sappi's latest The Standard, which showcases all the various techniques and methods for printing.

December Editions featured prints on paper by ADC Young Gun Andrio Abero, Paul Pope, ADC Young Gun Chris Rubino and Paula Scher, designers who have produced their work through a variety of limited edition printmaking processes. Printmaking has been the backbone of counterculture art and design movements for decades, and even in today's digital age, the process is still very much alive amongst many young designers. The group show December Editions provided a platform for viewing a group of prints rarely seen beyond books and digital manifestation.

THE ART OF SOCIAL MEDIA
JUNE 8TH, 2010

"The Art of Social Media" was a collaborative event between the Art Directors Club and the Social Media Society, highlighting innovative visual and performance artists who utilize social media as a source of inspiration and as a method of showcasing their art. The event featured the work of Matt Held, a fine artist, whose portraits are inspired by the profile photos of his Facebook fans (courtesy of Denise Bibro Fine Art Gallery) and Justin Gignac, a multi-media artist and ADC Young Gun, whose nudes are inspired by ChatRoulette – the latest Internet phenomenon. The evening will concluded with live performances by subway rockers Michael Shulman and The Stumblebum Brass band.

ADC**PROGRAMS**

SoDA unCONFERENCES
NOVEMBER 3RD, 2009

UN**CONFERENCE**

The Society of Digital Agencies (SoDA) held the latest in their ongoing series of "unConferences" at the Art Directors Club, "A Conversation with Industry Peers on the Hottest topics of Digital Marketing " where attendees of all kinds came to share ideas, network, and spend an afternoon engaged in conversations unique to the digital agency industry. A cocktail hour was held at the end.

CLICK CONFERENCE
OCTOBER 1ST, 2009

DIRTY WEEKENDS
OCTOBER 10TH, 17TH, 24TH, 2009

Creative Review is at the heart of digital creativity – defining and showcasing innovative digital from the traditional to the obscure. After a successful 2008 stint they returned to the ADC to set up shop for a day of digital creativity. Click New York provided a platform for US creatives to reveal the secrets behind some of the year's most influential digital campaigns. The event had a great lineup of speakers that included Chloe Gottlieb, Rob Reilly, Michael Lebowitz, Patrick Burgoyne, Lars Bastholm, Benjamin Palmer, Tom Ajello, Vivian Rosenthal, Vincent Morisset, Jason Zada, ADC Young Guns We Should Do It All, Gareth Kay, Ty Montague and Khoi Vinh.

AAU ALUMNI RECEPTION
OCTOBER 28TH, 2009

3 Saturday afternoon workshops led by Steve Haslip, creator of the Dirty Weekends series, took groups of 30 back to the art of making. Mark Making featured broom drawings, drawing, machines and calligraphy. Printmaking featured potato printing and screen printing and the 3D Construction workshop used paper, cardboard, found objects, images, and string. ADC members attended for free.

FOOSBALL EVENT
NOVEMBER 13TH, 2009

In its sixth year already, the annual World Graphic Design Foosball Championships took place at the ADC where a field of over 60 graphic design teams from far and wide battled for the coveted one-legged challenge cup trophy.

DESIGNISM 4.0
NOVEMBER 18TH, 2009

ADC held its annual forum exploring the responsibilities and experiences of creatives and designers to drive social and political change through their work and career focus.
The focus of Designism 4.0 was the business models that drive social change, effectively providing careers and generating revenue while also doing good for the world. Guest speakers include Blake Mycoskie, Chief Shoe Giver of TOMS Shoes; Bill Drenttel, partner, Winterhouse Studio and Design Observer; Paula Scher, partner, Pentagram and 1998 inductee in the ADC Hall of Fame, and Mark Randall, principal, Worldstudio.

BERLIN SCHOOL OF CREATIVE LEADERSHIP'S
JANUARY 17TH - 23RD, 2010

JEFF JARVIS LECTURE
JANUARY 20TH, 2010

The Berlin School of Creative Leadership is a not-for-profit organization dedicated to research and leadership education for executives in creative industries such as advertising, design, entertainment, interactive, journalism, media and marketing. At the heart of the Berlin School is the Executive MBA in Creative Leadership, a part-time program with 5 separate 2-week modules in Berlin, London, the US and Asia. The first week of the Berlin School's 2010 US module took place at the ADC in January with a guest lecture line-up that featured Jon Kamen, Stefan Sagmeister and Bob Greenberg.

ADC played host to the Berlin School of Creative Leadership's President's Lecture featuring Jeff Jarvis, Associate Professor & Director of the Interactive Journalism Program at City University of New York's Graduate School of Journalism. Jeff, author of the influential media book "What Would Google Do?", spoke about new and better ways to gather, share, and verify news and the radically different and improved relationship between journalists and the public they serve. (During his lecture Jeff discussed product versus process journalism and the shift he argues is necessary from a longstanding myth of perfection and mistake-free news to a "beta culture" in which news and public information are acknowledged to be imperfect, incomplete and ultimately best shaped through collaboration.) ADC members were given access to seats to the lecture for free.

ADC**PROGRAMS**

YOU TUBE SHOW & TELL LAUNCH
MARCH 25TH, 2010

ADC PAPER AND PRINTING EXPO
APRIL 13TH, 2010

YouTube Show & Tell is a gallery-style brand channel that showcases the best marketing examples. Show & Tell was debuted at this speaker event which included cocktails and a conversation about great marketing that generates interest for brands and how YouTube is becoming a canvas for marketing creativity. Danielle Sacks, senior writer at Fast Company, moderated the Q&A with the panel of creatives from Goodby, Silverstein & Partners, The Martin Agency, The Buddy Group and Fullsix Group.

ADC held their annual Spring Paper Expo in April which featured paper companies including Appleton, Arjobex, Cordenons, Crane, Curious, FiberMark, Gould, Gmund, International, Legion, Mohawk, Neenah, New Leaf, Riech, Sappi, Scheufelen, Taylor Box, Yupo joined by printers Aldine, CMYK, Innovation and Precise Continental. More than 515 creative professionals from the New York metro area enjoyed meeting new vendors, collecting great samples, and connecting with each other over drinks and hors d'ouevres. The response to the evening was so overwhelming positive that the ADC has added a second Paper and Printing Expo, to be held September 23, 2010.

BOULDER DIGITAL WORKS: EVOLVE!
JUNE 7TH, 2010

A new integrated projects-driven graduate program in media and business design at the University of Colorado Boulder called Boulder Digital Works unveiled their new website, from partner Modernista!, at the ADC with a presentation and party during Internet Week NY. Within this changing digital world is a compelling need for a greater supply of multi-disciplined thinkers, problem solvers and leaders. Founded by the University of Colorado and MDC Partners, Boulder Digital Works is driving and accelerating this change by developing talent with the technical, intellectual, entrepreneurial and collaborative expertise necessary for success in the 21st century digital media space. Top digital minds from companies like Crispin, Porter + Bogusky, BBH, Yahoo! and Apple spoke about their partnership with BDW to create the next generation of digital talent.

MAKING IDEAS HAPPEN: SCOTT BELSKY
MAY 11TH, 2010

DESIGN CAN CHANGE THE WORLD
MAY 11TH, 2010

Drawing on the research in his new book, "Making Ideas Happen," Behance Founder & CEO Scott Belsky gave an overview of key tips and insights for pushing ideas forward. He touched on the three crucial components of creative execution – organization, communal forces, and leadership capability – and review a series of best practices shown to be effective across industries. The morning presentation kicked off with 30 minutes of coffee & networking and concluded with Q&A session.

Adobe hosted a speaker event featuring Emily Pilloton, founder of Project H Design which connects the power of design to the people who need it most, and the places where it can make a real and lasting difference. Emily had just finished a nation wide roadtrip covering 6,300 miles, showcasing 40 products in the Design Revolution Roadshow that have been designed to change the world. She discussed their findings and their initiatives and how it relates to design. The event concluded with a networking hour with the audience.

ADC**EDUCATION**

SATURDAY CAREER WORKSHOPS
OCTOBER 17TH, 24TH, 31TH NOVEMBER 7TH, 14TH, 21ST
MARCH 20TH, 27TH, APRIL 10TH, 17TH, 24TH

ADC GRANDMASTERS
NOVEMBER 16TH, 2009

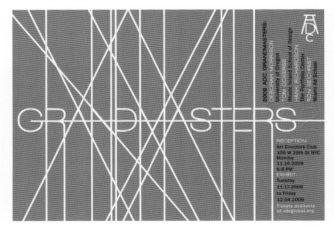

Every semester, the ADC, together with the School Art League and the New York Department of Education, offers a series of Saturday Career Workshops for talented, high school juniors from under-served New York City public schools. Leading visual arts professionals introduce students to careers in visual communications, while helping students build competitive portfolios for art school applications.

For the second year ADC bestowed its GrandMasters Award on 4 outstanding educators whose careers in creative education have impacted and mentored generations of students and whose legacy is a far-reaching network of industry leaders and professionals in Advertising and Design. The program salutes those who have dedicated over 10 years of their teaching careers to establishing and raising standards of excellence in visual communications.

THE NATIONAL STUDENT PORTFOLIO REVIEW
MAY 3RD - 5TH, 2010

On May 3rd, 4th and 5th ADC held its annual National Student Portfolio Reviews in Design, Advertising and Interactive Media featuring 250 of the nation's top graduating seniors from over 35 schools. ADC received record numbers of reviewers seeking exceptional, fresh talent. This year's reviews were chaired by Van Rais, Senior Associate at Linpincott; Rob Rasmussen, CCO at Tribal DDB; Trevor Eld, Creative Director at R/GA and David Lee, Senior Creative Director, TBWA\Digital Arts. Students received encouragement and feedback and many left with interviews and even job offers from the foremost professionals and creative recruiters in New York.

SVA GRAPHIC DESIGN PORTFOLIO EXHIBITION
MARCH 29TH- APRIL 9TH, 2010

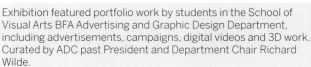

Exhibition featured portfolio work by students in the School of Visual Arts BFA Advertising and Graphic Design Department, including advertisements, campaigns, digital videos and 3D work. Curated by ADC past President and Department Chair Richard Wilde.

PARSONS ILLUSTRATION SENIOR SHOW
MAY 10TH - 14TH, 2010

Annual exhibition featured work by seniors of the Design BFA Illustration Program featuring "Obsessions", their Senior Thesis projects and "Superheroes and Villains", a special collaboration with 826NYC/Brooklyn Superhero Supply Co.

ADC**HENRY WOLF**

HENRY WOLF PHOTOGRAPHY WORKSHOP
JULY 12TH - 16TH, 2010

The week of July 12th - 17th, 2010, ADC held its third-annual Henry Wolf Photography Workshop, an introductory photography course designed to give New York City public high school students the opportunity to meet and learn from top photographers and producers.The program is generously supported by a 10-year grant from the Henry Wolf Foundation.

Approximately 25 juniors from 12 NYC public high schools were given a hands-on overview on the art and trade of photography from five experts in the field. Each student received a digital camera to shoot their assignments and to take home after the workshop.
In addition to shooting assignments, the students learned basics of Photoshop editing techniques. Students were also taken to the Aperture gallery, ICP and the Metropolitan Museum of Art to view and discuss professional work.

Tom Starkweather was the lead instructor for the workshop and was joined by fellow photographers Will Mebane, Christopher Lane (YG5) and Aaron Taylor. New to this year's workshop was a video production component, led by Emmy Award-winning producer Elizabeth Hummer of Hummer Productions. With the students, Elizabeth expanded the idea of the narrative told by a single still image into one told by a 30-second "one-shot/one-take" image.

NY high schools participating in the workshop were Curtis High School, Murry Bergtraum High School, Port Richmond High School, Staten Island Technical High School, All City Leadership Academy, Brooklyn Technical High School, Tottenville High School, H.S. of Art & Design/(Frank Sinatra H.S), Jamaica High School, School for Excellence, Bryant High School and Bronx Leadership Academy High School.

This annual educational program from the ADC was created in honor of Henry Wolf, the famous graphic designer and photographer who, as art director of Esquire, Harper's Bazaar and Show magazines in the 1950s and '60s, held great sway over American magazine design.

ADC**YOUNG GUNS**

APPLE STORE YOUNG GUNS SERIES ——————————

SEPTEMBER 28TH, 2009
New York City Apple Store
Speakers: Menno Kluin and
Graeme Hall

OCTOBER 26TH, 2009
New York City Apple Store
Speaker: Julien Vallee

NOVEMBER 23RD, 2009
New York City Apple Store
Speaker: Justin Gignac

DECEMBER 2010

FIVE PLUS FIVE
SEPTEMBER 16TH, 2009

YOUNG GUNS 7 EXHIBITION OPENING
OCTOBER 21ST, 2009

In partnership with Adobe, the ADC brought back "FivePlusFive."
Five Young Guns pick five creatives they admire; all ten present
their work, pecha-kucha style - 20 slides, 20 seconds each - 400
seconds to tell their story.

The evening was moderated by Matt Lambert.

On October 21, 2009, winners of Young Guns 7 were announced
and honored with an opening party and exhibition at the ADC
Gallery. The party also marked the release of the Young Guns
7 Annual, published exclusively for ADC by Moleskine custom
editions. There were 50 winners and the exhibition ran until
November 6th.

FEBUARY 22ND, 2010
New York City Apple Store
Speaker: Stewart Smith

San Francisco Apple Store
Speaker: Ed O'Brian

Santa Monica Apple Store
Speaker: Will Staehle

Chicago Apple Store
Speaker: ALSO

London Apple Store
Speaker: Adam Simpsom

MARCH 22ND, 2010
San Francisco Apple Store
Speaker: Jennifer Lew

Santa Monica Apple Store
Speaker: Yo Santosa

Chicago Apple Store
Speaker: The Little Friends
of Printmaking

London Apple Store
Speaker: FX&MAT

Paris Apple Store
Speaker: Yves Gleyn

JUNE 28, 2010
New York City Apple Store
Speakers: Garland Lyn and
Ting Ting Lee

London Apple Store
Speaker:Stewart Smith

Santa Monica Apple Store
Speaker: Florencio Zavala

JULY 2010
New York City Apple Store
Speakers: Michael Schachtner
and Julia Neumann

FIVE PLUS FIVE
JUNE 10TH, 2010

YOUNG GUNS 8 CALL FOR ENTRIES OPENS
MARCH 24TH, 2010

Call for Entries for Young Guns 8 launched on March 24 with a party at the ADC Gallery. Attendees were invited to "make their mark" on the gallery wall. This year's Call for Entries was designed by Justin Gignac of Young Guns class 5.

5 Members of Young Guns 7 class picked 5 creatives they admire.

Speakers included: Wesley Allsbrook + Adam Scmidt
Brian Close + Shoplifter, Matt Smithson + Hayley Morris,
Dora Budor & Maja Cule + Micah Lidberg,
Qian Qian + Kevin Grady

ADC**TRAVELING EXHIBIT**

The Art Directors Club representative program is in its inaugural year and has sought out individuals or organizations from around the globe engaged in Advertising, Design, Interactive/Digital Arts, Photography, Illustration, Media, Education and Communications that will help promote global awareness of the club as well as the prestigious honor of winning an ADC Cube.

The program offers representatives a unique and rewarding opportunity to be an integral part of the continued global success of the Art Directors Club.

BUENOS ARIES, ARGENTINA
SEPTEMBER 14TH - 28TH, 2009

ADC REPRESENTATIVES

ADC Representatives are instrumental in a number of areas: finding hosts for the annual traveling exhibition; suggesting key individuals to participate on the jury panel for the annual awards competition; acting as ADC's official exclusive representative in his/her country by distributing ADC press, Call for Entries, deadlines and jury information; and helping ADC connect with the advertising, design, education and visual communications industry in his/her country.

Alina Alexandrescu
Romania

Eduard Cehovin
Bosnia and Herzegovina
Croatia
Macedonia
Montenegro
Serbia
Slovenia

Meera Chandra
United Kingdom

Pancho González
Bolivia
Chile
Colombia
Ecuador
Peru
Uruguay

Jiri Janoušek
Czech Republic

Tautvydas Kaltenis
Lithuania

Ken Tsai Lee
Taiwan

Minoru Morita
Japan

Velina Mavrodinova
Bulgaria

Claudia Neri
Italy

Angela Ng
Hong Kong

Baohua Ren
China

Anne Saint-Dreux
France

Pippa Seichrist
Sao Paulo, Brazil
Berlin, Germany
Miami, Minneapolis and San
Francisco, USA

Harmandar Singh
Indonesia
Malaysia

Guillermo Tragant
Argentina

Dominique Trudeau
Montreal, Canada

Niwat Wongprompreeda
Thailand

SHANGHAI, CHINA - CCII
DECEMBER 6TH - 30TH , 2009

TAIPEI, TAIWAN
NOVEMBER 1ST - 13TH , 2009

BEIJING, CHINA - CCII
JANUARY 5TH - 30TH , 2010

ADC**TRAVELING EXHIBIT**

SANTIAGO, CHILE
MARCH 15TH - 30TH , 2010

LJUBLJANA, SLOVENIA
APRIL 23RD - MAY 3RD , 2010

NOVI SAD, SERBIA
APRIL 23RD , 2010

PODGORICA, MONTENEGRO
APRIL 19TH - 30TH , 2010

MARIBOR, SLOVENIA
MAY 13TH - 30TH , 2010

ADC**ANNUAL AWARDS**

89TH ANNUAL AWARDS JUDGING
FEBRUARY 17TH - MARCH 23RD, 2010

Judging commenced in mid-February! The Art Directors Club happily welcomed an impressive international group of creatives to judge Design, Interactive, Advertising, ADC Design Sphere, ADC Hybrid and the Nissan Student Brief competition. Leading the charge was Design Chair Chris Campbell, executive creative director, Interbrand (NYC), Interactive Chair Dave Bedwood, creative partner, Lean Mean Fighting Machine (London), Advertising Chair Luis Miguel Messianu, president, chief creative officer, Alma DDB (Florida), ADC Hybrid Chair Rob Reilly, partner, co-executive creative director, Crispin Porter+Bogusky (Colorado) and ADC Design Sphere Chair Karen Welman, creative partner, Pearlfisher (London).

ANNUAL AWARDS EXHIBITION
JUNE 3RD - 30TH, 2010

ADC**ANNUAL AWARDS**

89TH ANNUAL AWARDS PRESENTATION
MAY 19TH, 2010

The ADC 89th Annual Awards was presented on May 19, 2010 at the SVA Theatre at the School of Visual Arts, 333 West 23rd Street, New York. This year marks the first time the club has ever presented a best-in-show ADC Black Cube, which was introduced last year, and the first time in 12 years that ADC has made such a selection. In addition, ADC named recipients of this year's Agency of the Year, Network of the Year, Design Team of the Year, Interactive Agency of the Year and School of the Year honors, based upon cumulative points for this year's winning work.

ADC Cube presenters were a who's-who of top industry leaders, including ADC past-presidents Bob Greenberg, chairman, CEO, global CCO at R/GA, Paul Lavoie, chairman, TAXI and Bill Oberlander, EVP, CCO-New York, Cossette Communications, as well as ADC past-presidents and ADC Hall of Fame laureates George Lois and Richard Wilde, chair, BFA Advertising and Graphic Design Department, School of Visual Arts and founding partner, Wilde Design.

ADC**PARTIES**

89TH ANNUAL AWARDS AFTER PARTY
MAY 19TH, 2010

The after-party, with hors d'oeuvres by Gabrielle Hamilton of "Prune" and signature cocktails by Alex Ott. Featured a surprise performance by Twin Sister, and award winning work of the past and present projected on gallery walls.

ADC REBRANDING PARTY
NOVEMBER 4TH, 2009

ADC HOLIDAY PARTY

DECEMBER 13TH, 2009

The annual Holiday Party featured a group exhibition of prints on paper December Editions, hors d'ouevres, cocktails and the debut of the 88th Art Directors Annual. ADC board members, ADC Young Guns, members and new friends gathered for this festive evening and at the end of it ADC had collected over 300 toys and children's books and a cash donation to benefit The Children's Aid Society.

ADC gathered together Annual Award and ADC Young Gun Cube winners, Board members, Hall of Famers, and ADC members to celebrate the unveiling of a major rebranding developed by Trollbäck + Company. The new ADC branding accentuates the club's commitment to currency and relevancy while also embracing its origins and heritage. Party attendees inlcuded several ADC Young Guns, Paul Davis, Carin Goldberg, Ivan Chermayeff, Brian Collins, Ann Harakawa, Seymour Chwast, B. Martin Pedersen, Noreen Morioka, Kevin O'Callaghan, Jakob Tröllback and Janet Froelich...to name a few.

89TH ANNUAL AWARDS SPONSORS

Adobe
Corbis
Earthcolor
Sappi
Fast Company

SPECIAL THANKS

Ace Hotel
The Actualizers
Aldine
Alex Ott
The Cleaver Co.
Goose Island
Jerry Wong
Prune
Scott Ballum, Sheepless Co.
Twin Sister
Two Twelve

CREATIVE - CALL FOR ENTRIES MATERIALS, GALA INVITATION
Publicis New York
www.publicis-usa.com

EXHIBITION DESIGN
Lucas Stoffel

EXHIBITION INSTALLATION
David Ogle

GALA EXHIBITION REEL / PRODUCTION
Lucas Stoffel
Michael Waka

EVENT PHOTOGRAPHER
Ric Kallaher

ADC ADMINISTRATION

Olga Grisaitis
Director

Jen Larkin Kuzler
Awards Manager /
ADC Annual Editoral Director

Jenny Synan
Director of Technology

Kim Hanzich
Information Manager

Alison Davis Curry
Director of Development

Lucas Stoffel
Awards Coordinator /
ADC Annual Editor

Erin Biggerstaff
ADC Young Guns Manager

Regan Murphy
Event Coordinator

Flora Moir
Education Coordinator/Digital Archivist

Max Dunfey
Membership Coordinator

Hugo Verdeguer
Facility Associate

Michael Waka
Awards Associate /
ADC Annual Assistant Editor

Carlos Ochoa
Design Associate

Kyle Eggers
Design Intern

Jack Mello
Media Contact
201.981.5617
jack.mello@gmail.com

89TH ANNUAL AWARDS STAFF

JEN
LARKIN KUZLER

LUCAS
STOFFEL

KIM
HANZICH

JEN
MCCLELLAND

KRIS
HOOVER

WHITTNEY
SUGGS

MAX
DUNFEY

MICHAEL
WAKA

ADC BOARD OF DIRECTORS

Doug Jaeger | President

Rei Inamoto | First Vice President
Global Creative Director, AKQA

Brian Collins | Second Vice President
Chairman/Chief Creative Officer, COLLINS

Stephen Smith | Treasurer
Partner, Stephen M. Smith & Co.

Chee Pearlman | Secretary
Principal, Chee Company

David Angelo
Chairman/Chief Creative Officer,
David&Goliath

Roger Baxter
EVP/Chief Strategy Officer,
Publicis in the West

Scott Belsky
Founder and CEO, Behance

Craig Dubitsky
CEO, 20-10

Rob Feakins
Chief Creative Officer/President, Publicis
New York

Janet Froelich
Creative Director, Real Simple

Ann Harakawa
Principal/CEO, Two Twelve Associates

Rick Kurnit
Partner, Frankfurt, Kurnit, Klein & Selz

Noreen Morioka
Partner, AdamsMorioka

Benjamin Palmer
CEO, The Barbarian Group

Rob Rasmussen
US Chief Creative Officer/NY Executive
Creative Director, Tribal DDB Worldwide

Anthony Rhodes
Executive Vice President, School of Visual
Arts

Jakob Trollbäck
President/Creative Director, Trollbäck +
Company

ADVISORY BOARD PRESIDENT

Paul Lavoie
Chairman, Taxi

ADC PAST PRESIDENTS

Richard J. Walsh 1920-1921
Joseph Chapin 1921-1922
Heyworth Campbell 1922-1923
Fred Suhr 1923-1924
Nathaniel Pousette-Dart 1924-1925
Walter Whitehead 1925-1926
Pierce Johnson 1926-1927
Arthur Munn 1927-1928
Stuart Campbell 1929-1930
Guy Gayler Clark 1930-1931
Edward F. Molyneux 1931-1933
Gordon C. Aymar 1933-1934
Mehemed Fehmy Agha 1934-1935
Joseph Platt 1935-1936
Deane Uptegrove 1936-1938
Walter B. Geoghegan 1938-1940
Lester Jay Loh 1940-1941
Loren B. Stone 1941-1942
William A. Adriance 1942-1943
William A. Irwin 1943-1945
Arthur Hawkins 1945-1946
Paul Smith 1946-1948
Lester Rondell 1948-1950
Harry O'Brien 1950-1951
Roy W. Tillotson 1951-1953
John Jamison 1953-1954
Julian Archer 1954-1955
Frank Baker 1955-1956
William Buckley 1956-1957
Walter R. Grotz 1957-1958
Garrett P. Orr 1958-1960
Robert H. Blattner 1960-1961
Edward B. Graham 1961-1962
Bert W. Littman 1962-1964
Robert Sherrich Smith 1964-1965
John A. Skidmore 1965-1967
John Peter 1967-1969
William P. Brockmeier 1969-1971
George Lois 1971-1973
Herbert Lubali 1973-1974
Louis Dorfsman 1974-1975
Eileen Hedy Schultz 1975-1977
David Davidian 1977-1979
William Taubin 1979-1981
Walter Kaprielian 1981-1983
Andrew Kner 1983-1985
Ed Brodsky 1985-1987
Karl Steinbrenner 1987-1989
Henry Wolf 1989-1991
Kurt Haiman 1991-1993
Allan Beaver 1993-1995
Carl Fischer 1995-1997
Bill Oberlander 1997-2000
Richard Wilde 1997-2000
Robert Greenberg 2002-2005
Paul Lavoie 2005-2008

GOLD CORPORATE MEMBERS

Leo Burnett

SILVER CORPORATE MEMBERS

TBWA\CHIAT\DAY

CORPORATE MEMBERS

Hill Holliday
Wiley
K's Project
Martha Stewart
Pentagram
Publicis
St. Martin's Press
Two Twelve

ACADEMIC MEMBERS

AAU School of
Advertising

AAU School of Web
Design and New Media

College for Creative
Studies

School of Visual Arts

Virginia Commonwealth
University Brandcenter

INDIVIDUAL MEMBERS

UNITED STATES

Hassan Abdul-Hameed
Leif Abraham
Christiano Abrahao
Ruba Abu-Nimah
Gaylord Adams
Haydn Adams
Peter Adler
Charles S. Adorney
Richard Agerbeek
Joe Alexander
Wesley Allsbrook
Emily Anderson
Jack Anderson
Gennaro Andreozzi
David Angelo
Frank Anselmo
David Arnold
Michelle Arrowood
Christopher Miles
Astillero
Mark Avnet
Robert O. Bach
Ronald Bacsa
Priscilla Baer
Damon Bakun
Ethan Baldwin
Lindsay Ballant
Mike Ballard

Giorgio Baravalle
Jensen Barnes
Don Barron
Robert Barthelmes
Liz Bauer
Dawn Bauer
Mark Bazil
Allan Beaver
Christian Behrendt
Jeremy Belk
Rodger Belknap
Archie Bell, II
Fernando Bellotti
Felix Beltran
Elizabeth Benator
Edward J. Bennett
Jerome Berard
John Berg
Barbara Berger
Jacob Berlow
Candace Bexell-
 Oukacine
Danilo Biagioni
James Biber
Tim Bierbaum
Michael Bierut
Robin Bilardello
Bruce Bildsten
Tai Blanche
Robert H. Blend
Andrew Boal
Danilo Boer
Janina Boesch
Bryan Boettger
Carole Bolger
Laura Bonetti
Jeroen Bours
Harold A. Bowman
Shiri Bracha
Al Braverman
Ivan Brewster
Brian Brindisi
Tricia Broadfoot
Ed Brodsky
Ruth Brody
Robert E. Brothers
Brian Brown
Craig Brown
Michael Christopher
 Brown
Kelly Brozyna
Bruno E. Brugnatelli
JW Buchanan
Melissa Buchanan
Dora Budor
Ona Burns
David Byrd
Stephanie Cabrera
Marsha Camera
Jon Cammarata
JulieAnn Cannizzo

Wilson Capellan
Ryan Carl
Chris Carlberg
Maria Carmanno
Thomas Carnase
Andreina Carrillo
Mike Carsten
Vicente Casellas
Jesse Casey
Nicole Casper
Stephanie Casper
Lisa Champ
Chia-wei Chang
Terri Chang
Anthony Chaplinsky, Jr.
Christopher Chase
Jack Chen
Jennifer Chen
Sy-Jenq Cheng
Ivan Chermayeff
Stephanie Chin
Yong Choe
Yon Joo Choi
Song Chong
Mary Choueiter
Greg Christman
Shelly Chung
Stanley Church
Seymour Chwast
Maggie Ciavarella
Elfe Cimicata
Eduardo Cintron
Herbert H. Clark
Thomas F. Clemente
Jon Clifton
Joann Coates
Sheila Cobb
Josh Cochran
Fernanda Cohen
Alexa Cohen
Karen Cohn
Brian Collins
Nolan Constantino
Erin Convy Hasek
Lane Cooper
Andrew Coppa
Anna-Lisa Corrales
Andres Cortes
Sheldon Cotler
Niko Courtelis
John Cowell
Dailey Crafton
Meg Crane
Gregory Crossley
Dulcinea Cuprill
Lisa Curesky
Renato D'Agostin
Scott Dadich
Flory Danish
David Davidian
Simone Davidson

Paul Davis
Randi B. Davis
Myrna Davis
Roland de Fries
Gabriel De los Rios
Mario de Toledo-Sader
Ericson DeChavez
Joe Del Sorbo
Omar Nikolai Dela Cruz
David Deutsch
Pete Deutschman
Stewart Devlin
John F. Dignam
Linda Dillon-Iribarren
Paul DiNovo
Ceil Diskin
Christina Dittmar
Nate Dolce
Edward Donald
Marc Dorian
Enrico Dorizza
Kay E. Douglas
Nina Dubin
Craig Dubitsky
Donald H. Duffy
Spring Dunn
Ryan Eanes
Kimberly Easley
Bernard Eckstein
Mark Edwards
Andrew Egan
Stanley Eisenman
Cecilia Ekmark
Eric Elms
Keith Endow
David Epstein
Lee Epstein
Gabriel Escobar
Jeff Faust
Rob Feakins
Roxanne Feldman
Michael Fenga
Anthony Ferrara
Lauren Festine
Blanche Fiorenza
Carl Fischer
Bernadette Fitzpatrick
Katie Flanagan
Donald P. Flock
Chris Ford
David Foster
Stephen Frankfurt
Mike Freeland
Christina Freyss
Janet Froelich
Diana Frurip
S. Neil Fujita
Yoko Furusho
Leonard W. Fury
Danielle Gallo
Jay Ganaden

Brian Ganton, Jr.
Gino Garlanda
MC Garofalo
Tom Geismar
Steff Geissbuhler
Efi Georgiou
Karan Gera
Michael Gericke
Janet Giampietro
Elena Giavaldi
David Gibson
Justin Gignac
Monica Gil
Alan Gilleo
Frank C. Ginsberg
Bruce Gionet
Sara Giovanitti
Bob Giraldi
Milton Glaser
Erin Gleeson
Tom Godici
Felipe Godinez
Bill Gold
Carin Goldberg
Roz Goldfarb
Ana Gomez Bernaus
June Gonzales
Timothy Goodman
Derek Gordon
Ora Gordon
Michele Gorham
Jason Gorman
Mariana Gorn
Eric Goud
Ray Graj
Renata Graw
Geoff Green
Jack Griffin
Christopher Griffith
Glenn Groglio
Raisa Grubshteyn
Rich Gustke
Robert Hack
Motoko Hada
Kurt Haiman
Laurent Hainaut
Emily Hale
Graeme Hall
Carl Hammond
Keith Hart
Sarah Haun
Kasia Haupt
Sagi Haviv
Luke Hayman
Alexander Heil
Karl Heine
Steven Heller
Louis Hernandez
Lea Marie Herrington
Nancy Herrmann
Elana Hershman

James Hickey	Katherine Knab	Ryan Mauro	Bhavika Parekh	Glenn Rosko
Michelle Higa	Andrew Kner	William McCaffery	Cynthia Park	Charlie Rosner
Stacy Hirschheimer	Henry O. Knoepfler	Dana McMahan	Shawn Park	Richard J. Ross
Jessica Hische	Ros Knopov	Ahmed Mekky	John Passafiume	John Rothenberg
Charles Hively	Gary Koepke	Kevin Melahn	Juston Payne	Mort Rubenstein
Ralph Hockens	Tomas Kohoutek	Michelle Melton	Chee Pearlman	Randee Rubin
Marilyn Hoffner	Dennis Koye	Scott Meola	Margarita Peces	Chris Rubino
Sara Theresia Hofmann	John Kudos	Adele Merlo	Sean Pecknold	Don Ruther
Derick Holt	Jesse Kuhn	Olga Mezhibovskaya	Jessica Perilla	Stephen Rutterford
Michael Holtermann	Hiroshi Kumatani	Andres Miguel	Harold A. Perry	Thomas Ruzicka
Bryan Houlette	Rick Kurnit	J. Abbott Miller	Mike Perry	Kate Ryan
Brent Huffman	Anthony La Petri	Michael Miranda	Ben Peterson	Jill Sabato
Mario Hugo	Pinar Lacroix	Susan L. Mitchell	Robert Petrocelli	Dan Saelinger
Nadia Shireen Husain	Cristina Lagorio	Samantha Mitchell	Theodore D. Pettus	Robert Saks
Rei Inamoto	Robin Landa	Nick Moore	Allan A. Philiba	Kimberly Sall
Brian Inatsuka	Brian LaRossa	Tyler Moore	Jessica Philpott	Robert Salpeter
Christopher Italiano	Diana Lau	Ben Morahan	Alma Phipps	James Salser
Harry Jacobs	Oliver Laubscher	Grace Moreno-Vasquez	Pablo Pineda	Greg Samata
Doug Jaeger	Mark Laughlin	Noreen Morioka	Ernest Pioppo	Monica Sanga
John E. Jamison	Paul Lavoie	Jean Morley	Rodrigo Pires	David Santana
John Jay	Amanda Lawrence	William R. Morrison	Mary Pisarkiewicz	James Santiago
William Jennings	Sal Lazzarotti	Louie Moses	Carlos Pisco	Yolanda Santosa
Phillip Jennings	Gina Lee	Will Mosgrove	James Plattner	Michael Sausa
Rose Jensen	Michael Lee	Greg Moy	Robert Pliskin	Yusuke Sawairi
Patricia Jerina	Jee-Eun Lee	Oliver Munday	Rico Poon	Sam Scali
Peninna Jeruzalmi	Caroline Lee	Monica Murphy	Carla Popenfus	Ernest Scarfone
Paul Jervis	Henry Leutwyler	Brian Murphy	Michael Posso	Michael Schachtner
Mariah Jochai	Alex Lin	Gino Nave	Laddawan Prawatyotin	David Schaefer
Ilene Joel	Ruy Lindenberg	Barbara Nessim	Chuck Pyle	Paula Scher
Judy John	Andreas J.P. Lindstrom	Julia Neumann	Theresa Raffetto	Randall Scherrer
Brown Johnson	Keelin Linehan	Sophia Nicolay	Dave Ragan	Michael Schiffer
Jeff Johnson	Lourdes Livingston	Lauren Niebes	Brandon Ralph	David Schimmel
Margaret Johnson	Matthew Llewellyn	Joseph Nissen	Enrique Ramirez	Klaus F. Schmidt
Heather Lynn Jones	Rebecca Lloyd	Seungkuk Noh	Christine Raniets	Michael Schrom
Spencer Jones	Quintin Lodge	Barbara J. Norman	Benita Raphan	Eileen Hedy Schultz
Elias Jones	Sarah Loffler	Roger Norris	Ali Rashidi	Patti Schumann
Lars Jorgensen	George Lois	Frankie Norstad	Rodrigo Redondo	Mary Jo Scibetta
Michael Jovel	Brandon Lori	David November	Samuel Reed	Stephen Scoble
Matthias Kaeding	George Lott	Kevin O'Callaghan	Matt Reinhard	Cindy Scudder
Kenneth Kaiser	Jodi Luby	Wendy O'Connor	Herbert Reinke	William Seabrook, III
Kelly Kam	Fredrik Lund-Hansen	Niall O'Kelly	Chad Renfroe	J.J. Sedelmaier
Tim Kan	Valerie Luttner	Bill Oberlander	David Rhodes	Leslie Segal
Walter Kaprielian	Liz Macfarlane	Rahul Odedra	Anthony Rhodes	Sheldon Seidler
Anna Kardaleva	Richard MacFarlane	Kelly OKeefe	Marc Ricca	Tanisa Sharif
Masashi Kawamura	David H. MacInnes	John Okladek	Stan Richards	Susannah Shepherd
Norman Kay	Lou Magnani	Lauren Omanoff	Hank Richardson	Michael Shirley
Nancy Kent	Lisa Maione	Takashi Omura	Keren Richter	Elsa Kawai Siew
Inna Kern	Jay Maisel	Lysa Opfer	David Riedy	Karen Silveira
Taylor Kieburtz	Vanessa Mannino	Theresa Ortolani	Jason Ring	Louis Silverstein
Satohiro Kikutake	Jon Mannon	JB Osborne	Arthur Ritter	Todd Simmons
Hoon Kim	Greg Mar	Cristina Ottolini	Emma Victoria Robinson	Milton Simpson
Sunghee Kim	Alison Marana	Andy Outis	Klajdi Robo	Devan Simunovich
Esther S. Kim	Jacob Maraya	Lisa Overton	Luis Roca	Leonard Sirowitz
Kitae Kim	Joe Marianek	Nina Ovryn	Thomas Rockwell	Kristin Sloan
Andru Kim	Leo J. Marino, III	Onofrio Paccione	Breonna Rodriguez	James C. Smith
Christina King	Norma Jean Markus	Majid Padellan	Edel Rodriguez	Christopher Smith
Duane King	Chris Martin	Juan Carlos Pagan	Odoardo Rodriguez	Stewart Smith
Alex Kirzhner	Joseph Masci	Ben Pagel	Johanna Rogers	Jiyeon Song
Tim Kitchen	Lucia S Matioli	Brad Pallas	Andy Romano	Harvey Spears
Judith Klein	Bob Matsumoto	Benjamin Palmer	Joel Rosado	Christopher Spohr
Hilda Stanger Klyde	Lauren Matsumoto	Vasilis Papadrosos	Jamie Rosen	Sandy St. Jacques

Mark Alan Stamaty
Mindy Phelps Stanton
Elizabeth Stein
Doug Steinberg
Karl Steinbrenner
Peter Stemmler
Keith Stentz
Lea Stepken
Daniel E. Stewart
Colleen Stokes
Bernard Stone
David Stonehouse
D.J. Stout
Lisa Strausfeld
Charlotte Strick
William Strosahl
Gerhard Stubi
Emily Suber
Jessica Sudalnik
Baekkyu Suh
Emily Susen
Maiko Suzuki
James Talerico
Jack G. Tauss
Graham Taylor
Nichola Taylor
Barbara Tejada
Mark Tekushan
Jim Temple
Mitzie Testani
Anne Thomas
Yi Yang Thoo
Damian Totman
Gael Towey
Victor Trasoff
Jakob Trollback
Valerie Trucchia
Ling Tsui
Vinny Tulley
Mark Tutssel
Dino (Ntino) Tzouroutis
Katsuhiro Ueno
Khoi Uong
Andrea Uva
Robert Valentine
Elizabeth (Ackerman)
 Valins
Carlo Van de Roer
Andre Bean Vaseghi
Marcos Vaz
Denise Velez
Diane Painter Velletri
Alec Vianu
Frank A. Vitale
John Vitro
Jason Vogel
Semjon Von Doenhoff
Marine von Koenig
Kay Wakabayashi
Dave Wallace
Joe Walsh

Michael J Walsh Jr
Nai Wang
Yifan Wang
Diksha Watwani
Jessica Weber
Susan Weil
Roy Weinstein
Craig Welsh
Robert Shaw West
John White
Rodney White
Richard Wilde
Christoph Wilhelm
Christopher Williams
Jackie Wilzoch
Ben Wiseman
Steven Wohlwender
Laury Wolfe
Roger Wong
David Wong
Timothy Woods
Jon Wyville
Betsy Yamazaki
James Kyungmo Yang
Seong Im Yang
Chieh Yen
Zen Yonkovig
Won You
Yeonjae Yuk
Cagan Yuksel
Mark Zapico
Vito Zarrillo
Emily Zier
Jeff Zimmerman
Ron Zisman
Bernie Zlotnick
Alan H. Zwiebel

ARGENTINA
Marina Caminal
Marcos Girado
Guillermo Tragant
Guillermo Vega

AUSTRALIA
Jay Benjamin
Peter Bosilkovski
Dan Forrestal
Tim Jetis
Ivana Martinovic
Jesper Nielsen
Jake Smallman
Suzy Tuxen
Adam Yazxhi

AUSTRIA
Tibor Barci
Mariusz Jan Demner
Lois Lammerhuber
Silvia Lammerhuber
Stefan Müllner
Franz Merlicek

Roland A. Reidinger

BAHRAIN
Nermin Habib

BELGIUM
Marcel Lennartz
Tuuli Sauren

BRAZIL
Filipe Cavalcanti
Doda Ferrari
Joao Carlos Mosterio

CANADA
Jean-Francois Berube
Rob Carter
Karim Charlebois-
 Zariffa
Gerard Cleal
Sylvain Dumais
Louis Gagnon
Joel Harding
Carlos Huezo
Doug Jackson
Wally Krysciak
Anita Kunz
Sterling Lorence
Jarold Muino
Ric Riordon
Ross Rodgers
Fernando Salvador
Lucio Schiabel

CHINA
Han JiaYing
Merlin Yu Lu
Zhiqiang Wang
Uran Wang
Lai Yajun
Hei Yiyang

COLOMBIA
Santiago Rivillas

CROATIA
Iva Babaja
Boris Bengez
Jelena Mihelcic

DENMARK
Kamilla Blæsbjerg
Lars Pryds

FRANCE
Thomas Cabus
Jeremie Fontana
Milan Janic
Mat Letellier
Anne Saint Dreux

GERMANY
Frank Aldorf
Siggi Eggertsson
Michael Eibes
Kahen Grace
David Grasekamp
Harald Haas
Rudy Halek
Sascha Hanke
Oliver Hesse
Michael Hoinkes
Philipp Hubert
David Kamp
Amir Kassaei
Christoph Kirst
Claus Koch
Oliver Krippahl
Olaf Leu
Nicolas Linde
Andreas Lueck
Helmut Meyer
Joel Micah Miller
Lothar Nebl
Gertrud Nolte
Simon Oppmann
Friedhelm Ott
Frank Philippin
Achim Riedel
Damian Rodgett
Sven Ruhs
Eva Salzmann
Hans Dirk Schellnack
Wolf Schneider
Doerte Spengler-Ahrens
Joerg Waldschuetz
Detlef Wintzen
Joerg Zuber

HONG KONG
David Au
David Chow

ITALY
Andrea Castelletti
Moreno Chiacchiera
Stefano Colombo
Valerio de Berardinis
Alessandro Demicheli
Pasquale Diaferia
Viviana Leveghi
Debora Manetti
Gab Marcelli
Cristina Marcellini
Lorenzo Marini
Claudia Neri
Riccardo Pisani
Milka Pogliani
Giorgio Rocco
Carlo Simonetti

JAPAN
Kan Akita
Takashi Akiyama
Masuteru Aoba
Hiroyuki Aotani
Katsumi Asaba
Norio Fujishiro
Toshiya Fukuda
Shizuka Fukuda
Shigeki Fukushima
Mioko Hara
Morihiro Harano
Keiko Hirata
Seiichi Hishikawa
Tomoyuki Hishiya
Kazunobu Hosoda
Ttsuki Ikezawa
Kogo Inoue
Takumi Inubushi
Masami Ishibashi
Keiko Itakura
Naoki Ito
Takao Ito
Yasuyuki Ito
Toshio Iwata
Takeshi Kagawa
Shuji Kakoi
Hideyuki Kaneko
Satoji Kashimoto
Mitsuo Katsui
Shun Kawakami
Yasuhiko Kida
Yoshikyuki Kikuchi
Yuki Kimura
Takashi Kitazawa
Kunio Kiyomura
Pete Kobayashi
Ryota Kojima
Akiko Kuze
Asakura Makoto
Shin Matsunaga
Chie Mitsuyama
Kaoru Morimoto
Minoru Morita
Kentaro Nagai
Keisuke Nagatomo
Hideki Nakajima
Kazuto Nakamura
Shintaro Noda
Sadanori Nomura
Reio Nunoyama
Yoshimi Oba
Kuniyasu Obata
Toshiyuki Ohashi
Gaku Ohsugi
Yasumichi Oka
Hiroshi Saito
Hideo Saitoh
Michihito Sasaki
Akira Sato
Tamotsu Shimada

Hidemi Shingai
Yusuke Sugimori
HIrotaka Suzuki
Yutaka Takahama
Masami Takahashi
Masakazu Tanabe
Soji George Tanaka
Yasuo Tanaka
Norio Uejo
Takuya Umemoto
Katsunori Watanabe
Masato Watanabe
Takanori Watanabe
Yoshiko Watanabe
Akihiro H. Yamamoto
Hiroki Yamamoto
Yoji Yamamoto
Seitaro Yamazaki
Masaru Yokoi
Yasuhiro Yuasa

KOREA, REPUBLIC OF
Hae Jin Chang
Jin Hyun Kim
Han Lee
Hansol Oh
Alfred S. Park
Kum-jun Park

LATVIA
Toms Skabardis

LITHUANIA
Andrius Kirvela

MEXICO
Luis Ramirez

NETHERLANDS
Ben Bos
Pieter Brattinga
Richard Vijgen
Wim Vos

NEW ZEALAND
Toby Curnow
Aaron Edwards
Dean Poole

REUNION
Boutin Fabrice

SERBIA
Dejan Vukelic

SINGAPORE
Morris Lee
Hal Suzuki

SLOVENIA
Eduard Cehovin
Tanja Devetak
Loni Jovanovic

SOUTH AFRICA
Waldo Zevenster

SPAIN
Jaime Beltran
Verónica Fuerte
Raul Goñi
Javier Gutiérrez Gil
Angel Montero Barro

SWEDEN
Susanne Ekelund
Andreas Kittel
Mats W. Nilsson
Kari Palmqvist

SWITZERLAND
Florian Beck
MC Casal
Bilal Dallenbach
Andreas Netthoevel
Dominique Anne
 Schuetz
Rene V. Steiner
Philipp Welti

TAIWAN
Alain Fa-Hsiang Hu

TURKEY
Pinar Barutcu

UNITED KINGDOM
Eze Blaine
Paul Brazier
Laura Carlin
Daryl Corps
Sonya Dyakova
Daniel Fisher
Dominic Goodrum
Paul Grizzell
John Hegarty
Anna Karlin
Johnny Kelly
Domenic Lippa
Kate Nielsen
Harry Pearce
Sean Reynolds
Adam Simpson
Bianca Wendt
Greg White

VENEZUELA
Jeanny Ponce

STUDENT
Christine Aaron
Jacob Abernathy
Christopher Abrams
Bambang Adinegoro
Oliver Adriance
Hyung Ahn
Jeffrey Aikens
Amanda Aliperti
Art Amaya
Jason Arias
Norihiro Asano
Amanda Askea
Paweena
 Attayadmawittaya
Robert August
Rodger Austin
Seyoung Baek
Kristie Bailey
Sungwoo Bang
Jennifer Bapties
Jarrod Barretto
Alyssa Bascom
D. Saije Bashaw
Eric Baum
Michelle Becker
Sharar Behzad
Victoria Bellavia
Katie Jo Benjamin
Aksana Berdnikova
Robin Birnbaum
Nathan Blackburn
Katherine Bose
Jacob Botello
Elisa Breuer-Penello
Terrance Brown
Meagan Burns
Tiago Cabaco
Alexis Caban
Carolina Caicedo
Francis Callaghan
Richard Carbone
Andreina Carrillo
Iric Catbagan
Annie Chan
Elizabeth Chan
Lauren Chan
Jonelle Chandler
Justina Chang
Jennifer Chen
Yi-Chen Chen
ZongYue Chen
Meiling Chen
Everett Ching
Yong Joon Cho
Yooln Cho
Erica Yujin Choi
Hannah Choi
Julia Coelho
Josh Cohen

Lindsey Cole
Yusmary Cortez
Maria Cosma
Justine Cotter
Ryan Crispo
Melanie Crump
Kathryn Davenel
Kadeem Davis
Mary Day
Will Decher
Kelly DeChiaro
Christine Dempsey
Eric Dennis
Luke Derivan
Amrithi Devarajan
Mira Deverich
Anne Di Lillo
Philip DiBello
Vu Do
Samuel Dolphin
Marisa Domenech
William Donahoe
Pedro dos Santos
Manali Doshi
Jeffrey Dryer
LoÔc Dupasquier
Sebastian Ebarb
Kevin Eichorst
Nora Elbaz
Ariel Elias
Shao-Ann Fang
Kristie Fenning
Kissa Fernandez
Josh Fiebig
Nicole Fleisher
Katrina Ford
Mark Forsman
Vincent Garbellano
Joseph Gaston
Alicia Gearty
Lauren Geisler
Donald George
Lynne Gerde
Grant Gold
Juan Pablo Gomez
Milena Gonzalez
Robert Gonzalez
Amanda Gonzalez
Pablo Gonzalez Castro
Rose Gordon
Marie Graboso
Adam Grabowski
Amanda Green
Rose Greenstein
Michael Griffith
Ligia Guerra
Shawfay Guo
Tara Gupta
Anoj Gurung
Danielle Guzman
Lauren Gwaley

Jungseon Ha
Megan Haase
Caitlin Haden
Stephen Hadinger
Joe Hagel
Alex Haglund
Raihana Halim
Joe Hall
Natalie Hammel
Nick Hansen
Grace Harris
Nana Hatori
Jarrod Higgins
Joe Hollier
Michael Hollingsworth
Kyung Sun Hong
MinJi Hong
Jeff Hornung
Fumiko Hosotani
Nazmul Howlader
Genevieve Huba
Kirstin Huber
Aimee Hunt
Tim Hurt
Jeeyoung Hwang
Jung Su Hwang
Grace Ilori
Sarah Inglis
Christina Irving-Bell
Virginia Ivey
Molly Jamison
Kayla Jang
Maria del Mar Jaramillo
Darshan Jasani
Lee Jensen
Danny Jimenez
Byeolyi Jin
Micah Jones
Hope Jordan
Jae Sung Jung
Fatimah Kabba
Jamie Kakleas
Lilit Kalachyan
Aramazt Kalayjian
Callie Kant
Neslihan Kaplan
Karen Khouth
Anna Kim
Ji Won Kim
Jiwon Kim
Min Kim
Sejin Kim
Yebyul Kim
Yuna Kim
Eunah Kim
Ye Sung Kim
Ian Kirk
Elisabeth Kjormo
Griffin Klement
Stuart Knowlan
Peter Kondratowicz

Lauren Kosteski
Adam Kostman
Jarek Kowalczyk
Emily Kowzan
Sarah Kraus
Joyce Kuan
James Kuczynski
Elizabeth Kuehnen
Mike Kuhn
Ki Won Kwak
Zarina Rose Lagman
Tiffany Lam
Susan Land
Richard Langhorne
Talia Ledner
Deuk Gyu Lee
Hanso Lee
Hyun Hwa Lee
Ji Soo Lee
Min Jung Lee
Seo Jeong Lee
Sheila Lee
Vanessa Lee
Yong Soung Lee
Woojin Lee
Sherry Leung
Mario Licato
Alicia Lo
Brianna Lohr
Bianca Londono
Mee Lor
Nina LoSchiavo
Julia Lovallo
Amy Love
Yi-Fan Lu
Tess Lundgardh
Dana Lynn
Wen Chi Ma
Hollis Maloney
Amrita Marino
Liana Marqueen
Lance Marxen
Leigh McCarron
John McClaire
Maureen McFee
Nasser McMayo
Nicholas McMillan
Dylan Meagher
Jacopo Miceli
Tyler Mintz
Ekta Mody
Flora Moir
Amanda Molnar
Jieun Moon
Amanda Morales
Angela Moramarco
Michelangelo Moran
Erin Murphy
Meaghan Murray
Hye Jung Na
Yumi Nakamura

Teresa Naranjo
Hamon Nasiri
Honarvar
Christopher Nelson
Alexis Nera
Carmen Ng
Justine Ngai
Mike Nichols
Kali Nickless
Paulina Niewinska
Nathan Nowinowski
Derek O'Leary
Senem Oezdogan
Nak Kyu Oh
Allyson Otis
Sheena Paguia
Lisa Papa
Deva Pardue
Soon Park
Su Jung Park
Sonia Patel
Vijay Patil
Stan Peresechansky
Ruben Perez
Lauren Perlow
Simon Philion
Karolina Pietrynczak
Brandi Pittman
Renina Powell
Sarah Ratinetz
Lindsey Reay
Jenny Reci
Alana Renfro
Samantha Ridgway
Alexander Ridore
Jay Rivera
Raul Rodiles
Olga Rodionova
Ana Paula Rodrigues
Denisse Rodriguez
Heather Rosen
Naomie Ross
Michelle Roy
Yevgeniya Ryaboy
Heather Ryder
Jin Ryu
Bryan Saffe
Fitgi Saint-Louis
Eileen San Felipe
Kate Sanders
Jennifer Schubert
Barbara Schwartz
Bari Schwartz
Hillary Scott
Zehra Sen
Megs Senk
Kanan Shah
Lana Shahmoradian
Vladislav
Shargorodsky
Hilly Sharon

Emily Shields
Dong Hwi (Thomas)
Shim
Hyewon Shim
Julie Shim
Jarwon Shin
Marie Shirato
Tal Shub
Johanna Silfa
Erica Silverman
Hem Partap Singh
David Sloan
Catherine Small
Matthew Smith
Morgan Sobel
Dahee Song
Aleanna Sonnylal
Joshua Souter
Matthew Spicer
Curtis Steckel
Scott Steidl
Erin Stelmaschuk
Chris Stephens
Marc Andrew
Stephens
Alex Stikeleather
Jennifer Stopka
Kevin Su
Minjung Suh
Michelle Sukle
Vjeko Sumic
Yun Gui Sung
Erin Swanson
Christine Szeredy
Junko Takano
Eida Tan
Lingxiao Tan
Tonianne Tartaro
Joe Taylor
Nicole Tenbieg
Andrew Teoh
Sarah Teubner
Sarah Thomas
Dana Tiel
Julia Tiller
Eddy Tsai
Akira Uchinokura
Andreas Unteidig
Diana Uvaydova
Manuel Lucas Valadío
Christine Valerio
Billy Veasey
Julia Veinberg
Sylvia Villada
Saritha Vuppala
Tine Wahl
Shaung Wan
Devin Washburn
Dayne-Arron Watai
Diane Wilder
Arielle Wilkins

Rachel Willey
Jared Williams
Jeremy Williams
Michael Wilson
Adam Wolinsky
Allen Wong
Carmin Wong
Youmin Woo
Hayato Yamane
Jin Yong Yang
Ying Ying Yang
Kimberly Yau
Chiu Hung Yip
Hana Yoo
Soomin Yoo
Jeane Yoon
You Jung Yoon
Dami You
Jane Youn
Jameson Young
Yuan Yuan
Tim Yuen
Samantha Zahabian
Dana Zahavi

INDEX

Matthew Carter

Art Directors Club Hall of Fame

The essence of your genius is your ability to perfectly balance the aesthetic and functional requirements of typeface design. From your early apprenticeship as a punchcutter to creating the seminal Galliard® and Charter® typefaces—and now the new Carter Sans™ family—you have proven yourself a master of both the art and craft of type design.

All of us at
Monotype Imaging

Monotype Imaging

ADC **FUN FACTS**

FOOD & DRINK

INDIAN FOOD LUNCHES:

TWO HUNDRED AND FORTY

CUPS OF STARBUCKS:

CHIPOTLE RUNS:

FORTY EIGHT

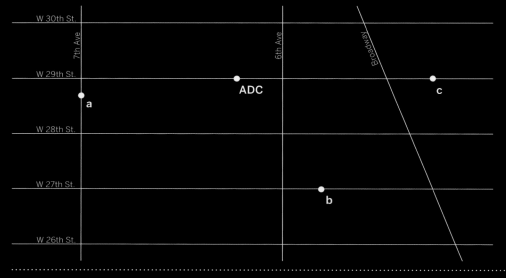

W 30th St.

7th Ave

W 29th St.   ADC   c

a

W 28th St.

6th Ave

Broadway

W 27th St.

b

W 26th St.

a. BEST HAPPY HOUR:

GINGER HOUSE

b. MOST EATEN PIZZA JOINT:

WALDY'S PIZZERIA

c. BEST PLACE FOR
A LUNCH MEETING:

THE BRESLIN*

* MOST INTERESTING
MEAL EATEN:

TONGUE SANDWICH

MOST UNAPPEALING ADC INFUSED VODKA: JALAPENO PEPPER

AT THE ADC

NUMBER OF DOGS THAT  VISITED THE ADC

MOST PLAYED VIRAL VIDEO:

KEEP F----ING THAT CHICKEN

MINUTES SPENT
WATCHING R. KELLY'S
TRAPPED IN A CLOSET:

FORTY FIVE

BIGGEST
ORGAN LOST:

APPENDIX

AVERAGE
TEMPERATURE AT THE
ADC DURING WINTER:

50°

NUMBER OF YEARS
HUGO HAS WORKED
FOR THE ADC:

THIRTEEN

NUMBER
OF ELECTRIC
HEATERS USED:

13

WORST
MISPRONUNCIATION
OF HIS NAME:

FECUNDO

NUMBER OF
BABIES BORN:

ONE

ADC ANNUAL

MOST BOTCHED ADC PASSWORD:

GLOB@L92
GLOBE@L29
GLOB_@_L29
BLOB@L29

HOW MANY TIMES KEYNOTE CRASHED:
COUNTLESS

AMOUNT OF TIME SPENT MAKING THIS ANNUAL:

320 HOURS

PRODUCTIVITY LOST DUE TO SUBWAY DELAYS:

1,857 MINUTES

HOURS SPENT ALPHABETIZING: SIXTY-FOUR

ADC GALA/AWARDS

NUMBER OF PANT-LESS PARTY GO'ERS:
ONE

NUMBER OF ADC STAFFERS WHO WORKED ON THE 89TH AWARDS:

BEST COCKTAIL SERVED AT AN ADC EVENT:
THE KIM

NUMBER OF JURORS:
FIFTY SEVEN

FURTHEST DISTANCE TRAVELED BY JUROR:
8,098 MILES

NUMBER OF TIMES THE GALLERY WALLS WERE PAINTED IN 1 YEAR:

NUMBER OF COLORS USED:

We LOVE

Netdiver (ISSN-1911-866X)
http://netdiver.net

EXCEEDS EXPECTATIONS

With more than 150 new features, Adobe® Creative Suite® 5 Design Premium software gives designers the productivity and speed enhancements they expect, and the unprecedented ability to create interactive content without writing code.

Download a free trial at adobe.com/go/trydesignpremium

STAY
CONNECTED
TO THE MOST
TALENTED
PEOPLE
IN THE
INDUSTRY.
ArtDirectorsClub

DO YOU HAVE WHAT IT TAKES? THE ART DIRECTORS CLUB